A SHEARWATER BOOK

Fishcamp

Fishcamp

Life on an Alaskan Shore

Nancy Lord

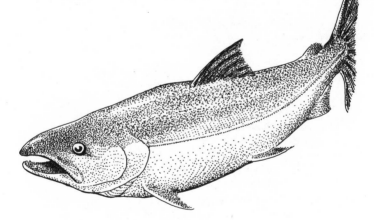

Illustrations by Laura Simonds Southworth

ISLAND PRESS / Shearwater Books

Washington, D.C. / Covelo, California

A Shearwater book
published by Island Press

Copyright © 1997 Nancy Lord
Illustrations copyright © 1997 Laura Simonds Southworth

All rights reserved under International and Pan-American
Copyright Conventions. No part of this book may be repro-
duced in any form or by any means without permission in
writing from the publisher: Island Press, 1718 Connecticut
Avenue, N.W., Suite 300, Washington, DC 20009.

Shearwater Books is a trademark of The Center for
Resource Economics.

Library of Congress Cataloging-in-Publication Data

Lord, Nancy.
    Fishcamp: life on an Alaskan shore / Nancy Lord.
        p.   cm.
    Includes bibliographical references (p.   ) and index.
    ISBN 1-55963-525-8 (cloth)
    1. Cook Inlet Region (Alaska)—History. 2. Cook
Inlet Region (Alaska)—Biography. 3. Cook Inlet
Region (Alaska)—Social life and customs. 4. Natural
history—Alaska—Cook Inlet Region. 5. Fisheries—
Alaska—Cook Inlet Region. 6. Lord, Nancy.
I. Title.
F912.C6L67   1997
979.8'3—dc21   96-52052
                                                   CIP

Printed on recycled, acid-free paper ⊛

Manufactured in the United States of America

10 9 8 7 6 5 4 3 2 1

For Ken

Contents

A Few Words About Words

The reader will note that I use the word *fisherman* through-out this book, applying it to both men and women. Although I as much as anyone would like a gender-neutral word for those of us who fish, none has yet been adopted by those who so de-fine themselves. A fisher, most men and women who fish com-mercially will tell you, is a furry animal related to the marten. *Fisherfolk* sometimes suffices in the plural, but *fisherperson* and *fisherpeople* seem unusually awkward. For now, I choose to use the word that people who fish call themselves, with full recog-nition that women as well as men live the life and do the work of fishing.

In naming animals and plants, I've again chosen common usage. The five species of Pacific salmon we catch we most often refer to as kings, sockeyes or reds, pinks, chums, and sil-vers. For consistency's sake, I've relied on these and chosen *sockeye* over *red* to use throughout. Elsewhere in the fishing world, kings are often known as chinooks, pinks as humpies, chums as dogs, and silvers as cohos.

The people native to the region about which I write were formally called the Tanaina and are today known as the Dena'ina. (The apostrophe serves as a glottal stop.) *Dena'ina* means "the people." Alaska is home to many indigenous peoples commonly grouped into Indians, Eskimos, and Aleuts and referred to as Natives.

And last, I have taken the liberty in my narrative to change or obscure a very few names of people and places in order to protect their privacy.

Preface

Summers, I live at fishcamp. June through August, Mondays and Fridays, my partner, Ken, and I catch and sell salmon that pass by our beach on their way to spawning streams. The rest of the week and during parts of May and September, we mend nets, comb the rocky shoreline for useful poles and cottonwood bark, and do a thousand camp chores and projects. We live quite happily in a tiny cabin at the top of the beach among the eagles and mosquitoes, our growing collection of agates and circle rocks strewn everywhere around us. We put up our personal supply of smoked and canned salmon, and from the middle of July on, our teeth turn black with blueberry stain.

The fishing on the west side of Alaska's Cook Inlet is poor, for complex reasons having to do not with depleted fisheries but with nuances of fisheries management, competition from the offshore fishing fleet, even the changing coastline itself. Other fisherfolk have abandoned these shores for more lucrative locations. In a dozen miles of coastline, we have only three remaining neighbors; they are old-timers a generation or more beyond us, men too old to begin afresh anywhere else. Stubbornly, we stay—because making a living is less important to us than living where we want to be, in an environment where what we do for work fits comfortably into the overall life of the place. We live with fish and with others who live with fish—not just our human neighbors but also seals, bears, magpies, wind and waves, tides, boats, stories of the past, dreams and wishes and fears: all those things animate and inanimate, tangible and intangible, that make up the community in which we find ourselves at home.

It wasn't long ago when such living within the natural world was the rule rather than the exception, when most people were farmers, shepherds and cattle drivers, loggers, cheese makers and butter churners, builders with wood and stone, fisherfolk. Before that—in fact, for ninety-nine percent of the time humans have lived on earth—they were hunters and gatherers. Our ancestors knew where they fit into a world that was larger than themselves and what the connections were between weather and food, predator and prey, wonder and cruelty. Their understanding, though lacking the cold precision we expect today from Western science, was no less legitimate for being contained instead within elaborate sets of myths, their own cosmologies.

It doesn't take much checking of demographics or popular culture to recognize the extent of today's estrangement between people and nature, work and the natural environment. For most Americans today, nature is what's on television's nature programs, or it's a vacation spot, preferably sunny. Half of this nation's eighth-graders, I read recently, aren't even aware that the sun rises generally in the east and sets in the west.

Commercial fishermen are among the lucky few who are privileged not just to visit wild places but also to participate in the life of those places, to live in relationship to other creatures and to mystery. Even in Alaska we're very likely anachronisms, doomed to pressures from fish farming, competition from sport fishermen, and habitat destruction. And yet it seems to me that the best chance for humans to regain a healthful connection to the earth, seas, and air will come not from worshipful distance but from the authentic integration of work and life that's known on fishing boats and beaches and in woods and fields. I'm speaking not of exploitive, industrialized work but of personal, sustainable work that's responsible to place and others, the kind that's part of a larger whole.

Aldo Leopold said that the best definition of a conservationist was probably written not with a pen but with an axe. "It is a matter of what a man thinks about while chopping, or while deciding what to chop. A conservationist is one who is humbly aware that with each stroke he is writing his signature on the face of his land." Such humble awareness is, of course, easier to come by when cutting a tree by hand, not bulldozing down forests, and when catching fish one at a time, not hauling them by the ton onto factory boats. For loggers and farmers and commercial fishermen alike, it's possible to use wisely the places where we live and what we find in them, but only if we also choose wisely the marks we make. We hold the power to destroy, but we must remember that we can never create anew.

If we're to live with nature, a part of it instead of apart from it, the question is, for me, reasonably clear. How shall we do this? By what moral authority, what tribal understanding? What are those things we'll want to think about as we take axe or chain saw, fishing net or pole or shopping list in hand? Some well-intentioned folk would drape laurels around the bears and the whales yet ignore the jellyfish and mosquitoes, forget the fallen trees and microscopic phytoplankton, even disregard people. Many others, of course, recognize only the value of other humans, get their fish out of tuna cans, and don't know or even wonder what a tuna looks like or where it lives or what it or a salmon or a whale needs to live.

I ask my questions in the spirit of inquiry, without credentials of the scholarly kind. I'm not a biologist or naturalist or a historian, anthropologist, ethnologist, or philosopher. I can't claim even a generational relationship to the place that means the most to me; I came to it only as an adult, not yet twenty years ago. Although I've tried to learn from Native American cultures, particularly the Dena'ina Athabaskans native to the Cook Inlet area, my understanding is that of an outsider; my own heritage is Anglo-European, by way of New England and a "liberal" education augmented by wide—though not nearly wide enough—reading in many disciplines.

What I am mainly is a person who catches fish, someone with a basic belief in the importance—the necessity—of paying attention. Although the specific out-of-the-way place and uncommon way of life I care about may be no more significant than any other, I hope in these pages to show, by the example I know something about, what even one place and its infinitely varied life contributes to the connections among us all and to the wholes we call "world" and "culture."

We are, after all, all aboard the same blue boat. As far as we know, it's the only one sailing the heavens that's equipped with what we need to survive, and it's really not all that large. John Muir's famous dictum becomes more apparent each day: whenever we try to pick out any one thing, we find it hitched to everything else in the universe. Wherever our places are and whatever we do in them, perhaps we might all begin to pay more attention to the little and big things that do indeed connect in profound ways to all the rest, miles and eons and cultures apart.

Acknowledgments

I'm grateful to many people for encouraging me with this project and for helping me think more clearly about the material herein. These good folks got me started on individual pieces that later folded into the book: David Burks, Bob Pyle, Carolyn Servid, Ron Spatz, and Annie Stine. These readers reviewed parts of my first draft and gave kind correction and advice: Alan Boraas, Gladys Elvsaas, George Hayden, Deborah Kaufmann, and Tom Kizzia.

My friend Sue Silverman was a most valued reader and advisor from the beginning. When I most needed it, Lidia and Fred Selkregg generously provided two months of quiet time on another shore. Later, the Anderson Center for Interdisciplinary Studies provided additional time, support, and camaraderie; I'm particularly grateful to Gary Holthaus and Judith Tannenbaum. I owe a great deal to my agent, Elizabeth Wales, and to my editor, Laurie Burnham, for advice and counsel. Many, many others have helped with my general education, teaching me the names and habits of things and ways of seeing and connecting, an attitude of living.

As Gary Snyder has said, books are our elders, too, and so I thank as well the authors of the many books that have guided me. A selected reading list follows my narrative.

I could not have written this book without the nurture and enthusiasm of my parents, Betty and Bob Lord, and my partner, Ken Castner; to them I give my greatest love and thanks.

Fishcamp

PART I

Beginnings

Beach Time

It's spring, and Ken and I are eager to get to fishcamp. The ice has been off the lake in town for weeks already. The second day of May we pack up—stuffing leafy raspberry canes into the back of the floatplane—and fly north. The hills beneath us are still snow patched; the inlet, when we cross, empty and gray. After an hour our cabin appears as a welcoming white dot, but the shoreline is crusty with old ice; then we're over the lake behind the camp, and it's still locked solidly in winter. The lake ice is blotchy, softening in ash-colored circles, but there's no open water on which to land.

We're too early and can only overfly the storm-scoured edge of the inlet, checking the line of closed camps and overturned skiffs, the highway of bear tracks along the beach, the paucity of drift logs. We fly home again, shivering.

✧ ✧ ✧

We come again two weeks later. On the open, black-water lake, a pair of snake-necked trumpeter swans stand out like marble statuary; I can't take my eyes off them the whole length of our descent and landing. As we taxi, we see the beavers' new work, a stew of gnawed sticks at the end of the lake. The hill behind our parking spot is open to the sky, as though it's been clearcut. When we've unpacked and tied the plane, we walk the area. The beavers have taken down, limbed, and hauled away all but the heavy trunks of a dozen birch trees, and they've knocked over a number of spruces right along with them. The pointed stumps ooze a thick slathering of sap, and the ground is littered with piles of wood chips. Fiddleheads are just emerging from the ground, alders are budding, and spiny devil's clubs are swelling at their tips; the whole place looks green tinged, as though outlined with a chartreuse crayon. I breathe deeply of air that smells like water and cool earth. There are no mosquitoes in this calm before spring's heated explosion.

Renewal. Return. Time slows. Moments fill with the big-throated trills of a courting warbler, the fall of a brown alder cone, my beating heart. The trail leads home.

✧ ✧ ✧

We go quietly, unannounced, loaded with our groceries and books, raspberry canes and a pot of chives, my computer. In the still snow-patched, not-yet-leafed woods, we can see clearly around us. We don't worry about surprising hidden and unsuspecting animals.

At the first of the two beaver ponds, when I glance across at the sunny knoll that I've always thought looked like a place a bear would be, there stands, in fact, a bear.

"Bear," I say in a flat voice to Ken, who's walking in front of me but hasn't yet spotted it.

He stops but still doesn't see it. "What color?" he asks. He means what kind—the smaller but often bold and unpredictable black bear or the larger, shyer, very fast and skull-crushingly powerful brown bear, the coastal grizzly.

"Brown." I'm afraid he'll scare it, so I add, as quietly as I can, "Let's just watch."

Only water and air stand between us—perhaps fifty yards' worth—and the bear is in wholeness, caught out on its own business. A young adult, it's as handsome as a rangy boy but with an outsized, balloon-shaped head. Its deep brown fur is sleek and ripply, elegantly plush and full of light. The bear splashes at the edge of the pond, digging a root or trying to catch something or perhaps only playing, slapping water. It stands upright and drips, and then it's gone, crashing into brush. It never looked our way. My back foot finishes the step forward it began seconds, epochs, earlier.

It's not fear I taste in my mouth but something icy and metallic, like the back side of a cold mirror. I never see a bear in the wild without having a profound sense of *presence*—the feeling of witnessing not just a large, beautiful, and potentially dangerous animal but something akin to a parallel culture. I tend not to be romantic when it comes to animals, but this much is true: I feel less as though I've just spotted a wild creature than that I've glimpsed the secret life of an undiscovered tribesman in an unexplored corner of the world. I understand with gut emotion why people cling to beliefs in yetis, sasquatches, and abominable snowmen. There is something here that transcends reason and biology, that reaches through time and space and entire belief systems.

Bears, after all, resemble us in a way that's unique among animals. I don't mean that they resemble us as chimpanzees and other primates do. The connections are different; they have to do with power and quiet authority, with who we think we are or wish we were, with origins that aren't evolutionary but spiritual. It's not coincidental that indigenous cultures the world over have held the bear in a special sort of awe, that they consistently speak of bears in kinship terms and treat them with utmost respect. The bear is like us yet is not us. Perhaps the bear is our connection back to something lost and still treasured, another way of knowing. The bear is nature and culture, together.

✧   ✧   ✧

We continue through the woods to the top of the bluff where the creek runs over; below us, the inlet's gray waters pour past our rock-strewn beach. We splash our way down the creek, stumbling over rocks and ducking alder branches, to the clearing with our smokehouse, to the cabin. We find the stashed ratchet and screwdriver and remove the nuts and screws that have kept the cabin door secure against bears. The plastic bag of repellent cayenne pepper I left tied to the door handle has been ripped open, probably soon after we left in the fall, when there were still provocative smells around. But the cabin is intact, windows boarded, chimney capped.

A dark wing-flash folds into the birdhouse that's nailed to the top corner of the back wall. The swallows have beat us back and are already moved in.

Inside, the cabin is dark and cool and musty smelling, like damp rugs and fishing clothes and mildewed paperbacks. All around the one room lie our familiar things, just as we left them—worn-out camp shoes in the middle of a sandy square of carpet, outboard motors in the corner, favorite mugs in the dish rack, several copies of last year's tide book scattered across the table. Hip boots and come-alongs hang from nails in the rafters like aged sides of meat and instruments of torture. There's my set of Russian knives with their bright painted handles, and beside the stove, a comforting amount of dry firewood and four full buckets of coal. A note we left explains how to operate the VHF radio and asks that anyone who uses the cabin please close it up again. No one has been here. No one ever has, after we've left and before we've returned.

Ken turns a switch to check the batteries. They're full, charged by the solar panel on the south side of the cabin.

We drop our packs and head down to the beach. Storm tides the previous fall, before the beach was iced in, have taken their toll. We lost more beachfront, including all of a hefty breakwater we'd built two years before, with posts sunk deep into clay and a spruce we'd split down the middle and bolted into place as cross-boards. Most of the hundreds of rocks I'd carried up the beach, one and two at a time, to fill in behind the breakwater are gone, washed away, along with part of our steps, our fish-cleaning table, and the poles to our net rack.

I think of the photograph we have of our cabin when it was new, twenty-odd years ago. The cabin stood well back on a gentle slope then, the beach in front high and sandy. Today, viewed from the beach, the cabin rises steeply on what's become a point, fortressed only by the levels of cement work and rocks and fill behind the curved remains of a recycled wooden skiff—the protection we add to every year.

The story's the same all along our beach—higher tides, the bluffs eroding back and back, clumps of alders and hunks of clay first undermined, then tumbled down, like icebergs calved from a glacier. On rainy nights, sometimes we hear them fall—the thud of cabin-sized tangles hitting the beach, the crack of a boulder bouncing into other rocks. The high tides immediately set to work stripping away the movable material and redepositing it down the beach and into the gritty sea.

This steady erosion is a result, I think, not of global warming and rising water but of long-term geological subsidence and simple gravity, a gradual leveling. Alaska's 1964 Good Friday earthquake rearranged coastline, lifting some areas and flooding others; the land here is quite likely still sinking, so the tides reach higher. In any case, Cook Inlet flows through a drowned glacier-carved river valley; from the moment the glacier melted, the inlet's been getting wider and shallower. Because our camp lies on the end of a point, beaten by storms from all directions, the carving-away effect is particularly dramatic. Our closest neighbor, tucked into the beginning of the bay north of us, has seen more sand and drift fill in against his shoreline, and our neighbors on the south side complain of bars building up below them and deflecting salmon from their fishing sites.

The sand, hard packed by recent tides, is solid under my feet; my rubber boots barely dent its swept-clean surface. The tide is well out and still falling, exposing the rock reef that curls out before our camp. White water foams over the reef's end, and the outer rocks are strangely pale; the winter's ice sheets must have scoured them of the rockweed that grew so luxuriously there a year ago. Under a broken sky, the inlet looks leaden, cold. The rip cuts close toward the point, the water there pitching into frothy peaks. I feel the pull of the water; from now on we will live largely by its schedule, the rhythm it sets. *Tide.* The very word derives from the Old English for *time.*

A neat-feathered eagle soars past, moving into the wind, riding an air current just above and offshore of the bluff. It turns its golden eye on me greedily as though it recognizes the sort of creature I am, one of the kind that sometimes leaves offerings.

I walk a little north of our camp and look up the steep-sided bluff where patches of leafing alders hang by tenuous toeholds and swallow nest holes line a crack in the clay face. A landslide begins as I watch—sand slipping from a vertical spot near the top, picking up pebbles as it falls, the rubble of it dinging onto the beach in a cloud of dust. Sand and clay, layers of gravel and seams of coal, embedded rocks and granite boulders—it's hard to think of all that, some of it a hundred feet

high, as having once been underwater. And yet its makeup insists. Some time in the past the ocean level was much higher,
or some force—earthquakes or glacial rebound—lifted the
land. Certainly this whole region was under ice during five or
more different glacial periods; the number and particularly the
diversity of rocks attest to a great deal of long-distance scrap-
ing and pushing. The last scouring can't have been so long
ago, judging by the thin layer of rooty earth that overhangs
the top of the bluff. The trees that grow there aren't very big,
and when they do grow tall they have a tendency to blow
down, exposing wide but shallow root systems that have
proved insufficient anchor.

The land lifts and wears down again, lifts and wears down
again. The process takes millennia, and it happens before our
eyes.

The winter's sea ice, too, has helped rearrange the landscape. Shoved about by tides and currents, it gripped and
dragged substantial rocks with it. Just in front of the cabin,
there's a boulder we've never seen before, the size of a laundry
hamper. The slabs of ice haven't been gone long from the
beach; all along its top edge the sand has a quilted look, raised
and depressed in odd patterns that collapse when we walk on
them, so delicately were the grains arranged by the shrinking,
fracturing ice.

The inlet itself faces me bare and wild, featureless. Summers, I know it by landmarks—buoys marking each of our fishing locations. During fishing season my eyes move from one
orange buoy to the next, knowing each distance, each relationship to the tideland below, to shore. But now the coastline
looks like a foreign country, a blank map. The whole of the
beach and its waters have a fresh, unoccupied look, a sense of
having been wiped clean. Its plain beauty would best be shot
in black and white, and then not in whole vistas but in small

details: the wave-sculpted hollow behind a boulder, a round white stone balanced on a slab of slate, the texture of water swirling in a back-eddy and running over a reef.

Across the water, on the shore ten miles distant, sunlight gleams on the white sides of massive round tanks filled with liquefied natural gas, and a refinery puffs a fibrous, steamy cloud. To the north, a line of oil-drilling rigs, each a spangled island with a golden flare, churn into a depleting field. The rigs have been in the inlet longer than we have, and when the wind blows from that direction their hums and pounding become a part of our beach, too. We live in the shadow of their possible blowouts and pipe burstings and tanker groundings just as we live in the shadow of active volcanoes, but we hope to outlive them, to one day see them safely dismantled and removed, when they've sucked the way-down dinosaur depths dry.

✧ ✧ ✧

Off up the beach, Ken searches the drift along the bank for lost belongings or new treasures while I follow the tracks of two bears, sow and cub. They're browns, I know from the print of the sow, which not only is large but has fat toes that butt up against each other in a fairly straight line, and claw marks well out in front. (A black bear's toe tracks have more space between them and form an arch, and its curved claws don't extend so far.) The cub is small—this year's—and it hardly weighs enough to make more than a scratchy impression in the sand. Their line of travel is leisured, with short steps winding back and forth, the cub in its mother's wake.

A glint of light, a certain pale orange color, catches my eye. I stoop to collect my first agate of the year. It's not very big—smaller than a marble—and rather plain, with pitting on one side and a smooth, jelly-bean, end, but it's interesting in the way that all beach agates are interesting: because each is different from every other and because it's always possible to find some but not many.

The eagle, the wild look of the inlet, the bear tracks, now the agate—all remind me of a story Ken likes to tell, one he heard originally from an Inupiat Eskimo who lived in two worlds—corporate America and the wisdom of his people. Ken tells it in long-drawn-out detail, but a short version goes like this: A man is walking on the beach and picks up a pretty stone to rub. A genie appears and offers him three wishes. The man says, "I want to be rich." Whoosh! The next thing he knows he's in a large corner office in a tall building with thick carpets, wood paneling, and an array of expensive artwork on the walls. He's wearing a custom-made suit and gold jewelry, and his bankbooks, overflowing with digits and dollar signs, are open in front of him. The man says to the genie, "No, this isn't right. I want to be *rich.*" Whoosh! He's in an elegant penthouse apartment with a rooftop garden and helipad. The bed has silk sheets and in it is a very, very beautiful woman. Servants open expensive wines to go with the caviar. "No, no," the man shouts, "I want to be *really, really, rich!*" Whoosh! The man is back on the beach, surrounded by water and sky and clean air, jumping fish, drift logs, and the smells of willow and sea salt.

I show Ken my agate. He looks it over and hands it back, feigning disinterest. Now begins our summer-long contest. "Stay away from my line," he growls as he picks a contour of the beach to walk—a band of lightly washed gravel between areas of packed sand, the best prospect. He has the sharper agate eye and more aggressive instincts, but I have my own tricks. I usually store extra agates in my pocket to add to my count when we finish our walk and compare numbers.

Agates are the simple wealth of the beach. Always they jangle in our pockets like coins, always when we meet neighbors we dig into our pockets and compare our finds, our best agates, as pleased as if they were nuggets of gold. We trade. We give them away and feel generous when we do. We teach all visitors to look for the opaque shine, to tell an agate from a piece of quartz, to develop the scanning eye that can locate the tiniest shard in a pile of gravel. At the cabin, we set our agates on the table, move them around like chess pieces, and after a time deposit them in a candy jar. When the jar overflows, we pour its contents into a five-gallon bucket on our porch, a bucket that's now four and a half gallons full. The best agates—the red ones, the ones with swirling lines or crystals, the ones that look like lips and teardrops—stay on the table and windowsill and are handled and admired again and again all summer. We think of them as valuables, though in the real world of commerce they're very nearly worthless. Once in a shop that sold rocks and shells I found agates for sale—a penny apiece.

This attention to agates—just few enough and just shiny enough—may be inherent to this area of the inlet, or it may be something passed down from neighbor to neighbor, old-timer to newcomer. I know only that our neighbors collected agates before we did and that old-time Dena'ina, the original people of this place, believed that lucky agates fell from the sky. When they walked on the beach they looked for marks indicating where agates had rolled after falling, and those agates, when they found them, gave them good luck.

Long before I read of this Dena'ina belief, Ken and I used to remark at the way agates are typically found on top of sand and gravel, never buried within, as though they'd rained from the sky. Scientific creatures that we are, we explained away this curious fact by guessing that they have less density than the rest of what forms the beach. We also wondered whether they popped from the clay bluffs and rolled onto the beach instead of riding in on the waves.

We observe agates as we observe fish, and after years of spotting, handling, and contemplating them, we put together our own theories about their origins. We decided, from their irregular shapes and pockmarks, that they formed inside something else and that their crystals and layers suggest something molten that cooled. Sometimes they contain black specks, like insects caught in amber. We noticed other agate aspects: that their accumulation doesn't depend on the roughness of the water; that they're more common north than south of our camp; that high tides turn over fresh, more fertile hunting surfaces. Still, for all our looking, pulling apart of hunks of clay, and smashing of suspicious rocks, we've never discovered an agate that wasn't simply laid out on the beach, like a gift.

When I finally found a book about agates, they became no less mysterious. They do, in fact, form in gas pockets in volcanic rocks or, sometimes, in cracks or fissures. They're typically made of chalcedony, a very fine-grained quartz, and they appear as loose stones when natural weathering softens and crumbles the rock around them. The exact manner in which agates form is still under debate, involving arcane theories best left to mineralogists. I'm less interested, in any case, in the science than in the lore. Marbodus, an eleventh-century French bishop, believed that agates made their bearers both agreeable and persuasive. The ancient Greeks and Romans both recorded tales of agates' talismanic qualities: the stones were believed to have the power to cure the bites of poisonous spiders, to turn away tempests, and to make wrestlers invincible.

❖ ❖ ❖

Without discovering any more agates, Ken and I reach the black rock, a turning point for our evening walks. We circle it and head home again, and I feel myself make the last slip of gears, the final adjustments into beach time. All the "stuff" of my winter life—the phone calls and desk work, the comings and goings and attendings-to, all the half-panicked rushing and tidying through the last weeks—seems like another, less consequential keeping of time and priority. I take a deep, cool breath. I'm on beach time now, driven only by the tides and the fishing openings and the need for looking closely at things, in their own good time.

Beach time is, for me, akin to *kairós*, the Greek for sacred time, in contrast to *kronos,* chronological time. This is a distinction I learned from Father Michael Oleksa, a Russian Orthodox priest who's lived among several Alaskan Native cultures and teaches classes in cross-cultural understanding. People in traditional cultures consider time differently from those of us raised on Western standards, who learn to be "on time," not to waste time, and sometimes to "kill" time. These concepts have no meaning in Native cultures, where time just *is*. Such people aren't interested in using time well or efficiently or in dividing it between work and play. What matters is doing things that are significant, such as gathering food, mending a fishing net, and telling stories. One doesn't rush to get these things done; it's the process, not the product, that's important, and the longer one spends in the *kairós* kind of time, the better.

In winter, I can't stand grocery shopping more than once a week; I don't like the bother, the inefficiency, of buying one thing one day and something else two days later. But in summer, I'll spend half a day tromping the woods to find a cup of blueberries and a week tending my smokehouse for a batch of fish. To bathe, we start by making a fire on the beach, take most of an afternoon and evening to heat water, and then soak ourselves while we watch the tide move and birds fly. Is that a good use of time? We don't even think about it. We know this is what we do on the beach, how we live the richness of our lives. Time preparing the tub or picking berries is sacred time, as close as I ever get to religion.

✧ ✧ ✧

That evening, our first of the year back at camp, Ken and I play Scrabble, something we do only in summer, only at camp. First, Ken finds the records for the previous summer and points out that of thirty-five games I won only five, or one out of seven. I don't mind that Ken's the better player because I know he wouldn't play if he didn't win. I'm not a Scrabble slouch; I play *aa* and *oe* and *qoph* with the best of them, and our two scores together routinely top 700 points.

We play Scrabble and eat popcorn and chocolate kisses and then go to sleep on our flannel-covered futon to the sounds of the creek and the incoming tide. The wind shifts in the night. We haven't yet added an extra length of stovepipe to lift the chimney over the roofline, so coal smoke blows back down the chimney and into the cabin. At two in the morning I run down the beach with a shovelful of coals, sparks flying in the wind, my comfy, old no-longer-elastic long underwear falling down around my knees. I throw the coals into the water, where they hiss and go dark. The tops of the waves catch what light there is, pushing it in overlays like lace onto the sand. Somewhere out there the king salmon are quietly passing.

The Weaving of the Web

Salmon have always been central to this place, from whatever ancient moment of glacial retreat opened the waters to wandering spawners. Before they took this particular north-ward turn, they'd long evolved in the icy North Pacific to home in on particular rivers and lake systems, each species and stock custom matched to exact conditions and demands. They buried fertilized eggs in gravel and then died, releasing nutrients for the next generation and for the general wealth of the planet. Eggs hatched. Smolt swam to sea, circled there for one year or several, and then made again the same long trek back to the waters of their birth.

As I begin on the net repair I didn't get done in the rains of last season's end, I think of how essential salmon must have been to the coevolution of humans in the same environment, all around the North Pacific. The Native Americans who first lived on this shore came from inland mountain areas where they would have known salmon in rivers and lakes. Perhaps only six hundred years ago, ancestors of those who would call themselves Dena'ina—"the people"—established the only branch of Athabaskan Indians anywhere to live at tidewater. Although they eventually came to surround Cook Inlet, their first coastal touch was probably not far to our north. I've often wondered what that must have been like—to have been brought up short by wide ocean water and then to have discovered what it could provide.

And the waters of Cook Inlet did, and do, provide. Herring and hooligan, an oily smelt, arrive with spring, and then come the five species of Pacific salmon—kings, sockeyes, pinks, chums, and silvers trailing on into the fall. The seals and beluga whales that feed on the fish would also have offered themselves to the first people, another source of oil and meat, fur and hide and sinew.

The Dena'ina were probably never all that numerous—before white contact, there were perhaps five thousand in an area the size of Ohio. They adapted their inland ways to their new environs, adopted tools and technologies from Alutiiq Eskimos to their south, and reasonably prospered. They lived by fish, and when the runs failed or they couldn't catch what they needed or the winters lasted too long, they starved.

This morning I've laid out our nets—piles of corks stacked to one side, lead-weighted lines to the other, green web stretched between—in a sandy spot at the top of the beach. Now I settle myself onto an overturned bucket and take up a leadline near its end, where the worn hangings that hold the web to the weighted line have broken. I cut the old twine loose.

I've never cared for the domestic arts of sewing, knitting, crocheting, darning, embroidery, and macramé, but I like net mending. It must, of course, be done, so there's that satisfaction to it—closing holes, making the nets whole again, leaving no unnecessary opportunity for a fish to slip through. There's the puzzle part of it, too—the challenge of finding the pattern in the web and, diamond side by diamond side, filling it in. And then there's the meditative quality—the fact that as my hands work, I sit or stand or kneel in quiet contemplation of the world around me.

These gillnets are a part of my life, as familiar to me as squares and levels are to a carpenter, as cookware is to a chef. Each one has its own qualities, its independent history. This first one, with blue corkline and 33 *f* marked on its last white cork, is one of our longest nets—nearly the regulation thirty-five-fathom maximum. It's one we bought from a neighbor, who hung the web between the corklines and leadlines in his own style, distinct in its knots and spacings and tension. The old web has had several years of wear, but it isn't quite worn out yet. Next year, maybe, we'll rehang this one; that is, we'll strip all the old web from the two lines it hangs between—the corkline, which keeps one side of the net afloat on the water's surface, and the leadline, which pulls it down—and rehang new web. Ken or I will sit on the hanging bench for many hours, catching three loops of web with the hanging needle, measuring a four-inch distance, and winding and tying, on down the whole long net, one side and the other.

We have, then, an intimacy with every net and every aspect of every net. There's the one with the heavy white corkline and the one with a leadline that's too light and flags out with the current. On this other net there's a missing cork; we cut it off after a bear's bite left holes that snagged web. This one, with the thin blue line, was part of a long Bristol Bay net Ken bought years ago. Here's a net we seldom use, with an old-style leadline—actual lead weights fitted over the line instead of being contained inside the weave. Here's the net with the short corkline end, where Ken cut it the time my glove got caught in a knot, pinching my finger. Here's mending done by our former neighbor, with dark twine and tying that starts not at a corner but at a tail, in the middle of a diamond.

None of this coloration, detail, and history is, of course, appreciated by anyone but Ken and me. Whenever guests try to help us with nets, even with something as simple as restacking them on the beach after we've dragged them from the boat, I'm reminded again of our peculiar, in-country feel for lines and web. Outsiders can't see how to find an end, or they catch their buttons and shoes in the web, or they lean over awkwardly as they slowly pull the leadline and pile it in messy loops.

Once a visitor accompanied us in a boatful of nets and, in the midst of all those gillnets, asked us what we use for bait. It hadn't occurred to him that there were other ways of catching fish than with bait on a hook or in a pot, and he was blind to what lay at his feet. And why not? What need had he ever had in his life to look at fishing nets or to contemplate how they worked? I'm sure I'm equally unseeing and uncomprehending of much of what accompanies other lines of work, other people's lives. I am, for example, a fool before an ATM machine; that's a technology I don't need and don't use.

❖ ❖ ❖

I tie my last knot on the leadline, snapping it tight against the back of the plastic needle, and cut it short. The new twine is shockingly white against the worn, silt-stained hangings. I take my needles, twine, knife, and scissors to the other side of the net and restack corks, looking for more broken hangings. I stop when I come to a small hole in the web, cut loose the ragged ends, take up the mending needle. I tie the thin nylon strand to one corner, measure it to the next point, tie it, bring it to the opposite corner, and then snap that last knot over itself. These "three-bars" are the most common holes, and quick to close with half a diamond.

Our art and practice begin here, with mending nets, and continue through every aspect of what we do in order to fish.

The nets stack into bins in the skiff, laid neatly to pull out over the stern, corks clattering. We set them from shore, with one end dry, into the inlet, and offshore, from reefs and in eddies, along fixed lines we call setlines and to anchored buoys. Like invisible curtains or a flexible chain-link fence, the nets hang down across the current. Salmon swim into them, passing their heads through the open diamonds of the mesh and getting stuck at their gills. They can't back out.

The art is in the picking, too—the way we pull net across our skiff, Ken and me on either side in bow and stern, snapping web from gills, shaking fish into the bottom of the skiff. As the tide moves up and down the beach, as the current swings from flood to ebb, we move nets to different locations. Later, we deliver our catch to a moored scow, pitching sockeyes into one tote, silvers into another. A tender comes and ties up to the scow, where its crew weighs each load, and its skipper leaves us our pink receipt. The fish travel on ice across the inlet to a plant we still call a "cannery," though no canning is done there anymore. Our salmon are gutted, frozen, and shipped, mostly to Japan. They're beautiful when we catch them and, we hope, still beautiful when presented on a garnished platter.

We do these things with salmon whenever we're allowed by law, regulation, and emergency order—normally every Monday and Friday through the short summer season.

So much has changed here since the days when the first Dena'ina caught salmon in weirs and basket traps and with snares and dipnets made from spruce roots. Captain James Cook sailed through the inlet in 1778; then the Russian fur traders arrived; then came the American canning industry, which scooped up all the salmon it could capture in giant traps that worked day and night in all kinds of weather, as long as the salmon ran. The Dena'ina saw their lands overrun, their food taken, their culture despised; they went from fishing for food to fishing for cannery pay or to doing other wage work when they could get it.

It wasn't until Alaska's statehood, in 1959, that the profligate salmon traps were banned, but by then a new fleet of driftboats trailing gillnets had begun fishing the inlet, chasing the schools and catching salmon in the deepwater rips before they made their way to shore. Overfished runs collapsed. The state limited commercial fishing with a permit system; only those fishermen who earned enough "points" based on experience and dependence were issued initial permits, and no one else could sell fish without inheriting a permit or buying one from someone willing to give it up. Fishing seasons, openings, and gear were further restricted. Hatcheries were built, lakes fertilized, obstructions cleared from streams. Other "user groups"—particularly sportsmen—demanded allocations. Fisheries management became much more sophisticated, involving sonar counters to track river escapements, test fishing, scale sampling, the partitioning of Cook Inlet into management divisions and subdivisions. By the late 1970s, the inlet was experiencing record salmon runs.

This, then, was the situation Ken and I stepped into in 1978, as two more fishermen to land on this shore and try to make a life around catching and selling salmon.

✧ ✧ ✧

So much has changed, and yet what we do here, along this beach, is what people have always done here. From shore, from rowed dory, from speedy aluminum skiff—food fishermen, cannery fishermen, independent fishermen have all caught salmon one at a time, have held those silver, kicking beauties in their hands as we hold them in ours. Although the web I'm picking through now is nylon, manufactured by machine in Japan, I still patch it in the time-honored way, diamond by diamond. Our corks are hard, light plastic instead of actual cork or cedar, our buoys tough plastic balls instead of sealed wooden kegs, but the nets still hang in the water and gill fish.

I stand to refill a needle, winding twine end to end while the spool rolls in the sand. Fishing's the same honest work it's always been, for hands and backs and minds, for sustenance.

It's physical work, yes—often hard. I beat up my body pulling anchors and nets and diving in and out of the boat like a seal, just trying to stay on my feet as we work the skiff in breakers that dump green water over the bow. I get seasick and vomit over the side. Other days, the inlet's a sunny millpond; the nets set without a snag right down the line and then explode with fish.

No fishing day is ever like any other: always the tide, the weather, the fish are different; always there's something we can do smarter, something more to look at. One day we spot an eagle snatching a gull in midflight, find a thick piece of Asian bamboo, and examine a salmon with deformed, gargantuan, kissy lips.

Tuned to this life, I always know the stage of tide and whether the tides are building or falling from one day to the next. At night, even at the bottom of sleep, I know the water; I know whether it's coming in or going out, how rough or flat it is, whether it's bringing us fine new sand or berms of gravel or whether it's gnawing deeper around the beach rocks. Some days, I spend hours stripping or hanging or mending nets with only the gulls cruising past, dried rockweed picked and eaten from the web, the snap of hot knots in my callused hands.

✧ ✧ ✧

When we began fishing in Cook Inlet, we had more company on this side—other fishcamps strung all along our shore, a mile or more between them. Our neighbors came from all kinds of backgrounds and held varied connections to the life.

There was a family of Dena'ina-Aleut-Norwegian heritage, another Dena'ina man whose grandfather had been the caretaker of a local fish trap, and two families of Inupiat Eskimos originally from Alaska's far northwest coast. There were white people whose working lives stretched back to territorial days and a couple of brothers with fresh-from-the-South drawls. Old people crept about on diabetic legs, and small children scrambled up the bluffs to carve their names in clay. We had among us seal hunters and skin sewers, a shoemaker, a Native corporation leader, an artist with work in major museums, boatbuilders, house builders, homemakers, oil-field workers, and a biometrician. All these folks were also, of course, fishermen, for whom summers at fishcamp were an integral part of their lives around which fit all else they did for work, family, travel, home, and inspiration.

Today, up and down the beach there are long distances between fishing nets. Empty cabins are boarded up and sliding into the sea. Most of the people are gone, and life here lacks the texture all those human lives and their activities contributed. For a variety of reasons, most of them economic, the fishing life here is no longer so attractive, or so tenable.

Most of the inlet's setnetting effort now takes place around the major rivers on its east side. There, nets are spaced regulation distance apart—often closer—all along the shore and then outward into the inlet, offshore and offshore again, in leapfrog fashion. Crammed together like that, they still fill with fish—many more than we catch on the west side. During the peak season, when salmon are rushing for the rivers, the fishermen there get extra fishing time—days and nights strung together, one extension after another. They hire fish-picking crews who work in shifts like factory workers, six hours on and six off. They use trucks and tractors to move boats and nets, to shuttle totes of ice and fish. Mechanization makes everything easier, and those fishermen go home at night and on days off—not home to fishcamp but home down a driveway off a road, in a town. They take hot showers, make phone calls, go out to eat. They attend to other business.

✧ ✧ ✧

I pull through more net and come to a huge hole the size of a seal. I stretch web over the sand so that the hole lies flat, and then I take my scissors and begin trimming. The key to mending large holes is first to enlarge them, to cut them out until you can see starting and ending points, until the pattern of remaking the mesh is apparent. I cut tails and I cut good web, leaving sides and points to the diamonds, all around the hole, until I have only two corners where three strands join.

I tie to one of these and then begin, connecting to a point, to a side; judging lengths with my eye; pinching twine; circling strands with the needle; pulling loose more twine; snapping knots tight. Gradually the hole begins to fill with new diamonds. The only sounds are those of birds, breeze, water slapping, twine coming off the needle with a plucking like harp strings, the thoughts in my head. I kneel in the sand and weave, and at last I see the pattern of the closure; then I'm back to the final three-sided corner to tie off. The hole is gone, the web remade, but my satisfaction exceeds the simple task; in a very real sense, I feel myself woven right into the fabric of the net, into the whole, webbed life that surrounds me.

Two Lakes

Fishcamp life is of the moment, in sand and birdsong and a person's solitary being, and then, too, it reaches back in time, and forward, and outward.

Late in June my seventy-seven-year-old father and I sit on tree roots at the edge of the lake. I've offered to take him out, away from the mosquitoes, in the rowboat that sits overturned beside us, but he says he's happy where he is. Ken has already left with my mother in our small floatplane; in a few minutes, after delivering her to an airport water lane across the inlet, he'll be back to ferry my father. For three days, my parents have visited us at fishcamp, chewing hard-smoked salmon and walking miles of rocky beaches. Now they're on their way, beginning their return to the other side of the continent.

"God's country," my mother called her home country a week ago, when I was townside with my parents and she was telling one of my Alaskan friends—a poet who has lived much of his life in the deep quiet of Alaska's bush—where they were from. She was speaking of New Hampshire, and she meant no irony. She's lived there all her life, and to her that country is endowed with a vast and sublime nature.

Somehow, I failed to inherit her enthusiasm for the state of my birth. All my twenty years there I felt pinched by its small-ness, by my sense that the best of it had been used up, worn out, or trashed. What I saw around me were dying mill towns, the dead rivers into which they poured their poisons, the blank faces of people who had never imagined another life. I had, I thought, been born too late. In the north country, the only bears I saw were chained to platforms and fed peanuts and bubble gum stuck into pulley-raised canisters by tourists. The polished granite basins were fenced off, admissible only for a fee, and bridged, and ramped, and painted with graffiti.

As a fourth-grader, when I had to choose a state to report on, there was only one for me; my mother still has my folder with its Alaska flag cover. Inside it are the map I colored to show Alaska's geography and major products and the pages I wrote on its wildlife and Native people, how it became a state. Alaska was new, big, and invitingly wild; bears lived there, and walruses, and people who walked on snowshoes and ate whale fat.

Whatever romantic notions I had of Alaska never did wear off. At my first opportunity—after a year in college, during which I made my first trek west, to Colorado mountains so lovely they made me ache with desire—I headed off to Alaska with friends for the summer. Deep in the Brooks Range, I wrote in my journal that I'd come to the most beautiful and perfect place on earth.

My father, in contrast to my mother and me, would never gush over any country, any place at all. He's a man who shows little emotion and much practical consideration, and if some-thing doesn't need to be said, he usually doesn't say it. He's told me he's comfortable where he is, and so he is, sitting in the morning quiet, the sun just cresting the hill behind us and beaming between trees. His white hair, unruly at the moment, sticks up like the ruffled feathers of a bald eagle, and his cheeks, three days unshaved, look quilled by a porcupine. If he seems a little more frail than when I last saw him, he also looks relaxed, at ease in his life and on this occasion. He wears his heavy, old-fashioned binoculars around his neck; these are part of his outdoors attire, part of what he puts on for his daily walks along the edge of a New Hampshire lake. Yesterday he pointed out the remains of adhesive tape on the side—my name, in my mother's handwriting. I so clearly remember my pleasure in being allowed to possess those magnificent magnifiers the summer I attended a nature camp.

This visit marks my parents' third trip to Alaska, their second to fishcamp, their first flying in and off the lake. My father must believe this trip will be his last—if not to Alaska, then at least to share this particular place with us. It's not easy to get here, and the mile-long trail from lake to beach cabin is wet and brushy and, at its end, plunges down a slick, boulder-strewn streambed. So far the summer has been particularly dry, making travel easy, but when I mention this—what good shape the trail is in—my father looks astonished and shakes his head. The trails he knows back east are built, managed, and maintained or are old roads covered in pine needles.

I grew up on trails like that, and on hiking trails in the White Mountains—undeniable thoroughfares well marked with mileage signs and bridged and protected from erosion, with other hikers just up ahead and just behind. On those long marches I imagined I was elsewhere, in a wild, unmapped place where I needed to find my own way, where I might be surprised at what lay ahead.

How is it that we find our homes, that sometimes these are the places we're born to and at other times we need to search them out? How many times have I heard Alaskans say that when they first came to this state (or that mountain-rimmed town or that tucked-away rocky cove) they had the overwhelming sense that they had at last found their home? I suppose people say this elsewhere, too, perhaps everywhere, though I have a hard time imagining a person entering an

eastern city and making this claim with the same heartfelt enthusiasm.

To me, this sense of homecoming has to do with making
very elemental connections, with responding through our
senses to something we recognize on a visceral level—perhaps
only from deep within our DNA. We come from somewhere
else, but we recognize from some remote human memory, by
that condition evolutionary biologists have come to call bio-
philia, the smell of budding cottonwood, the purple brilliance
of fireweed fields, the snorting of bears, even the deep silences
and the dark of moonless nights: the constellation of sensory
impressions that defines our true home. We recognize it, and
we want it—we need it. We need it more than we need what
we're born to, the familiar, family. We may love our people,
but we can't stay with them, not in a place that doesn't touch
us on a deep enough level.

✧ ✧ ✧

"Who cut down the tree?" My father is studying the stump before us at the edge of the lake.

Who? Ken and I are the only people who come here, certainly the only ones who needed to make room to park an airplane. I tell him we did it; it had to be done. In a forest where
dozens of trees blow down every winter and others are felled
by beavers, our removal of this one twisted spruce seems to me
a small thing.

He acts surprised, nevertheless, that we would alter the
landscape.

One tree—a necessity. I am, perhaps, defensive. I'm well
aware of the legacy of human settlement, the old story. People
come to paradise and then they cut trees, they kill things, they
change the land and what grows on it and can be sustained by
it. Then it isn't paradise anymore; it isn't a place they want to
stay. But this isn't our story. We don't pretend to leave no
marks on this land, but we don't leave many.

The flattened stump, it's true, doesn't mimic anything in nature. It betrays our presence, as does the overturned rowboat we hauled up in pieces from the beach, the pack frame hung in another tree, and the airplane itself, parked at the end of the lake most of the summer. I think of other stumps in the woods across the lake, rotted and overgrown with moss, and how it is to walk through those woods and come upon those stumps, like ghosts. It's been twenty-five years since people lived back there, in a log cabin on the shore of a smaller lake. They cut the trees for house logs and firewood; the height of the stumps—some as high as my head—tells us how deep the snow was those winters. Rather than be offended by the old stumps, we readily accept them as history, human history as a part of the area's natural history. People lived here and are gone. They had a generator, a television set, a TV antenna high on a pole. The television is there yet; in its plastic casing, it's perhaps the most enduring of what remains. One side of the cabin's rotted roof is caved in; cans are rusted; bedding has been carried away in pieces and threads for the nests of birds.

I admit I'd feel differently about this place if other people were here now, if the drone of someone's generator carried across the water. For me, part of the beauty of this place is the privacy of it, the selfish possession of space. I stare down the length of the lake to mountains that rise as white and towering as cumulus clouds in the distance. There's not a person, so far as I know, between here and there.

I recall an occasion in New Hampshire long ago, one of our many family hikes in the mountains. The trail passed through an area, I was told, of "virgin forest." I remember being very impressed by this—the concept of a place that had not been disturbed, where the trees had never been cut. The woods were not remarkable in any way obvious to a child, yet I walked through them in a sort of awe, sure that I was in a sacred, untouched place, a place allowed to find its own perfection.

In Alaska, we take for granted that most lands are in a natural state, that this is the rule rather than the exception. This is not to say that the forests here are terribly old or that they aren't dynamic. Volcanoes and glaciers are still raining rocks on and releasing the landscape, and boreal forest species—a mix of alder, birch, spruce, and understory—compete in thin and acidic soil. From the air this land is a patchwork of lakes, bogs, meadows, and woods, the outlines of eutrophic lakes filling in, deciduous trees losing sunlight to taller spruces. We know that moose are new to the country, having migrated in only when the right mix of food and shelter became available—willows and birches to eat, spruce stands to shield them from winter's deep snows.

Behind us, I point out to my father a beaver-girdled spruce, the chips at its base as big as crackers. It's hard to imagine how tools as simple as teeth can do that kind of work, and I don't know why a beaver would even take on a pitchy spruce, except perhaps to whittle down and sharpen its incisors. All around the lake, the sharp-cut ends of alders glow like white labels, and leafy branches float in the shallows. Long-dead spruces, gray and smooth as flagpoles, stand in shallow water, victims of the beavers' industrious lake raising. A belted kingfisher sits in stately profile at the top of one, then loops into flight, raspy-voiced. Small trout flip among the yellow pond lilies, and I wonder if I shouldn't have urged my father to make a few casts from the rowboat.

"There's a beaver," my father says. Sure enough, one's streaming across the lake—small brown head, V-shaped wake. It crosses in front of us, a hundred feet off. We watch it navigate among lily pads and approach a bank overhung with alders.

My father asks, "Are there beaver houses on the lake, or are they bank beavers?"

I point down the lake. It's just possible to make out an old lodge, one dug out, presumably by bears, a couple of years ago. Across the lake, out of sight in a cove, there's an active house, and around the turn, also out of sight, lies another. At the far end there's one more, alongside the dam that separates lake from creek. There are many beavers here, in this lake and the next one over and in the new ponds they've built farther down the creek, along the trail. More beavers probably live here now than at any time since the first people came through the mountains and began to club them for food and fur. No one has bothered these beavers in a long time.

Every spring we see young beavers in the inlet, as incongruous in the sea as fish might be in trees. They're there only because there's no room for them in the lakes or ponds they were born to and they've set off in search of new territory. One day we watched one head up our creek, climbing rocks and slithering through pools; the next day we saw it come back down and plunge again into the salt. It must have been turned away by the crowds already here.

"We have beavers at home, but they're mostly bank beavers," my father says. "We don't see too many houses."

I wonder if this has something to do with safety, if tucking one's beaver-self inconspicuously under a bank is safer in New Hampshire than building an obvious house. Growing up, I learned that beavers were nocturnal animals that came out only at night to feed and work on their dams. At the nature camp I attended, we waited patiently in the dark beside a beaver lodge, hoping to catch a glimpse of its residents. When at last a beaver came out, it slapped its tail hard on the water—a warning—and then was gone again. When I arrived in Alaska, I was surprised to see beavers at all hours, to know them as neither nocturnal nor wary. They commonly swim to our rowboat to take a look at us; when we had a dog, the beavers and the dog swam together, playing a sort of tag for hours on end. It was many years before I learned that beavers became nocturnal in most of America only after they were hunted and trapped nearly to extinction. They adapted to their new circumstances either by learning safe behavior or by making a very rapid evolution: survival of those who slept late.

I'm glad that this beaver has shown itself to my father. I'd hoped he and my mother would see more wildlife on this visit. Before they came, we'd had for company a couple of sea lions, rolling and diving in the inlet and barking like foghorns. On the morning of the day my parents arrived, Ken and I stood in front of our camp and watched a young brown bear stroll up the beach at low water. It came to our running line and was puzzled by it, stepping around the two lines and then biting at one. As it continued toward us, involved with the line, unaware it was being watched, I noted its pigeon-toed walk, knife-point claws clearly visible with each raised foot. Then Ken said, "How close are we going to let it come?" and we both, together, raised our arms and said, "Here we are. Hello." The bear brought up its head and stepped to the side. Only when it got downwind of us, when it must have inhaled a whiff of our unlikely and disconcerting odor, did it suddenly startle and break into a near run. Its fur was golden-brown, and it moved like something liquid, a smooth pouring of light and texture.

The beaver's recrossing the lake now. Perhaps it has fed on underwater weeds; perhaps it was only reconnoitering. In any case, it knows we're here. It looks at us with an indifferent curiosity, as a cat would. It dives once, without slapping its tail.

In New Hampshire, my parents are pleased to live now beside a lake that serves as a city water supply. The government owns most of the surrounding land, and trespassing is discouraged. My father skates over the ice in winter and keeps track all year of the bird life that comes and goes. When I visit there we walk the closed roads and an old railroad bed, and he stops to scan the waters for loons and the occasional blue heron.

There's broken glass in the water and there are cairns of beer cans stacked up after every sunny weekend, and the last time I was there someone had left a used plastic diaper in the middle of the road. Now and then, my parents foray with garbage bags to pick up litter. They love that lake, deservedly, but I always find myself wishing for bears in the woods instead of so many people and dogs, bird cooings and the kerplunkings of turtles off logs instead of the sound of trucks downshifting on the highway.

When I read Thoreau as a teenager, I was heart-struck by his comparison of Massachusetts to a book with the best pages missing or the sky with some of the stars plucked out. In his day, the eastern forests had been leveled, and Thoreau complained in his journal that the area around Concord no longer supported any wolves, bears, moose, deer, porcupines, or beavers.

I might, I realize, have understood that by my time the regrowth of forests had already changed Thoreau's grim assessments, and I might have stayed on my home ground and worked for continued restoration. I thank those who have. It's largely to their credit, along with wood-product economics and the resilience of natural systems, that today's eastern woods again shelter the missing creatures on Thoreau's list, all except the wolf. Cougars have been spotted in recent years in New England, and wolves may not be far behind, even as other threats—the spread of second homes, shifting weather patterns—develop.

In my youth, though, only that one stand of untouched forest moved me and, another time, a family visit to a heron rookery on an island. I remember thick forest and tall trees, nests that blocked the sun, screeches and a heavy thudding of wings. The ground was crusted with guano, eggshells, matted feathers, and dead unfledged birds. I dreamed of this place — primeval territory, a stepping back to the beginning, dark and smelly and wild—for a long time with a sort of awed horror, a longing for deep mystery. I dream of it still.

✧ ✧ ✧

During their visit, my parents both remarked about the work Ken and I do, what they refer to as "hard physical labor," as though they can't believe we willingly engage in it. My father's people, I remind myself, came from Welsh coal mining, and I know he feels lucky to have advanced from both that and his own father's store clerking to become a physician. On his previous visit, after we'd had a particularly good day of fishing, he shook his head and said that for the same amount of money, he'd much rather do a couple of hysterectomies.

My parents, I suspect, wonder at more than why we choose what seems to them such a tough line of work. The attractions of our modest cabin are, I'm sure, largely hidden to them. The walls are plywood, the floor's stained with outboard motor oil, and dead flies tend to accumulate along the back edge of the table. The pots and pans are bent (a bear walked on them, but I don't mention this to them), and the only refrigeration comes from the cool earth under the cabin. Our clothes are threadbare and rusty with old salmon blood, and our jackets are missing snaps. It's a small, grubby place, and if we lived like this anywhere else in the country we'd be thought poverty-stricken. But this is fishcamp, and we're rich with the simple pleasures of collecting odd stones, licking the grease of smoked king salmon strips from our fingers, and reading in bed while the surf pounds at our doorstep. When we hot-tub in the rain, we lie with our eyes just at water level and watch the raindrops bounce off the surface. Would I live anywhere else? I can't think of where.

The beaver's back again, streaming directly toward us this time. It coasts to a halt twenty feet off. Only its head, with rodent stare and twitchy ears, extends from the water. My father and I sit silently, motionless except for brushing away mosquitoes.

Bored with us, the beaver at last swims away. Though we're still in shadow, the sun has cleared the trees behind us and shines down on the lake with a blue, freshwater glow. Dragonflies with cellophane wings dip over the surface. In the distance, a woodpecker taps against a tree. I feel the calm, the sense of all being right, and I know it's this same sense my father seeks and finds on his own lake each time he stops to watch the surface of the water ripple or brighten or smells a freshness in the breeze. This we have in common, my father and I: our two lakes. Most likely I would never have come to this place, felt the need for what is here, if he hadn't shown me in his own quiet way what to look for, not just in lakes but in forests and fields, on the tops of mountains, in myself.

Partway down the lake, something catches my eye, and I point. A moose is swimming across, as smoothly as the beaver but with a higher profile—an ungainly head crossing the water like something being floated on a platter. Its long, narrow ears flick wildly forward and back, trying to shake off mosquitoes. The beginnings of antlers show themselves as knobby spikes high on the animal's forehead.

The moose has only just reached the far side, where it stands in the shallows to shake itself like a large dog, when the sound of the plane comes from behind the hill. Then the plane itself floats in over the lily-strewn neck of the lake and lands.

We hug good-bye and I see my father off, buckled safely in. When all is quiet again, I turn and make my way back down the trail. My mother, I know, will be worrying that I'll be eaten by a bear. Back in New Hampshire, she'll continue to clip any newspaper article that mentions local wildlife—the occasional moose that fixates on someone's cow, an eagle spotted somewhere, a single salmon reintroduced to an urban river—as though this will seduce me back. Homeward, I whistle my bear protection, "The Teddy Bears' Picnic," again and again.

When next I see my parents, it will be on their ground. My father and I will circle their lake and look for birds, and I'll enjoy the looking, perhaps spotting a loon or a heron, listening to the chatter of red-winged blackbirds, poking under dead leaves for the first pink mayflower blossoms. I'll think again of beavers and how the young ones go out to find new, roomier territory, and I'll be glad to have learned, growing up, what it was I needed in a place and then to have been allowed to find it. I know that throughout my life, my parents have only wanted me to be happy, and I trust that they understand, if not always why, at least that I am.

Putting Up Boat

At the end of the season, the fireweed blossoms are closed clear to their last spiky tops, and geese straggle into overhead vees. Mornings and evenings, unless there's a good wind, the gnats come out; they chew at the skin on my wrists and along my hairline. Ken and I catch the only not-too-rough tide in several days to beach our skiff, and then we crank it up over a berm and pull its drain plug for the winter.

Every year when we do this, I think of our neighbor Charlotte Hayden. When we first came to the beach, she confided in me that this was her favorite time of year—when the boat was put up. Each fall I understand a little more of what she meant. We survived another season. Nobody on the beach drowned. No boats were lost; all potential disasters were averted. I will no longer need to strain my eyes to check our moored skiff at first light or to worry as I lose sight of it behind the big fall-storm swells. We are out of the water, and we are indeed lucky in this world.

Charlotte's been dead for ten years, but in some ways I feel closer to her each year, almost as though I were becoming her. These nearest neighbors of ours—George and Charlotte Hayden—have acted as elders to Ken and me, teaching us the ways of the beach, and although we haven't always wanted to do things *their* way, we have perhaps become more like them than we ever intended.

As usual, this year we're the last ones on the beach—Ken and me and George. George's two-man hired crew is gone, and his visitors, too, and the bum knee that's bothered him all summer goes back and forth between just hurting and not working at all. Together, we pick a day to put up his boat.

✧ ✧ ✧

The aluminum dory's already on the beach when we get to George's camp, a mile and a half away. The tide had still been coming in, and sloppy, when George beached the boat, and he'd taken waves up through the motor well. The stern sits awash, and everything he's pulled from the boat—gas tanks, oars, his traveling tarp, a tote of raingear and boots, anchor, mooring buoy—lies on the beach. The gas tanks were swamped before he unloaded them, and his two outboards might have taken a couple of wave-overs, too.

We go to work. The task is simple, really. We have a puller that's like a heavy-duty come-along, and we attach its cable to the boat's bow and then crank, swinging the handle back and forth, back and forth. The boat, far larger and heavier than our own, advances bit by slow bit up the beach.

It all takes time. The boat needs to be lined up with the dock beside the cabin, and this means pulling from one point and then another and shoving the boat sideways with poles we jam under it. It needs to be on rollers, which we cut from beach logs, but it's so heavy it presses the rollers into the sand, and we shovel out the sand that builds up as berms. The boat's weight cracks to splinters one dry cottonwood roller and then another, and we cut larger, sturdier ones from spruce. We move rocks out of the path. We set up a come-along to pull the stern to one side. Ken cranks and then I crank, and then

Ken cranks again. George limps around, fetching lines and shovels and putting things away. We talk and joke, loudly so George can hear. We take off the smaller outboard to lighten the load. We place another roller under the bow and keep cranking. We stop to watch a landslide of dusty dirt fall down the bank on the far side of the creek.

I think of the times I've crossed the inlet in George's boats, catching a ride back from town or going with him for groceries and parts. Once on a clear day, from the middle of the inlet, we exclaimed over Denali towering on the horizon a hundred seventy-five miles away. Usually we were beaten with spray, and always we had to negotiate the rips—those areas where the currents bang together in sharp, pitching waves that can swallow a smaller boat and where submerged logs and other scrap collect.

We bully and crank the dory some more, and I consider the business of getting around. Back when their only propulsion was legs and strong paddling arms, and later, when outboards were all of nine horsepower, people traveled the inlet and its beaches more than they do today. The first time our southside neighbor, Gladys Elvsaas, came here, back in 1939, she and her husband were long-distance boating from the southern inlet to Anchorage with a load of beaver and muskrat pelts; later, she would walk ten miles or more to exchange *Redbook* and *Good Housekeeping* magazines with other women on the beach.

Overhead, another de Havilland Beaver drones. These big planes, from flying services across the inlet, have become a fixture of the summer's airspace, crossing back and forth all daylight long. They carry sport fishermen to inland lakes full of sockeyes and, now, to upriver sections of the Kustatan, where their paying passengers sit in lawn chairs at the river's edge and hurl lures at silver salmon. The "sports," as George calls them, fly in and out the same day, each hauling home the limit of salmon. They cover distances without, I think, really traveling. They are transported.

George's dory slides forward another inch. I'm getting to know each grain of sand along its path.

Like watching for fish to hit a net, like mending nets, like filling buckets with beach coal, putting up boats is not only a ritual of the beach but an act of *kairós*-time contemplation. Clouds move slowly across the sky; waves beat at the shoreline; George's wind sock flutters. A lone glaucous-winged gull glides past. I peel off my sweatshirt and feel the air on my arms. I know this ritual. It has history and purpose, a way of doing and a way of being. It's part of what we do here, one of the many neighborly conditions of living in this place. My mind moves back and forth through space and time. I think about splashing through rips, about Charlotte and Gladys, and about Doris, before our time, who used to winter up beyond the lake and periodically snowshoe or sled down to Gladys's camp to bake bread in her large oven. When Gladys returned in the spring, she'd find socks stuffed around her windows where Doris had tried to block the frame-rattling winds.

✧ ✧ ✧

Putting up a boat was how we began, after all, the first time we came to the beach, in 1978.

We came once by chartered plane and stayed for about an hour, looking over the camp and the beach. Although it was still only August, the fisherman whose place it was had left for the year, and we didn't see anyone else. We went home and bought the cabin, the fishing locations, the necessary permit, a dinky wooden boat, and a pile of wet nets. What we knew about fishing Ken had learned in a week of helping friends at their camp farther down the inlet; I knew fish only from working at a salmon hatchery and kayaking among the seine boats that fished an adjacent lagoon.

Still, we'd moved to Alaska five years earlier with fishing in mind. From our college rooms on the East Coast, we'd studied maps of the state, narrowing our choices to coastal towns, to coastal towns we could drive to, to towns where commercial fishing was a main industry, to coastal fishing towns that were small but not too small. I was the one who was determined to move to Alaska; I had, I think, always known I would, but ever since my visit to the state's interior two years earlier, my resolve had been absolute. Ken was less monomaniacal about our relocation or its permanence, but since we wanted to be together, the only issue was exactly where we'd land. Ken, in particular, thought he'd like to fish, while I was most committed to finding a community where the landscape would stun my eyes every single day. We picked two towns that seemed to meet our criteria and wrote for their weekly newspapers and to their chambers of commerce. We got a nice note back from one of the chamber secretaries, full of small-town pride but warning us that there really wasn't any work to be found there. We bought a no-frills pickup truck and built a camper on the back, and when school was out we drove straight to that town in ten days.

It turned out to be the right place for us. When we're not at fishcamp, we live there still.

There weren't many jobs—that much was true. We didn't become fishermen but did whatever we could that would allow us to stay where we wanted to be. For me, that meant cracking crab legs and sorting shrimp at the cannery, and then cleaning rooms in a hotel, and then trying to stay awake nights at the weather service, where I filed hourly temperature and wind reports. Ken helped out at a fledgling sports shop and changed the recordings at a volcano-monitoring station. Nights, he worked the desk at another hotel. At first we lived in our truck; then we house-sat at an off-road homestead. Eventually we bought the sports shop business and then its building and lot, and then we built a new, larger building. We ran that business, without employees or pay, six days a week for five years, in addition to always working, between us, at least a couple of other jobs. Finally we had our grubstake.

We worked hard in those early years, but we were young and we expected to. Ken and I had in common, as well, stubborn beliefs in our own capabilities—we were certain we could do just about anything we wanted to, if we just did it. Neither of us suffered any concerns about "career paths"; that was not what we were up to in stitching together our lives.

There were, of course, moments when I stood behind our store counter and wondered why I was there instead of out in the Alaska I'd come for, putting to use the boots and skis we sold. There were moments in our partnership, too, when Ken and I infuriated each other. We were still so young; in some ways we were still being formed—tempered, maybe—by our environment and by each other.

✧ ✧ ✧

So it was that we finally came to fishing. We chose setnetting because it was something we could do together, and we chose the west side of Cook Inlet because it was somewhere we could get to but still far enough away, in roadless Alaska.

We returned to the beach in September, shortly after our initial look, to dry the nets we'd just bought and figure out what we'd need for the next season. On our first day, we walked north on the beach to a substantial red-and-white building with a plume of chimney smoke and met George and Charlotte. They were the last fishermen on the beach that year.

George is a big man, and he was wearing what we would come to recognize as his trademark white dress shirt, slightly frayed, which set off the bronze of his face and forearms. Thick, white hair curled onto his forehead, which—from being shaded by his hat—was paler than the rest of his face, and his eyes were a watery, seagoing gray. He was, I thought, an icon of a fisherman, and it was clear from his first hand-shake that he belonged to his life, to the beach and the fish-ing. Charlotte might have been anyone's kindly grand-mother—a little thin, a little stooped in the shoulders, content to let George talk while she heated water and gazed from the window at their dory bucking on its mooring.

We had tea and cookies with them and learned a first few things about our fishing sites and what we could expect from them. They'd been George and Charlotte's sites before they'd sold them, and when they were theirs, George told us, they were the best producers on all their long beach. (Only later would we learn they were also the hardest to fish because of the current and rocks and that George referred to our beach as a "young man's beach.")

George took us into the back part of the building—a work-shop stuffed with old leadlines, wooden corks and kegs, and tools I couldn't even imagine a use for—and showed us a huge pressure-canning retort. Their camp was a former cannery where, in the 1940s, they'd put up in hand-packed cans the catch from a dozen nets fished six days a week, day and night. Back in the kitchen, George told us a story about a fisherman who, when asked what he'd do if he had a million dollars, said he guessed he'd just keep fishing until it was all gone. Char-lotte looked slightly pained—whether from hearing the story so many times or from knowing the truth in it, I couldn't guess.

They were finished fishing for the year, and we agreed to come back on a calm day later in the week to help put up their boat. When we left, George handed us a package of smoked salmon wrapped neatly in newspaper and said, "Welcome to the beach," words that seemed at the time to be both a vow of friendship and a sort of blessing. They were in fact both, and over the years George and Charlotte and their children and grandchildren and, later, George's second wife, Lorraine, have all been good to us, and so has the beach.

And so it was that our first act as new fishermen was helping to put up George's old wooden dory, the *Running W*.

✧ ✧ ✧

The *Running W* was old even then, and heavy. George had built her of his own design, which was, like many of George's efforts, unique. Her thirty-foot hull was shaped like a W, made to cut through the water like the usual V shapes but offering greater stability. Floorboards fit in to make a flat working surface, and openings on the sides allowed fish to fall under the boards, where they'd be stored until delivery time. Another feature was a pipe hole in its center, normally kept sealed. George used large rocks as offshore anchors for his nets, and he moved these with a winch he braced across the boat gunnels, over the hole. The line to an eyebolt screwed into the rock was passed through the hole and pipe, and the rock— sometimes as big as a washing machine—was winched off the bottom and slowly motored to its location.

George had an equally ingenious way of bringing in the *Running W* for winter storage. Using a come-along and log rollers, we cranked it partway up the beach. Then we turned it over, blocked it up, slid a huge, cylindrical metal buoy—one of George's scavengings—under it, and winched and rolled that up the beach, then up the ramp to the top of the dock.

That first year the whole operation, which took an entire day, was a mystery to me. I never grasped the mechanics of what we were doing, never anticipated the next step so I could be truly helpful. George would get a roller. Ken would tie a line. One of them would crank on the come-along. George would get a block for under the boat. He'd shovel. He'd get a pole and lever the boat sideways. Ken would attach another come-along and pull from another direction. They'd wrap a line around the boat. Charlotte watched nervously from the window, cigarette to her lips.

I felt caught in a male rite, something I decided must be linked to male chromosomes or hormones, something begun with Tinkertoys and Erector sets for which I had no natural ability and that I had failed to learn along the way of wanting to be a fisherman. It occurred to me that there were simple and essential things I didn't know and I would need to learn, things that might be hard to learn, even things about fishing I might never be able to master.

I went in to visit with Charlotte in the kitchen. She told me to sit, not to bother about the men; I didn't need to help. We talked about family and where we were from, about baking bread in peanut butter cans. I liked Charlotte and I liked what we talked about, but I was also keenly aware that her life in the kitchen was not what I expected, or wanted, for my life.

I went back out and tried again to help. The big boat turned gently over, with lines pulling it every which way, and it lifted as it was levered onto stacked wood blocks and gas drums until the cylinder, with paddle-shaped arms attached to its axle, fit beneath it. I was in awe of what time and a few physical laws, a few lines and sticks of wood, could do. I helped clear away the blocks and poles and rollers.

Charlotte fixed us lunch and dinner that day—meals she and George called dinner and supper. We ate like farmers, piling our plates with chicken casserole, bread and jam, green beans, peaches, watermelon pickles, and cake. The food was all home-canned, brought with them from Nebraska, where they wintered. Every year they traded, case for case, their vanload of canned salmon for Nebraska's best.

✧ ✧ ✧

This fall day all these years later, we crank up the *Proud Bow* inch by inch. From the first time we met him, George disdained what he called "tin boats" and said he wouldn't have one, but soon after we traded up from our shattered fiberglass model to a tough twenty-three-foot aluminum skiff, he did the same, only bigger. The boatbuilder he hired didn't have a lot of experience, though, and he apparently ran into trouble with George's design. It's an unhandy boat for fishing, with a bow so far off the water that George's helpers can barely lift nets over it. This year one of his crew went home with a ruined back before the season even got started.

We don't turn this boat over, and the puller we're using is a lot easier than a come-along, but it still takes time to bring the *Proud Bow* up the beach. The three of us do it together, although the roles have changed. Ken's in charge, setting up the lines, cutting rollers, and deciding when and how much to swing the stern. He does most of the cranking. I at least understand what we're doing and can anticipate the steps. I place the next roller where the bow will slide onto it and check the one that's about to spin out from under the stern. I get the shovel and dig away berms that build up under the rollers, and I clear away rocks. George makes suggestions, but he's comfortable letting us do most of the actual work, just as we're comfortable doing it. I tell him to be sure to see a doctor about his knee over the winter, and he says he might see a sports specialist.

George cooks us spaghetti and garlic toast, although he forgets that the toast is in the oven when he comes out again to help and it burns black. He apologizes to Ken for not having any watermelon pickles and opens a fresh jar of homemade dills instead. We sit at the table with lowered heads while he says his grace:

> *Grant us Thy grace, O Lord.*
> *Whether we eat or drink or whatsoever we do,*
> *May we do it in Thy name and to Thy glory.*
> *Amen.*

George's voice is soft and melodic, and the simple words rise and fall with a canonical resonance. George never varies this saying of grace; it's part of the pattern of his life, and of ours when we eat with him. Although my own spiritual life doesn't involve any sort of prayer, these familiar lines of George's never fail to remind me how fortunate we are to gather again at his table.

In the corner of the room, over the old rolltop desk and beside a clipboard full of pink fish tickets, hangs a photograph of a small, sturdy, fair-haired boy—perhaps two years old—kneeling over a net on the beach. He grips a mending needle firmly and enthusiastically in hand and wears a look that's at once determined and angelic. This picture, which has hung in that spot at least as long as we've been coming to the beach and probably more than twice that long, has always spoken to me about the good fit of life on the beach. Here, the photograph says, is a place that interlocks family and work and play, imagination and environment, learning by hands and learning by minds. At the same time, the picture always saddens me. The child is George's son, Buck, and although Buck loves the beach in his own way, he was also a slave to it all his youth. By the time Buck had finished and paid for college, he was also finished with fishing. A few years back, when he was between jobs, he and his wife and two of his children came back to try fishing once more, but there was no money in it, and his father was still the driven and driving skipper.

Same old story, I guess. The kid who grows up on the farm leaves for the city lights, and the city kid wants only to try living on the land. Had I grown up in this life, I really have no idea what I'd be doing today. I have a strong suspicion I would not be here. Buck has an older sister with even less attachment to this place.

While we eat, George keeps glancing out the window, watching for Grandpa, an old white-headed eagle he's befriended over the years. The bird typically roosts on a snag just outside the kitchen window and will practically feed from George's hand. We've sat many times at George's table when he's leaped up at the sight of Grandpa and run out to throw a fish head on the beach.

This mealtime, Grandpa doesn't show.

✧ ✧ ✧

The next day, we finish putting up George's boat. It takes pulling from one side and another to get it lined up for the ramp, and a lot of hard cranking. Ken moves behind the dock to pull from a monument of old cannery machinery, but when the boat's partway up the ramp, the old pile begins to creak and lean. We need to go farther back behind the camp, to anchor to a sturdier deadman, a boulder that won't move.

George thinks cable will be better than line, so he and I go off in his jitney to pick up a coil at Nick's, the cabin halfway between his place and ours where his help usually stays.

We bounce along in the skeletal, balloon-tired jitney, which has lost so much body to rust it's barely more than a seat on wheels, its exposed drive chain coated with sand. The last time I'd ridden with George was early in the season, when I went with him toward our camp to look for an anchor he wanted to borrow.

That time, as we had rounded a rocky corner, I spotted an enormous brown bear directly in our path, some distance away but headed toward us. I couldn't believe that it wouldn't have heard us coming and hightailed away long before either one of us caught sight of the other. I leaned close to George and shouted, "Bear!" At the same instant we both saw the second bear, a smaller one just behind the first, and George slowed the jitney. "I think we should turn back," I said, not sure that George would have the same idea. He began to circle through the rocks.

When I looked behind us, the large bear was still coming our way. In fact, it was gaining on us. We hit clear sand and picked up speed, and George waited for another day to borrow our anchor. Later, when Ken and I looked at the tracks, it was clear the sow had bluff-charged just long enough for her cub to climb the bank.

Today, our ride to Nick's is uneventful. George and I fetch the cable and head back. At Hightowers, where the cotton-wood trees grow, George points up the bluff. An eagle sits at the peak of a spruce, its white head brilliant against a patch of blue sky.

"Come on down, Grandpa!" George yells. He slows the jitney and makes a sweeping motion with his arm, toward the old cannery. "COME ON DOWN!"

The bird tilts its head, one old white-top regarding another.

✧ ✧ ✧

Finally the big aluminum boat reaches its balance point and tips forward onto the dock. It's up against the *Running W*, and we have to squeeze and shift to work it farther forward without knocking the old dory off its blocks or pushing it too hard against the cannery wall.

After our two days of intimate contact with the hard, gray aluminum of the newer boat, the *Running W* looks parched and tired. It's almost surely seen the end of its fishing days and maybe even had its final taste of salt. The last years he fished it, George treated it as though it were eggshell. He kept off the rocks and trained his crew to jump out in chestwaders to keep the boat from bumping shore. It got to be hard to work; nets caught on its old shoes and splintering underbelly. But it's a beauty still—the long curves, gunnels worn to a rich, buttery shine. I think of all the nets that have crossed that bow, all the hands that have gripped its rail, the loads of fish it's held. In the old days, George said, they used to catch a thousand king salmon in a season, and ten thousand "small fish." I remember the last time the *Running W* was painted—George's grandson Cade, Buck's son, was here on the dock, stroking it a bright, bright, blindingly bright orange.

I can't recall what year that was, only the image of a young Cade, all legs and hair, and the bright paint. The past for me is already starting to blur, one year and decade into another. Cade is a grown man living in Hawaii, and I feel a little creakier all the time in my knees and shoulders. I know better, too, than to ask George about dates. Five or ten or forty years all compute in his remembrances to "a few years back." Ken has taken to teasing him by doing the same thing. "That dock we built a couple years ago" refers to the only dock we ever built, our first summer, which was taken out by storms the same year.

We wouldn't build such a dock again because we learned that one won't stay in such a place. George knew that, of course, but he never advised against our effort. We might not have listened, and he probably wanted us to learn for ourselves and to find out, himself, if we had the mettle and the salt to lose docks and boats and whole seasons to the sea, to suffer the life of fishermen and not be defeated by it.

It's struck me recently that Ken has started telling stories like an old-timer, much like George, and that he tinkers with camp projects in a similarly relaxed way. They're different stories and different projects, to be sure, but there's more resemblance than I would have expected. I've noticed, too, that both Ken and George, big men, can move surprisingly fast when they need to, grabbing a net or hopping in or out of a boat. Ken is starting to lose a little of his hearing, an occupational hazard of spending so much time around motors; he will one day, I suppose, be as deaf as George. When I imagine us as an old couple, it's with me shouting to be heard, the same way both of us shout when we're with George, the way Charlotte shouted.

Watching George and Ken together, it comes to me that the source of any resemblances is nature more than nurture. We've learned from George, but more than that, we've stayed on this beach because the place fits us, just as it's fit George for fifty years. Ken's inborn nature agrees with the place and the life and is satisfied with what they offer. A more aggressive or desperate fisherman would have moved on; a slower or weaker one, or one with limited imagination, would not have survived. This is a place for using muscles, for tinkering, for scheming out new ways to fish a net. Each of the three of us made matches here; we agreed to live with the beach's rhythms and with its birds and bears and the neighbors we are. And then, of course, after the beach became home, the place itself continued to shape each of us, just as the sea rounds the edges of all rocks that roll into it.

I imagine Charlotte in the window, watching us winch the boat its final distance. In fall, her hair would be flattened under a kerchief, her permanent long ago grown out. My fingers go to my bandanna, which keeps my own overgrown hair out of my eyes. I know that behind Charlotte the next meal would be steaming on the stove. Very likely the canner would be knocking its way through yet another case of fish to take back to Nebraska. Charlotte would know by the cooker's sound, without even looking at the gauge, that the pressure was holding at ten pounds.

Charlotte, of course, lived in a different and more restricted age from mine, her life circumscribed by closely defined roles as mother, cook, and caregiver. She never fished as I fish but maintained the warm and well-fed home life of fishcamp. On stormy days in her younger years, she walked the beach and released nets from their inside ends, allowing the men to pick them up without coming ashore. Rarely, though, did we ever see her outside the kitchen, where she organized meal after meal, cookies after cake, washing and cleaning after sweeping.

Still, when I imagine her face in the window I see the tension it so often wore begin to dissolve, and I understand, as I never could have on that first fall visit or for many years after, what that means. As much as I love fishing, there's something particularly satisfying about putting up boats. Waves can smack rocks now, and I won't need to look. I can sleep at night without fearing frayed lines, rainwater to be bailed, the next day's weather. I can turn away from the sea.

Such concern about boats and boat safety, I know now, belongs to women. Men sleep at night—quickly, soundly, deeply. Deaf men don't even hear the surf. But women hear every change in the weather, just as they hear the faintest cries of children. Charlotte worried. I worry. That's our nature. If she were here today, we would look at each other and not need to say a word. Or we might. She might say, "This is my favorite time of year." Or I might. I might be the first to say it.

✧ ✧ ✧

Ken cranks on the *Proud Bow* while I stand to one side. Aluminum presses wood and the wood squeaks, a shrill, yielding protest. George tells us it's good; the boat is far enough back. A little more shifting and blocking, and at last we've got everything right.

PART II
More History of a Hard Place

A Crying Country

A Dena'ina story tells of a man who fell in love with a woman he found in the woods chewing spruce gum. He took her home and they lived together, but she ate only brush and sometimes she disappeared and came home soaking wet. One day he followed her and found her swimming with beavers. She was a beaver-woman. She led him into her beaver house and taught him to swim and to eat tender branches. When fall came she told him he could go, but he didn't want to. He became a beaver, and they lived at the lake after that. Now and then they changed into people, but most of the time they were perfectly happy to remain beavers.

I think about this story as I walk to the lake above our camp. Here, some distance down the outflow creek from the lake, the new beaver ponds have flooded the trail and opened the forest. Small purple violets tilt their heads to the light.

I stand below the first dam and touch a piece of it, a butt end of alder faceted with the cuts of chisel-wide teeth. I wonder: how is it possible that mud and sticks, none of them larger around than my wrist, can be holding back that eye-level expanse of flat, sun-glistened water? As I watch, fish surface with a sound like soap bubbles bursting, leaving tiny ringed ripples.

They're no more than finger length, rainbows that might have washed over the older dam at the end of the lake. Across the pond, a bush shakes; a bird I can't see is working through it, picking buds. Birdsong is everywhere—the wistful, burry tones of the thrush, the trilling of warblers. Water trickles through the dam like musical notes. A breeze rustles past, turning alder leaves to show their paler sides. With a crack of wings, two pintails take off from the far end of the pond and whistle across a cloudless sky.

A few years ago this was a shady forest of dark, lichen-streaming spruces and twisted birches, head-high thickets of devil's club, and mossy humps of moldering logs. Passing through on the trail, we could just hear the gurgle of the creek, buried somewhere within. Since then the beavers have spread from the lake, felling enormous trees and engineering new waterways. Their tail-flattened paths weave back and forth across our own.

Ken calls from up ahead. Always the pragmatist, he's checking out the blueberry bushes, examining buds, predicting a good harvest.

Yes, I'm coming. We're on an expedition, after all, to the lake and beyond. It's the time of year—that brief window between winter's snows and summer's explosive greenery—when it's possible to tramp in the country. Only now, before the end of May, can we leave trails behind and examine the broader landscape. We can cover distances and look at ground-level contours, see the shapes and history of the unadorned place. We are off to see what we can see.

I take a last look at the beaver pond. The Dena'ina hunted beavers, roasted their tails on sticks, and used their fur for hats and sleeping robes. They lived with beavers as we never will and knew beavers to have their own lives, as complete and legitimate as any others. It would not have been ridiculous to imagine a human choosing a beaver's life. This I think I understand, though I know little enough about the first people who lived on and around this point of land.

Kustatan—literally, "point of land." The Dena'ina name today affixes to the old village site a couple of miles from here on a south-facing shore, to the ridge that runs behind us, and to the silver-salmon river that flows out of the mountains to meet the inlet just beyond the village. To us, it also means the fishcamp and the bay and bar, the fishing sites, where our southside neighbor fishes, the area around the old village site.

For everything else it is, Kustatan is also almost surely the point of first contact between the Dena'ina and Europeans, the beginning of "history" in this part of Alaska, in 1778. Captain Cook's ship, oral accounts tell us, arrived like "a giant bird with great white wings," and one brave man from the village paddled out to the ship and came back dressed as a soldier, with a boatful of goods. The Kustataners called the people on Cook's ship and later ones the Underwater People, because they thought they came from beneath the sea. They might better have called them the Germ People, for the diseases they brought—smallpox, tuberculosis, and influenza. Epidemics decimated families and whole villages, including Kustatan.

❖ ❖ ❖

Near the end of the 1920s, the last villagers at Kustatan moved to another village to send their children to school. They went north, or—as traditional Dena'ina must have said—"upstream." Such was their directional system—established not by points on a compass but, more logically for them, in relation to the flow of water. Before compasses, people in more southern latitudes marked direction by the sun and stars, but in Alaska the sun crosses the sky in greatly varied places depending on the season, and summer nights are too light for spotting stars. Eskimos base their directional systems on positions of things relative to the coastline, and Athabaskans, including the Dena'ina, base theirs on the flow of rivers. Cook Inlet they knew as Big-Water River; they would have marked its directions as upstream, downstream, across, and so on.

This directional system of the Dena'ina was built into their entire language structure. After all, where they were and where they needed to go to find food and other necessities were dominant aspects of their lives. The emphasis their language gave to directions, placements, distances, and relative positionings might be compared to the complexity of verb tenses in the languages of cultures oriented more toward considerations of time and timing. It's a truly elegant and efficient language that can layer prefixes, roots, and suffixes into short and precise locational words.

As I move away from the creek, I think about how sensible the Dena'ina directional system still is, in many ways, for this place. Downstream the creek takes me home; upstream it takes me to the lake; upstream the lake takes me to another lake. Even before I knew anything about Dena'ina language or directions, Ken and I referred to the inlet as upstream and downstream because of the way the water flows in and rushes out on the tides. The way of speaking about the inlet was given by the inlet itself.

Languages, after all, belong to places in the same way that living creatures do. They're indigenous to the places that spawn them, both in the words needed to identify and address the particulars of that place and in the structure needed to survive there. Anyone who's ever studied a foreign language knows that even a modest familiarity with its vocabulary and grammar provides fascinating insights into the ways that a culture thinks about itself, what it values, and how it fits its origins. The differences between French, Italian, and Russian are very much the differences between the French, Italians, and Russians.

Language extinctions, then, are as tragic as the loss of any species of animal or plant. When we lose the language that belongs to a place and culture, we lose a way of knowing. And we *are* losing them, at a furious pace. Of the seventeen thousand languages once spoken in the world, only six thousand are spoken today. Most significant, nearly half of those six thousand are no longer spoken by children, and most of the rest are considered endangered. The "educated" peoples of the world communicate almost entirely in just seven main languages, as cultural and intellectual diversity dwindles. Michael Krauss, a Native language expert at the University of Alaska, predicts that within the next fifty years all but two of Alaska's twenty indigenous languages will become extinct.

At the time of European contact, the Dena'ina people spoke in five dialects. Three are still spoken, by perhaps a total of fifty or sixty mostly elderly individuals. The last fluent speaker of the dialect spoken here was Peter Kalifornsky, who died in 1993 at age eighty-one.

By all accounts, Kalifornsky—whose Russian name came from a great-great-grandfather who was taken by the Russians to their colony at Fort Ross, California—was an extraordinary man. A self-taught writer, teacher, scholar, and tradition bearer, he understood the significance of language to cultural identity and dedicated the last decades of his life to preservation of the Dena'ina language and beliefs. Although he was born across the inlet and lived most of his life there, he spent his boyhood years with an uncle on this side, not far from here. Elders trained him in the old-time ways, which apparently included a great deal of storytelling, spiritual instruction, and close attention to the natural world and the ways that people lived in it. Kalifornsky learned, and later taught, that everything has a life of its own—not just people and salmon, beavers and gnats, but every tree, flower, rock, and grain of sand, every wave, cloud, raindrop, and shift in the wind.

By the time Kalifornsky began his preservation efforts, in the early 1970s, Dena'ina had barely been spoken for half a century, erased by the American school assimilation process that forbade the speaking of any language except English. Until he worked one out with a linguist, the language didn't even have a written form.

Although I briefly met Kalifornsky a couple of times in his last years, what I've learned from him about traditional Dena'ina life I've learned in the usual Western way—by reading his books. The bible of these is A *Dena'ina Legacy: K'tl'egh'i Sukdu* (literally, "the remaining stories"), published in 1991 by the Alaska Native Language Center. These writings—with Dena'ina and English on facing pages—include traditional stories "from the time when animals could talk," historical stories, and Kalifornsky's own stories, told from his experience.

A page in A *Dena'ina Legacy* I often turn to describes a car trip Kalifornsky took through the Kenai Mountains and what he saw there. His words describing that landscape translate awkwardly into "ridge broken up into knolls, almost bare," "ridge with knolls pointing up," "ridge sloping to a point," "pointed-up mountain," "sloping mountain," and so on. He recorded another series of words for how trees grow: "they grow on the upper mountain slope," "they grow up the mountain in strips," "they grow up the mountainsides," "they grow through the pass."

It's common knowledge that Arctic people have dozens of ways of identifying and describing what we English speakers simply call "snow," but this same language precision surrounds every aspect of the mountains and trees and other environmental features that were so dominant—and important—in Dena'ina culture. As I walk these woods, I try to imagine such exact words in my vocabulary, to think about how their use would affect what I see, the intimacy with which I might know my surroundings and my place in them. I look at a fern and think "fern," but what if the word I thought were *uh t'una?* I would know then with particular clarity that I was seeing and thinking about the leafy part of the plant, in contrast to *uh,* the underground parts of the plant used for food. I might also think *etnen tselts'egha,* literally "ground's coiled rectum," and mean specifically the fiddlehead portion of the plant. With these words as my own, surely I would connect more strongly to the particular stages of fernhood and their applications to my life, would even find the humor in their associations.

Quite naturally, the Dena'ina have an entire lexicon of words to describe different kinds of streams, different kinds of trails. It makes a difference whether a stream is a river, a tributary, the outlet of a lake, a straight stretch of water, or a place of fast or slow current or whether it is covered with slush ice or overflow ice. Similarly, a trail was not just a trail; it was a packed-snow trail or a trail with snow drifted over it, an animal trail, a snowshoe or sled trail, a trapline trail or a trail used for getting wood. Although few of these words are spoken anymore, they've been preserved in their various dialects in a dictionary developed by linguist James Kari at the University of Alaska's Native Language Center.

The Dena'ina language is equally expressive when it comes to salmon and fish—not only in the names of the fish but also in specialized words to distinguish among dried fish, half-dried fish, a bundle of dried fish, fish dried in one day's wind, fish dried with eggs inside, fish dried ungutted, fish dried flat, smoked fish, half-smoked fish, the backbone of the fish, the fish belly, the fat, the fatty part just in front of the king's dorsal fin, the roe, dried roe, fermented roe, frozen roe, salted roe, and roe soup. If only I knew all these words, surely I would be that much more involved in the universe of fish and the vari-

ety of foods they give us. I wouldn't have to think about how
to describe something because a precise word for it would already exist, and I would know from the roots of words and
their specificity what was important, how one thing related to
another.

✧ ✧ ✧

Climbing uphill through a tunnel of alder, Ken and I straddle
the tracks of a moose in the center of the muddy path. We
whoop at the top, giving notice to any bears on the other side.
The lake appears, a cerulean blue, through the birch leaves.

In our life here, this is the only lake we know or need to
know, so we usually call it simply "the lake." One of thousands
of Alaskan lakes, it is not named on any map. When we began
to file flight plans with airports, Ken identified our destination
point as Hayden Lake, after our neighbor. George had told us
that other people sometimes called it that, though he never
had; in fact, when mapmakers sat at his kitchen table and
asked about local names, he hadn't mentioned the lake.

The traditional Dena'ina would have thought it extremely
arrogant to name a place or landmark after a person. Lakes
and creeks and mountains were themselves, not the property
of or secondary to people. Nor did Dena'ina in historical times
coin new names for pieces of the landscape; all necessary
names preexisted, reaching back through generations of oral
tradition. In fact, when Dena'ina place-names were collected,
a remarkable consistency was found among speakers from various communities and regions. Names were reported with care
and with obvious affection or concern for their associations. A
hill was known as Where an Animal Is Crouching because
from a certain vantage it looks like a large animal preparing to
spring. A hunting area was called Where Horns Are Gathered. The volcanic mountain I know as Mount Redoubt was
The One with Creased Forehead.

Dena'ina Shem Pete, before his death several years ago, recorded hundreds of place-names covering the vast area of upper Cook Inlet he'd hunted and fished and traveled all his life. A mountain ridge we can see from our camp was known as Ridge Where We Cry. He said about this place and its name: "They would sit down there. Everything is in view. They can see their whole country. Everything is just right under them. They think about their brothers and their fathers and mothers. They remember that, and they just sit down there and cry. That's the place we cry all the time, 'cause everything just show up plain."

The Dena'ina knew some of their lakes as Lake of Creek That Flows Swiftly, Grass Is There Lake, Overturned Trees Lake, Water Lily Lake, Lake in Which There Are Beaver Lodges, Down Feathers Lake, No-Good Lake. The lake above our camp would have had a name. It might, I suppose, have been Point of Land Lake.

✧ ✧ ✧

We cross the lake by creaking rowboat, escaping the first sluggish mosquitoes of the season. Ken rows; I sit in the stern and stare into black water, the sun hot on my head. *Plok.* I turn to see widening rings near the shore.

I look back at the dead, broken tree that always looks to me, especially in evening light, like an antlered moose. In that low spot just past it, twice, I've seen moose sunk to their knees, browsing. There, too, was where Ken once saw a giant blond bear with a dark streak down the middle of its back. Just beyond, the green-and-yellow airplane gleams from its face-out mooring. Its metallic colors hyperbolize its setting: vegetative background, the promise of water lily blossoms. The plane— like the snag, like moose and bears—is a part of this place, with a life defined in part by high wings, windows all around, a big engine, a military justification, an Arizona youth, and a hunt-guiding past. Its floats are the same age as Ken and me; its aluminum body is somewhat younger. The Birddog lands where few others will dare and spends most of the summer season tied quietly in the shallows. Often we find muddy bear paw prints along the tail, and twice black bears have climbed right inside—once breaking out the back window, another time opening the door.

Ken stops rowing, fills a plastic bag with lake water, and drinks from a corner of it as the water spurts from pinholes in its side. I trail my hand in the water, thinking *bena*, the Dena'ina word for lake. The distant mountain—*dghili*—are lost in billowy clouds. We cross the lily-padded narrows, and I look down the lily stems into darkness. Something Ken knows from flying: where there are water lilies, the water is deep enough to land a plane. The lake turns toward the beaver house that looks like a haystack, toward the beaver dam and lake outlet, toward the best of the blueberry bushes. This day we don't turn with it; we land on a point beside a clearing that will soon be filled with cotton grass.

Away from the lake, we hike into sun-dappled forest. We circle hollows of devil's club and climb over downed trees. Salmonberry bushes are already in bloom, pink petals wide and silk-smooth. Here and there, last summer's highbush cranberries are still hanging on, reduced to wrinkled red shells. The Dena'ina used all these plants. They ate the berries, but they also boiled the cranberry bark as a cure for upset stomachs and colds. They ate salmonberry shoots and flowers and made a tea from the leaves. This time of year, they ate the leaf clusters of the devil's club; year-round, they spit its chewed stalk onto wounds as a painkiller, wrapped fractures in its bark, and treated toothache with its root.

✧ ✧ ✧

We come, finally, to what we are looking for. The pit is deep—a depression in the ground perhaps four feet lower than the forest floor. It's not the pit's depth that's so remarkable but its exact rectangular shape: the outline of two rooms. One is perhaps fifteen by twenty feet; the other is a third that size. Rimmed with ridges of earth, they're joined by a break in the wall between them. Another break opens the large room to the outside.

I've been here once before, but I'm still taken by surprise. I want to hold my breath. This physical evidence—these holes in the ground, these ridges of earth—embodies what otherwise exists for me only in a mythic, nearly abstract sense. People who belonged whole to this country, in ways I will never come close to, lived right *here*.

The house that stood here long ago—before those ancient spruces now growing in its interior were even seeds—was semisubterranean, a Dena'ina winter house, or *nichił*, also known by its Russian name, *barabara*. I try to picture this one as it had been—dug into the ground but then framed with short walls of posts and logs, surrounded with sod and thatch, with a roof of overlapping sheets of birch bark or animal hides. Perhaps there was a window made of bear gut. The main room would have been the communal living space, lined with sleeping benches. The smaller room off the end would have been the steam bath, where heated rocks were sprinkled with water.

I try to see the *nichił* in snow, smoke curling from the hole in its roof, snowshoe trails beaten around it. I imagine the smell of boiling meat, sounds of people talking, babies. Winter was a time of rest. January was Month for Going About Singing.

Right now, with Egg Month just about turning to Salmon Month, this *nichił* would be silent, empty, with the countryside's new grass closing in around it. The people would be on the beach below, perhaps at Kustatan, perhaps closer to the point where we have our camp. They'd be living in less substantial shelters, feasting on fresh kings, and splitting and hanging salmon to dry in the smoke of an alder fire, beginning again the cycle of preservation that would see them through another winter.

Even hard-to-impress Ken is awed by the antiquity here— the amazing hold of the earth, this display of the work of man and woman softened by the work of rain and snow and the nibblings of voles, by gravity and sun and the slow accretion of carbon. For a few minutes we talk about what might lie under all the leaves and broken boughs, and I tell him what I once heard an archaeologist say about the old Dena'ina: they were "excessively tidy." Similar pits have been excavated centimeter by careful centimeter, and almost nothing in the way of artifacts or historical record has been found. Eskimos down the coast left a wealth of stone, bone, and clay artifacts behind, but the Dena'ina's wood-based culture recycled itself into earth and new trees. Dena'ina containers were made from spruce root, birch bark, and hollowed-out logs. The people walked about on wooden snowshoes, hunted beavers with clubs, and furnished their homes with grass mats. They did without stone lamps, lighting instead the tails of hooligan, an oily fish. They cremated their dead. The bones of water animals they returned to the water; those of land animals they burned or buried.

We could dig into the leafy, earthy bottom of this pit, but we would most likely find only fire-cracked rocks from the hearth or from cooking—cracked from being dropped, hot, into bark bowls filled with water.

Ken and I walk away on snapping twigs, moving farther into the woods. Everywhere I think I see unnatural depressions or two walls forming a right angle. I know that pits are here and I can't see them exactly or that what I see are only dead trees fallen and rotted, covered with moss. We pick our way through brush and over more deadfall. We break through spiderwebs and surprise small birds, and then we come to the rim of another pit. This one is deeper than the first and smaller:

two rectangular rooms of different sizes connected by a pass in the wall. There's no mistaking it for anything else.

I climb down into this second pit. At the end that slopes downward, the walls are as high as my head. Ken pokes around the rim for a few minutes and then, more interested in the hunt itself, continues bushwhacking for more pits.

I'm left alone to listen to the faraway cry of a jay and wonder at the breathlessness that still grips my throat. All my life I've been fascinated by abandoned living places. Cellar holes in New England's woods, the collapsed shed and bottle dump of a Colorado miner, Alaska's rotting-to-earth homestead cabins—all these have drawn me with their starkly melancholic beauty, the aesthetic of lichen-covered rock walls and weathered wood and the tarnish of an unearthed spoon. Mostly, though, I'm touched by the anonymity of what's left in the end. I always want to know: who was here and why did they leave? Was it the land that proved too hard? Weather? Economics? Did they meet with catastrophe of some sort, large or small and private?

Here, where there are only lines in the earth, and so close to my own door, the loss of inhabitants seems all the more poignant. I know so little, and there was and is so much that needs understanding. What became of the encyclopedias of knowledge that informed this exact place, akin to those of Peter Kalifornsky and Shem Pete?

To be sure, there remains the village to the north and, by the time Kalifornsky died, the beginnings of a lively cultural revival among other Dena'ina. Kalifornsky must have been heartened to see a new generation lay claim to some of what had been repressed, denigrated, and ignored for so long. His people have a language again, based on classes he began and that are continued now by others with his lessons and tapes. This learning is rewarded with college credits—even if for a time Dena'ina was categorized as a "foreign" language. A dance troupe of youngsters joyfully patches together remnants of traditional movements with songs and costumes. Others are reviving the skills needed for building fish weirs and moose-hide boats. It's not that any of today's Dena'ina are going to return to the life lived by their ancestors here in the woods, but that now they can acknowledge with pride that from which they came and are made. They can honor and adapt instead of reject.

When the city of Kenai observed the bicentennial of Russian contact a few years ago, it was the Dena'ina who insisted that the point of view of the people who were there to receive the Russians be represented. The commemorative mural painted on the side of a building views the historic moment from *onshore,* depicting the Dena'ina staring out at the Russians and their ships. The Dena'ina are drawn large and in detail; their faces are filled with emotions ranging from fear, confusion, and suspicion to wonder, amazement, and eager anticipation. They are individual and complex people, at home.

I'm well aware of the awkwardness of my situation. If the continuum had *not* been broken—if Dena'ina lived on this point still—there probably would not be room here for me. I would be like a beaver swimming in the ocean, nosing up every creek to try to find space enough to establish myself. I can't accept the notion that I never would have fit in—if not here, then someplace else in the north, somewhere I also don't belong except by sensibility and raw desire.

I shuffle my feet in the decaying leaves and consider a single spruce tree that snakes its roots over the edge of the pit. I think about how a more aware person would sense that tree—its smell and texture, the workability of its roots, the amount of dead wood it carries, its capacity to shelter one from a storm, the sound of wind in its branches, what creatures it provides homes for. Someone who observed it regularly would note changes in the tree and in each of its aspects—day to day, season to season, year to year. Its roots would be supple one time, stiff another; its resinous smell would increase in spring, and be strongest when the tree was trying to "pitch out" an attack of bark beetles.

Air cools my forehead and tangles my hair. I suck its woody smell through my nose and deep into my chest, where I picture it circling like a whirlwind in a cavernous space. *Air, tree, hole in the ground, myself standing still.* The barely cracked window in my brain seems to lift a fraction of an inch, and that much more light flickers in on my confused thoughts. I may be "getting" it, just a little—that concept of which Kalifornsky spoke, the idea that everything has a life of its own, a spirit. He didn't mean, of course, that every tree, rock, and breath of air contained a humanlike existence, something that popped in and out like an elf. Rather, in their dependence on the natural environment and what it provided, the traditional Dena'ina and other Native people experienced the trees, beavers, wind, and everything else with all their senses, as *felt* things. Those things, or parts of things, *had* spirit, that which could be known with the senses, and thus they *were*—fundamentally— spirits.

"Spirit" is probably the wrong word, confusing in its religious and ghostly connotations. We might better have translated that quality of felt aspect as suggested by Rupert Ross, a Canadian jurist familiar with the Cree and Ojibway—as something closer to essence, quiddity; that which is somehow mystical, magical, inexplicable; the animating principle, that which is *meta*physical or *super*natural, *beyond* the basic thing as it stands there in plain, unstudied sight.

I understand, yes, that there's something beyond considering each aspect of air or spruce as simple characteristics, static and nameable. If each part of nature exists in relationship to all other parts—varying with time, responding to all else, discernible by our senses—then even something as obviously "lifeless" as a rock can have a life.

My logical Western mind gets me about this far—however inaccurate, incomplete, and oversimplified—in understanding Native belief, and then I'm in over my head. I'm a product of cultures that stopped knowing the natural world by feel a long time ago. When Europeans changed from hunter-gatherer to agricultural societies, their survival depended no longer on knowing and being able to adapt to natural conditions but on manipulation and mastery. My ancestors let their spiritual lives wither like vestigial tails and developed instead mental lives focused on rational thought, involved not with felt life but with ideas.

And so it is more idea I grapple with now—that part of traditional Dena'ina cosmology that involved the ways attitudes and behaviors of people interacted with the spirits of animals, plants, weather, and the rest, and how the spirits of these things then responded with wills of their own. If respect were not shown, the fish would not come, the tree would not give good roots, the beavers would not offer themselves: these were the cultural understandings that enforced "proper" behavior.

As I understand it, in traditional Dena'ina society the ideal, the definition of living well, was staying the same, keeping all things in harmony. A person lived as his parents and grandparents lived, and he expected and desired his children and grandchildren to continue in the same patterns. The shape of existence was symmetrical, circular, revolving instead of evolving, and the goal was to turn over the place of living to the next generation in the same condition as it had been left by the last. It's no wonder, then, that Shem Pete could speak so movingly of Ridge Where We Cry. His ties there were more than personal; the land connected the past, present, and future, all the people who had lived in the country and all who would follow, on and on and on.

That, finally, is the part that clutches at my heart—the on and on and on. I know I'll never look down from a mountain or across any other geography and cry—not at how beautiful the wild country is or in generalized nostalgia for what's been lost but for those ties of which Pete spoke: brother and father and mother, history and place where "everything show up plain."

In my own history, and in American culture generally, I've seen little of that attachment to homeland. Four generations of my mother's people have lived in the same house, but the spirit has not, it seems to me, been one of commitment to the life of the place. Rather, a certain inertia is involved. I admit I've neglected—even rejected—the place I was born to and the life I might have found there in favor of this other place that speaks to me in a language of landscape. Call my choice incongruous, evasive, or something worse, and I won't try to defend it except to say I find it easier here than elsewhere to honor what I value. Here I find stories that make sense to me. Equally meaningful stories exist elsewhere, too, but I find them hard to sort out from all the "noise" of modern society, where so many people seem to plunge along with so little awareness of what it will take to leave a world fit for a future.

I'll never feel for myself what Pete or another Dena'ina could feel here, but I do feel for what has been lost by this *place*. The people who could do Pete's kind of crying here are few and far now, and the circular path, like all the old hunting and trapping and traveling trails through this country, no longer gets much tread. The culture has been diminished, and so, too, is the world diminished.

From the edge of the woods *tsik'ezlagh*, the golden-crowned sparrow, sings its three-note name, reminding me of the best I can do within my own heritage, my own inhabiting of this place. I can listen to what's here. I can look under my feet. Always, I can try to learn the connections, to live as much as I can—with whatever I can bring to it—a felt life.

Under the Tides,
Under the Moon

At the far end of our beach, more than two miles from our camp, I have one last eyebolt and buoy to put in to be ready for setting our nets when the season opens. I had to wait for the minus tide to hit bottom before I could wade from the beach to a rock pile where I replaced a plug with an eyebolt in a drilled rock and attached two lines and buoys—one I'll pull in and attach to a setline, one I'll leave as the inside anchor to an outside set. Now I rush across the rocky beach to the base of a long, curved, barely exposed reef, which reaches out and around a sort of water-filled trench it shelters. On the far end of it, there's another plugged rock—the final place I need to prepare.

The inlet is rough today, which means the water didn't suck out as far as it normally would on a minus-two-and-a-half-foot tide, and with the tide's turn the waves are hammering the reef, tossing up spray and surging through the breaks. I hesitate for a second to think about whether I have enough time to get to the end and back. Then, clutching my tote bag and the buoy attached to a coiled line, I scramble out the path of sea-rounded and mud-slicked rocks. It's like walking on the backs of turtles, and I never lift one foot until the other is firmly in place, which means I can hurry only so fast.

At the reef's end, water is already flooding around the rock. I brace a knee high against the boulder, grab the pliers and loosen the plug, and then unscrew it with my fingers and drop it into my bag. I squirt grease into the hole, screw in an eye-bolt, bang it tight with a hammer, grab the end of the line, tie it tight to the eye, and finish it with a bowline. I throw the buoy out into the water to pull the line straight, and I'm done. My leg is vibrating like a sewing machine, and the reef behind me is getting spottier.

Returning, I feel like Harriet Beecher Stowe's poor Eliza crossing a river by jumping from ice floe to ice floe.

I exaggerate. No slave trader is chasing me, for one thing, and my feet are always on rock. The surging water never even comes halfway up my knee boots. I'm in no danger of being stranded or swept away, but still, the power of the cold, pounding ocean is cautionary. The tides here are among the most extreme in the world, second only to Canada's Bay of Fundy.

Low tides here mean long stretches of exposed beach and a huge volume of water that first pours out and then floods back. Every few years someone gets stuck in the goopy mudflats near Anchorage and the tide sweeps in before help arrives. I don't mean someone's vehicle; I mean someone's *person*, legs stuck in the mud, water rising. From lowest low to highest high, the tides here move more than thirty vertical feet. Our smallest tides rise and fall ten feet.

Whenever I walk home after doing low-water work, I like to pick my way along the water's edge, just to look at whatever's exposed. For a place with a large intertidal zone, there's amazingly scant intertidal life. We have no tide pools teeming with crabs, darting fishes, or the festooned sea slugs known as nudibranchs; no rock walls paneled with colorful sea stars; no beds of mussels or layers of barnacles; no mats of algae and seaweed;

no swarms of feeding gulls; no fecund low-tide smells; no sounds of things popping, spurting, digging, or swishing. For long stretches there's only the slick gray mud and, here, in one low spot that's rapidly filling with water, the tips of army-green plants that look something like asparagus and are as rubbery as Gumby.

The sparsity of creatures is a consequence mainly of the inlet's mud and tidal currents. The waters carry such a load of roiling sediments that anything that needs to see to eat will have a problem, and anything that would live on the bottom must be able to survive the ground's being alternately washed away from under it and piled back on in suffocating layers. The migrating salmon we catch have already stopped eating; they have empty, atrophying stomachs and are packed instead with skeins of eggs and slabs of white milt. The inlet's prodigious clam beds leave off about twenty-five miles to our south, in clearer water.

The strength of the currents, even absent mud, is inhospitable to intertidal populations. Whatever stays here must have a good anchor-hold; otherwise it ends up far down the inlet, like anything we accidentally lose overboard. Cold temperatures and ice also place limits on what can live here. Ice brutalizes the coast in winter; if it can push around rocks it surely also scrapes them clean and imprisons, if not crushes, organisms that would share its space.

I pass a boulder and tear loose a clump of rockweed to eat. *Fucus*, bladder wrack, popweed, paddy tang, old man's firecrackers—it has many names, but its key to hanging on is a holdfast of tiny, tenacious roots that seem to work their way right into rock. The plant's bladderlike ends are like the filled fingers of gloves, swollen with a juicy liquid that contains its eggs and sperm. These tips have a good, green vegetable taste, slightly salted.

Here, out from the base of that boulder, where water's now

flooding in, Ken and I once found a pale sea anemone clutching a fish several inches long. The fish, which appeared to be
a small cod, was held sideways, belly-to, in the anemone's ten-
tacled mouth. Anemones—animals that look like flowering
plants—were described by Rachel Carson as resembling
chrysanthemums, their underwater tentacles waving like
petals. They capture their food by shooting stinging darts from
these tentacles, but I'd never imagined that they could trap
quarry as large as a cod. I tugged gently on the fish and it came
away easily, showing no sign of being eaten, no digestive juice
attack. I pushed it back against the anemone, which seemed
unresponsive and lethargic, and left the two of them alone, to
eat and be eaten or not.

Another time, on a minus-five-foot tide, one of those rare
occasions when the sea rolls back so far that I can walk a long
way offshore and still be onshore, I discovered a large colony
of anemones adhered to the low sides of the farthest reef rocks.
Fleshy and cylindrical, when they're out of water anemones
look, more than anything else I can think of, like the saggy
breasts of buxom old women, even to the point of having nip-
plelike ends. Some of the ends were simply knobby, while others were opened up, extending clusters of stamenlike tentacles. It was the colors, though, that wowed me. Some were
only dull tones of beige and tan, but others fairly pulsed with
fluorescent shades of red, pink, green, and yellow—solid and
in combinations. I'd wandered among them as in a flower garden, leaning sometimes to touch them, to pat their rubbery
sides. They shrunk from me, slowly, as though it took awhile
for the stimulus to connect with whatever passes for their
brains. In a sea of gray mud, I'd never expected to find such
extravagantly decked-out creatures. Later, I learned that the
species of reds and greens is known as the Christmas anemone.

Mostly, though, this beach of ours is spare, sparse—some
would say empty, even boring. For me, the limits are part of

the attraction: we get to know a few things well. The tide goes in and out in a predictable pattern; the rocks stay—for the most part—in their places; the kingfisher that lives up the creek rattles past. The rules of the beach are few and clear: stay out of the water; avoid going nose to nose with a bear; don't burn down the cabin. A boat or a plane passes and we look to see who it is. We note shifts in the wind for what they tell us about weather and the movement of fish. We know salmon because we don't also need to know cod, pollock, herring, mackerel, tuna, halibut, crab, shrimp, pigs, or cattle. There's nothing to be filtered out, and we don't. If we come upon a rubbery green shoot or an anemone or catch the occasional odd fish—a halibut or sculpin—in our nets, we stop to look it over. We pay attention to what we think we know, and then to anything that's new or different.

Instead of being beach fishermen, Ken and I could be boat fishermen. We could chase salmon, visit a different coastline or section of the inlet every opening, anchor in various bays, comb fresh beaches. We could know a little bit—maybe even a lot—about many different places. We could, but I frequently recall a Zen-like line of writer Richard Nelson's, something he'd synthesized for his own life after living among the Koyukon Athabaskans: "There may be more to learn by climbing the same mountain a hundred times than by climbing a hundred different mountains." I'm still learning from this couple of miles of spare beach; I'll still need to walk it many more times before I begin to understand even a fraction of its mysteries.

This low-tide walk, I'm content to look at rocks. Boulders and rocks and stones we do have, in glorious multiplicity: granite and slate and jadite, conglomerate and volcanic—as red as brick, as shiny as metal, as flat as coffee tables, and as round as cannonballs. They have holes worn right through them and big hunks of quartz stuck in their sides. They look sometimes like adze heads or stone lamps, although they're not; in fact, in all our years of looking, we've never found any such artifacts—not so much as a stone sinker or a projectile point. The one time we thought we'd found something—not even a worked rock but a bone handle to a knife—it turned out to be George's, something he'd lost twenty years earlier. The prehistoric culture here was thin and frugal, and the place itself casts everything to the sea, to be ground to pieces and washed away.

Partway back to camp I come upon a real find, my rock of the day. It's deep red, shiny, and smooth, with a very light pitting. It looks, in fact, like a museum piece, a cast metal sculpture. As high as my knee, it resembles a seal—or at least an artist's interpretation of the muscle of a seal's back when its head is turned. There's no doubt in my mind that this rock/metal/sculpture has been through fire—out the top of a volcano or through the atmosphere, a shelling from a far star. I've never seen anything like it, and it stands alone in a field of rocks to which it bears no resemblance, as though it must surely have fallen from the sky.

A little farther on, I stop to study the gray lines that divide black rocks into mosaics, dozens and dozens of winding curves and crossings and intersections, designs at once random and perfectly pleasing in their balance. They must be the trails of some variety of small, fleet-footed snail, but there are few snails on our beach and none in sight at the moment. Surely there are not enough to make all these lines? I can only guess that the snail tracks are extremely durable; the snails lay them down over time, perhaps mainly when they and the rocks are both underwater, and the tides fail to erase them. They are, in fact, of varying shades of gray.

Just as I'm thinking about how few snails there are, I come upon a largish, cream-colored one with a turreted shell. It's lying on its back in the mud, and I can see where it took a tumble from the side of a rock. It's hanging out of its shell, reaching for the ground and exuding a copious amount of snail slime, but it doesn't look as though it's close to being able to right itself. I pick it up, examine it closely all around, and then set it back down on rock, correctly oriented, and I think of something Annie Dillard wrote. "We have not yet encountered any god who is as merciful as a man who flicks a beetle over on its feet." There's no right and wrong in nature, she says. We people are moral creatures in an amoral world.

Then there's the Dena'ina story about the man and the mouse told by Peter Kalifornsky. The man was lazy; instead of helping his people catch fish and prepare for winter, he just walked around. As he was walking in the woods, he came upon a mouse. The mouse had a fish egg in its mouth and couldn't climb over a downed tree, so the man lifted the mouse over. Later in the winter his people ran out of food and were starving. The man walked to the foothills and came to the house of a giant, who, it turned out, was the mouse in another shape. The mouse-giant gave him fish eggs and small pinches of fish and meat and told him how to take the food home and dust it with feathers so it would become a large amount of food. Kalifornsky said that although laziness was bad behavior, the man was gentle and kind and did something good to help the mouse. That's why he was able to save his people from starving.

We are moral creatures in an amoral world, but that doesn't mean we can't yet draw moral lessons from that world.

✧ ✧ ✧

As I keep moving toward home, my eyes settle on rust spots, circular patches that bleed over the tops and sides of certain boulders and rocks. These are the human artifacts such as we have: our historical monuments, the marks of fishermen past, present, and—I suppose—future. Each rust patch, like those that helped me spot the two all-important rocks I just readied for fishing, surrounds a hardened steel casing drilled by hand into granite. The ones we use I know with a particular intimacy, and I see them with an eye that habitually checks buoys, lines, eyebolts, and knots.

It's these others, the record of unused rock anchors along the low-tide line, that interest me in a different way. I like to simply look at them and remember where they are, to note the particular stretch of beach they address and guess how someone fished there, or why, or whether we might again. Some of the old casings are nearly gone, bled out into the gritty granite. The plugs in others are rusted to a welded solidity, worn to hardened nubs. Some we know well. Some we drilled ourselves. Some we abandoned. Some abandoned us. Some of the smaller rocks, the ones that weigh only as much as compact cars, are ones George used to winch up and move out as anchors and then winch up again at season's end and move back in.

I step onto a rectangular drilled rock I've never seen before. Every bit of casing and rust is gone; all that remains is a perfect, fat-finger-size hole an inch and a half deep. I imagine a future archaeologist trying to make sense of this remnant of an earlier culture. A hole in a rock: if I didn't know fishing, did not have the whole picture, it would be hard to guess its origin. It's hard enough to imagine a person drilling a hole in a rock with two hands and a hammer, a pointy-teethed metal tube and a driving pin. The first time I watched George do it, I was amazed. Strike and turn, strike and turn. The collision sings out like a bell. The teeth grind granite to dust. The beach has rung with all this pounding. I've rung it myself.

Older even than most of the drilled rocks are the stakes, one more set of artifacts. Pounded deep into the mud and clay low on the beach, they were another way of anchoring lines and buoys. In their old age they're worn and stubby, a mix of dark, water-soaked wooden posts and corroded steel pipes. They tend to disappear and reappear as the beach shifts around them, sometimes seeming to rise up out of nowhere after years or decades. We used one of these found wooden stakes until just a few years ago, when it truly disappeared during a winter. Others we've struggled to dig out when they've been in our way, catching and tearing nets.

I'm looking at rocks and stretches of sand and mud, the geography that underlies the tides, the places where nets go and get hung up and turn in eddies, the places we steer our skiff in and out of and around. I see the lay of this land, and it's also a mapped history of the place, the chart of so many people trying so hard. There were times when this whole long beach of ours was crowded with fishermen, their nets as close to one another as the law allowed and often closer. Years ago at Kustatan, when canneries from across the inlet sent fleets after early kings, the flats thronged with two hundred or more fishermen. A cannery operated there, too, into the 1930s. I've seen photographs—a sign reading Kustatan Packing Company, a long building at tidewater, a group of workers celebrating the Fourth of July.

The tide's racing in, and by the time I reach the old line of pilings, only the uppermost of them still shows. I know how they lie under the water, though—a line of posts that march out under the surf. They're much thicker than stakes, six or more inches across, and they extend no more than a few inches above the sand. Their tops are polished smooth and are ingrained with sand that's been beaten in among the wood fibers.

The fish trap that belonged to these truncated pilings was one of hundreds that operated in state waters between the arrival of American salmon canneries in 1878 and the abolition of such traps in 1959, when Alaska became a state. This one—judging from the hefty size of the pilings and the fact that they're still here—would have been pile driven; that is, the logs would have been driven into the mud and clay mechanically. (Another type was a hand trap; its smaller poles, perhaps two hundred per trap, were set in place by hand each spring, removed for the winter, and reset in subsequent years.)

Salmon swimming along the shore here would have hit the fence of wire web that extended from one piling to the next and followed it into deeper water, through a cone-shaped weir, and into the box part of the trap. The net enclosure would have been rigged with numerous lines that lifted and lowered the bottom and sides with the tides and to "dry up" the fish so they could be pitched into boats and carried away to a cannery.

As a rule fish traps were extremely efficient, catching every fish that came their way with a minimum of effort. They overharvested salmon to a frightening degree, plummeting stocks rapidly toward depletion. They were, moreover, controlled largely by Seattle-based packing companies, which cared little about Alaskans or the long-term health of Alaska's fisheries. The canneries high-graded the choicest king and red salmon and threw away, dead, the species of lesser value as well as what exceeded their canning capacity.

More than anything, it was the greed and waste of the fish traps and their owners that led Alaskans to choose statehood. Throughout the 1940s and 1950s, Alaskans voted repeatedly and overwhelmingly either to abolish the traps completely or to transfer management of the depleting fisheries from the federal to the territorial government. In each case the power of the canned salmon industry thwarted any change, and Alaskans were finally forced into pressing for statehood in order to take control. To this day distrust of the federal government and outside influences dominates both the Alaskan psyche and the state's politics.

The trap on our beach, according to George, didn't operate for very long. The current was probably too strong here; the trap was abandoned long before he arrived in the 1940s. This was a beach that had been most easily fished with setnets.

In front of me the highest piling disappears under stone-rattling water, and I think of the men who sunk it so long ago. For a brief moment I imagine the beach as a construction site: men and barges, pile-driving equipment, some system of holding back—driving back—the water while they set the outermost pilings in place, everyone working at a furious pace to beat the tides. I see nets draped along the pilings, herding salmon into the trap, and men with rolled-up sleeves and toughened hands in the trap, peughing salmon with pitchpoles into dories. It's at once a semiromantic vision of a hardworking past and a nightmare of exploitation and destruction. Then, with a crack of wave on rock, it's gone, and I'm alone again on the deserted beach, with rough water rising.

✧ ✧ ✧

By the third week in August, the nights get dark. From bed, Ken and I watch a harvest moon rise over the eastern shore. We can only gape at its enormous beauty; it floats up over the land like itself magnified—huge and golden and in sharp relief. It looks so close that I can easily understand why the people of Europe—not all that long ago—believed that geese and swans flew there to winter on its tranquil seas.

I never think of the moon without also thinking of tides, and tonight I can't help wondering what the first Dena'ina to come to these shores made of the two. Although I'm unaware of any specifically Dena'ina beliefs about either the moon or the tides, certainly anyone living here would have readily observed the relationship—the biggest tidal ranges coming with the full and new moons, the smallest in between. The prescientific explanations I do know of, belonging to the Chinese and the Tahitians, are lovely to contemplate, for their logic as well as their poetry.

For the ancient Chinese, the moon was the spirit of water and the tides rose and fell with its moods.

In Tahitian mythology, a pair of gods created everything in the world but then became unhappy with the way things went from there. They cursed the stars, and the stars blinked. They cursed the moon, and it went out. They cursed the sea, and that was the cause of low tide. However, the earth's first woman, half goddess and half mortal, worked opposite those gods to try to save what they cursed. She brought back the stars so that they blinked *and* twinkled, rescued the moon a little at a time until it was full again, and pulled the tides until they reclimbed the beach. Ever since then, the stars, moon, tides, rain, and trees, and all the other things in the world that come and go or cycle through different stages, continue in those same patterns, balancing between the curses and the kindnesses.

Other ancients, according to Rachel Carson, attributed the tides to the breathing of an earth monster. Leonardo da Vinci tried to calculate the lung capacity of such a creature.

Big inhalation, big exhalation, regular and forever. I can imagine my predecessors on this beach assuming that the moon, with a will of its own, was simply following those breaths, signaling the tides. This signaling was surely helpful to them, as it is to us. "Uh-oh, the moon's getting bigger. We'd better move our stuff higher up on the beach."

I have to look beyond Dena'ina territory, but not too far, to find a regional story to explain the origin of the low tide. Not surprisingly, it stars Raven, that mythical creature of the Pacific Northwest and much of Alaska. In a cycle of Raven stories belonging to the Eyak people of Prince William Sound, "Raven and the Owners of the Tides" tells that in the beginning the tide was always high. Raven was hungry because he couldn't get to the food hidden by the water, so one day he took a prickly sea urchin to the house of the old woman who owned the tides and stabbed her bottom with the urchin's spines until she cried out and made the tide go down. After that, the tide always went up and down and Raven found enough to eat. In another version of the tale, from the same region, Raven acted more kindly. He visited the home of the old woman who kept the tides and asked her if she would make them go down so he could get some clams to eat, promising to fix her sore eyes if she would. She tried hard and eventually got the tide down, and Raven made her eyes better.

We modern folks know, of course, that the tides are a response of the earth's oceans to the gravitational pull of the moon and sun and, in theory, of every other planet and star. Before there was water, the earth's molten liquids were pulled back and forth; in fact, it's thought that the moon was formed when big sun tides and the earth's own oscillation combined with such force that a great wave was torn loose from the earth and spun into its own orbit.

These days it's the moon, because it's closest, that exerts the most pull on the earth's waters. When the earth, moon, and sun are lined up we get the greatest pull, and when they form a triangle, the least. The exact workings of the tides are enormously complicated, depending on such things as the distance from the earth of the sun and moon and their positioning north or south of the equator. Most significant, though, is that every body of water has its own period of oscillation; that is, although the force of the moon sets a particular basin of water in motion, the exact motion is determined by the shape and depth of the basin, and the movement of the water varies within it—less in the middle, more extreme at the ends.

Cook Inlet is a long, skinny, shallow basin—thus its extreme tides. A lot of water moves through the narrow entrance where it opens to the Gulf of Alaska and has only hours to fill all the way to its northern end. It's no accident that the Dena'ina name for the inlet was Big-Water River and that Captain Cook, in his inlet explorations, thought he was sailing up a river. A disoriented visitor to our camp, just flown in from Massachusetts, took one look at the inlet and asked, "What river is this?" The tidal current moves like a river—six to eight knots at our camp—and, curiously, as part of the inlet's counterclockwise circulation pattern, mostly runs *out*.

There is, of course, the water pouring out of rivers to add to the outgoing tide, but that alone can't explain why the outgoing tide at our camp runs much longer and harder than the incoming tide. Although the tide on our beach rises for roughly six hours and then falls for roughly six hours, at the same time it's rising on the beach, it's running out just offshore. Out of every twelve hours, the boat on the mooring is pulled up the inlet for about four hours and down for about eight, and when it's being pulled down, a wake forms behind it. Similarly, nets on most of our beach will fish well for only four hours of flood tide; for the other eight hours, they'll flag out in the current, their leadlines yanked right to the surface. There is no slack tide—only the moment when the tide turns from flood to ebb or vice versa. A net fishing in the shape of a crescent turns, cork by cork, from its outside to its inside end, first into the curve of an "S" and then into the opposite crescent.

✧ ✧ ✧

When I go out later that harvest-moon night, the moon hangs high, shrunken to a coin. Its cool, white light bathes the hillside, the ribbon of beach, the wide water. The skiff on the mooring is all sharp edges and glint. My shadow lays itself across the porch, so sharply defined I can see every kink in my hair. After a tub I slept on my wet hair, and now I look like

Medusa, or at least snaky-locked, like one might have looked had she sat for a cut-paper portrait and been snipped into a black silhouette. I extend my hand and cup light into its palm; the light has a quality like mercury—silver, rounded, both solid and liable to slip away. I spread my fingers, turn my hand, and watch its shadow thin to a blade.

In the inlet, salmon circle in bays or stall in current with wagging fins while they engage in fish sleep, or they move along the coast under the moonlight. When far out at sea, salmon migrations are thought to be ordered by electromagnetic forces, but once in the inlet and approaching their natal streams, salmon apparently begin to steer by some combination of rheotaxis—orienting to the flow of water—and an ability to detect subtle temperature changes and combinations of smells. A salmon's sense of smell is said to be thousands of times sharper than a dog's.

The moon plays a separate role in salmon movements, cueing them with amounts of reflected light about *when* to move. The largest migrations of salmon fry and smolt from freshwater into the sea correspond to the time of the new moon, when the moon floats invisibly between the earth and the sun. We say the salmon are moving under the cover of darkness to avoid predation, but the more exact truth is that they're driven by a growth hormone that readies them for salt water, a hormone triggered by the lack of light. Migrating adult salmon, meanwhile, tend to move less at night than during the day. Fishermen know this from monitoring their nets, and they know, too, that among the salmon species, silvers are most likely to travel in the dark. This may be because silvers are largely a fall fish, migrating late in the season, when the days are shorter, and so have adapted to needing less light.

I take a last look at the moon, the very same one that shone on the long-ago Dena'ina, on the pile drivers and fish peughers, on generations of salmon. It shone, too, and still shines, on Europeans and Chinese and Tahitians, on the Eyak who know about Raven. In our separate times and places, there isn't much we've witnessed together—only our single sun, the scatter of stars, that round or sliced or darkened orb moving through its phases, and the overarching vault of heaven. Tonight the moon, tugging quiet water down the inlet, has me in its hold. Millions of years after the ancestors of land dwellers first crawled ashore, my blood remains as salty as the sea. I am eighty percent water, and my cells bulge toward the moon.

Staying Alive

"It was a full-time job just keeping him alive." George has told us this probably a hundred times, every time he talks about Dick Langley, the man who built our cabin and fished our beach for ten years in the 1960s and 1970s. "But he never knew that. He just never knew at all."

Langley is coming this summer to visit. He hasn't been back since 1977, and he's bringing his wife and two children as well as a friend who fished with him for part of one summer and *his* wife and three children—nine of them, driving from California. Now that George has decided to sell his place, he has invited them for a last-chance visit.

We've never met Langley. We bought what had been his— the fishing locations, the camp, the old boats and nets—the year after he left the beach, from the man he sold them to, who had held them less than a year. But we feel we know him or something of him; certainly his presence has always been with us. Every piece of lumber in the cabin—every sheet of plywood, every two-by-four he'd had tendered in, already cut to size and ready to assemble—has *Langley* written on it in dark Magic Marker; we can't turn around, can't flip our futon, can't look under the cabin for a shovel without confronting the image of the man. We still wear his clothes and dry our-selves with his towels, and it was only a few years ago that we finally used up the many boxes of powdered milk he'd left be-hind.

Then, too, we know Langley through George's stories. We know that once at the end of the season when he left George's place after dark, he was chased by a brown bear into the inlet, right up to his neck. Minutes later, as he stood in George's kitchen, dripping wet, his only comment was, "The worst thing about this fishing is that you have to wait all winter to do it again." George insists he's never known anyone before or since who loved everything about fishing quite so unre-servedly, who was so relaxed about it all, so simply *fun* to be around.

But then, whenever we're tempted to make do with an old part, a temporary fix, an untrustworthy line, we remember George's head-shaking. Langley, he's also told us many times, would use any old scrap of beach-scavenged rope to tie his boat or anything else, and then he'd be surprised when it broke.

The day he announces the impending visit, George tells us again about the time Langley nearly drowned. It's my under-standing from what George has said in the past that this was why Langley left the beach—that he finally came too close to dying. It's also my understanding that it was his wife who had the good sense to insist he quit.

George's story is this: Langley rowed out to his dory on the mooring but, in climbing from the rowboat to the dory, some-how fell overboard. His wife saw the overturned rowboat being swept away in the current but couldn't see Dick. She ran all the way to George's, and she and George came back down in his boat to find Dick ashore, barefoot and in his underwear. He'd shucked his belt, pants, and hip boots before the boots could fill with water and pull him under.

I've known this story from, I think, year one. I think of it every time Ken or I make the passage to or from the mooring, with every step from one boat into the other. Ken makes most of these passages, and he won't wear any kind of flotation clothing. He likes to say that in Alaska's cold water, the only reason to wear a life jacket is so that your body can be recovered. He's right to the extent that those who die here don't so much drown as succumb to hypothermia. The cold saps a person's strength so quickly and thoroughly that it becomes impossible to swim or tread water or even to hold on to the hull of an overturned boat. But it's also true—as I never stop reminding him—that most people who die in cold water are not wearing life jackets. They disappear below the water, dragged down by water-filled boots and soaked clothing, and they don't come up again until their bodies bloat, if ever.

❖ ❖ ❖

To me, the story of Dick Langley's near drowning has always been emblematic of the human culture of this place—at least of that hard part of it that results from missteps, failure to pay attention, or simple bad luck. From Kustatan around our point and up past George's, along the beach and offshore as well as inland, so much of what has transpired here over the years, for human inhabitants no less than for other creatures, has had to do with trying to stay alive. There's tragedy enough to go around, and I'm sure I don't begin to know how much it is and how far it goes.

I do know that this has been a hard country forever, surely since the Dena'ina first arrived on these shores. When the land across the inlet became known to them as *Yaghanen*, The Good Land, it must have been so in contrast to this side—as a place of greater resources, smoother terrain, and milder climate. In *A Dena'ina Legacy*, Peter Kalifornsky recounts the story of a long-ago famine among the people at Kustatan.

"What they had put up for winter was gone. There were no moose or caribou. Black bear and porcupine were all that was left. It snowed repeatedly." According to the story, two men went to look for something to eat along the flats toward the river. When they stopped to drink at a slough, they fought over a last bit of dried fish, and one drowned the other. After that the slough was always known in Dena'ina as Where Someone Shoved a Person Under Water.

The abandoned village of Kustatan is today only depressions in the earth, and the cannery that fronted the beach into the 1940s is recalled only in the name of a fishing site—Cannery Set. Just the same, fishermen—Native and white, in greater or fewer numbers, in cutthroat competition and in kind neighborliness—have continued every summer to fish the beach and sandbars there and around our point and into the bay to our north. South to north, I know these heartbreak stories:

❖ One fall in the 1940s, a moose-hunting party from Kustatan hunted around the upland. They mistook for cow parsnip the deadly poisonous water hemlock, and two men died after eating portions of the plant. Water hemlock has been called the most violently poisonous plant in the whole North Temperate Zone; its victims suffer extreme stomach pain and convulsions.

❖ By our time, only one family fished at Kustatan. Some years earlier, one of the sons—a boy described to me as a tall kid with large hands—had drowned in the lake above their camp. He'd had a particular fondness for the lake and spent all his spare time there, rowing around in a punt. He fished for trout, followed the beavers, sang back to the loons. One day he didn't come home, and his family found the punt overturned in the lake. His drowned body was recovered later, but the family never pieced together what had happened, why the lake had claimed a strong boy who loved it and could handle the punt as comfortably as a part of his own body. In the unlikely event of a capsizing, he should have been able to swim his way clear.

✧   Our neighbor, Lou, fished the rock pile between Kustatan and our beach for about ten years. Of all the fishermen I've known, he is the one who most loved to fish. Fishing days, he'd be on the water hours early, looking and waiting, and he kept his nets in perfect repair. When we got together, he talked fish just as the most obsessive baseball fan talks baseball. After his wife left him and his teenage sons found girlfriends and work they liked better, he fished one summer with his ten-year-old, Emmet. One sloppy day we came around our point and spotted his boat against the beach, filling with waves.

Lou had come in on one of his setlines to set a beach net but had caught a wrong series of waves, and when the boat reared up Emmet hadn't been able to hold it with the setline. The line— which, as a good fisherman, he knew he should never let go— flipped him overboard, and then the boat turned and filled with the next wave. It rose up and crashed down, very nearly on top of Emmet.

When we found them, Emmet was dancing almost giddily along the beach, trying to stay warm in his soaking, stretched clothes, and Lou, a diabetic, was sitting on a rock with his back to the inlet, stuffing himself with cookies to bring his blood sugar level back under control. Dead salmon from their catch were washing up behind him like chunks of silvery wood.

Lou had swamped his boat a hundred times, destroyed props and torn up nets in the rocks, and never caught enough fish to begin to pay off his fishing debts, but it was the specter of losing his son under tons of boat weight that was more than he could take. He didn't fish again.

✧   Freddie Bismark once fished our point until a single storm wiped out his skiff, his motor, and all his gear. Afterward, his cabin fell into the sea.

✧   When we first visit George every spring, he gets out his guest book. No one comes to the beach without signing, and everyone signs every year.

One year I opened the book and turned to the end. As usual, I looked back up the page to see if we were the first visitors of the year, whether anyone had come in the fall after we left, and who'd visited the previous summer that I might have forgotten.

The last two signatures were from shortly after we'd left in September. They were the names of two men, each on a wide line, written in bright blue ink. George had penned in the margin next to them, connecting the two, *Drowned*.

I had known this already, had heard it on the news when it happened and had talked to George about it by phone during the winter; still, seeing the names and notation gave me pause.

The two young men, traveling in a skiff, had stopped and visited with George and then headed south to a bay where they planned to fish. The weather was still a little rolly after a storm, and they anchored their boat and began to row ashore in a dinghy. A woman standing on the shore saw the dinghy turn over but never saw the men come up, and when she went out in a kayak she still didn't find them. Their bodies were recovered later.

I stared at the signatures in George's book for a long time. They were so young looking, so politely set on the page, so blue. One pointed with a cramped slant; the other was looped with Catholic-school neatness. They were undoubtedly the last words the two men had written, the names they'd surely assumed they'd be affixing to fish tickets and checks and postcards from faraway places for many decades to come.

✧ At the north end of George's beach, at a place known as Coal Gulch, there's an old flat-roofed log house where no one has lived for a while. A fishing family by the name of Tapp spent the winter of 1963–1964 there. That was the year of the Good Friday earthquake, when spruce trees bounced their branches up and down against the earth and the Tapps, with their two small daughters, climbed the bluff to wait out a tsunami that never came. But mostly it was just a miserably cold winter in that uninsulated, poorly equipped cabin on an ice-heaped, blowy beach. As George tells it, they spent every day gathering wood and every night turning themselves around a barrel stove; even though the stove would burn red-hot, their backsides were cold, and water left on the floor froze. Ken Tapp lost sixty-five pounds.

✧   The next family up the beach from Coal Gulch had four sons and lost three to alcohol-related tragedies. The one who died at the beach put a drinking companion ashore and went to moor the boat. A neighboring fisherman saw him fall overboard. After a search involving people from up and down the beach and Coast Guard boats and helicopters, his body was found, rolling like a log in the surf.

✧   A tender loaded with our fish sank as it crossed the inlet, so fast the skipper barely got off a Mayday. He and his crew were res-cued from a small plastic dinghy belonging to George that they'd attempted to deliver to him earlier that day. George had told them to keep it until another time; he'd seen no other safety equipment aboard and thought they might need it more than he did.

✧   A single-engine plane, pushing for home, ran out of gas and went into the inlet very near our camp. No wreckage or bodies were ever found, but whenever I come upon a rubber boot washed up on the beach or a twist of riveted aluminum caught in the rocks, I think of the two little girls—the pilot's daughter and her friend—who were aboard. They are skeletons still strapped into their seats, and the pilot will never have another chance to re-consider the high price of gas in Port Alsworth.

✧   In the woods above our camp, a trapper's cabin not much higher than a coffin rots back to earth. The man's name was Slim Welch, and he's remembered for eating out of the same pot as his dog. Trapping was his first love, but he also fished at Kustatan. He once put a pistol in a man's face when he believed the other man's net was "corking" his own, intercepting fish he wanted for himself. So anxious was the other man to pick up his net and get out of the way that he cut his own anchor line. "Nobody fooled with Slim," someone who once fished with him told me, still chuckling.

Close by the old trapping cabin lean the gray and crumbling walls of a later and more substantial cabin that belonged to Jim

Haynes. Haynes, another Kustatan fisherman, tried to homestead above the beach. He dragged his cabin logs with a workhorse he brought to the beach on a barge and kept in a corral above Kustatan, where the old village used to stand. Children in the area would wait for him to go fishing and then release the horse from the corral and ride it. When the season ran out, Haynes shot the horse. He never proved up on the homestead despite attempting to fulfill the planting requirement by buying and sowing wild grass seed, to grow more of what was already growing on the hill. Haynes was also famous for bringing the first bathtub to the beach. He tried to tow it ashore with his skiff, but he had forgotten to put in its plug, so it filled with water and sank. It's still out there somewhere, along the Kustatan bar.

Not far from there, on the south side of a lake, lie the remains of yet another cabin, its roof fallen in, its logs disintegrating around strands of pink insulation and lengths of plastic-coated wire. At its center, under the sky, a television set bears witness to the slow collapse, the return to earth.

Here lived Chet and Doris, who used to fish where Lou fished, before Mark and Sandy but after the Nickanorka family. Their beach cabin slid into the inlet years ago. This cabin was their winter home, to which they came, like migrating birds, at the end of each fishing season. Here they faced southern sunlight, caught fish through the lake ice, and traveled on snow. It was how the Dena'ina had always lived, moving back and forth with the seasons, and Doris was Dena'ina, from the village farther north. In the butt ends of the cabin logs on either side of the door, .22-caliber shells had been pounded to spell out initials and dates— both sets of initials on one side with 1958 and just Chet's on the other, with 1973.

They've both been gone a long time now. They left the cabin in a hurry when one of them was sick, and they didn't pack much to take with them. With each year, parts of the cabin and all they left behind move outward and downward, like scattering bones.

The first time I visited the cabin, in 1984, half of the roof was still in place, with a bleached-white wooden sled laid across it.

Ptarmigan wings were nailed beside the door, and a moose rack was mounted above it. Inside, I looked through a spruce-root sewing basket and marveled at the work in a bedspread knotted from fine colored threads. There were more colors in it than I could count, and it unfolded to a great length, as though Doris had never wanted to quit. In a land of whites and grays, it must have held the very meaning of color.

I looked at the toothbrushes they'd left behind, at the ice cream maker and the single silver Christmas tree ball.

Now the ptarmigan wings are only tiny bits of fiber preserved behind nail heads, and the moose antlers lie on the ground, lichen covered and vole gnawed. The sewing basket's rotted to nothing, freeing its hard buttons, and the bedspread is nowhere to be found—no doubt integrated, with scraps of insulation, into a thousand bird nests.

The woodshed's still full of rotting firewood; the cribbed well is full of cool water. The dog's house is collapsing, but the dog's chain remains attached to the tree.

That first time, I'd looked at the dog's chain tied to a spruce and how the tree had grown around it, burying the chain and toughening over it like scar tissue. Where the chain dropped to the ground, it disappeared into needles and leaves, the soil that had built up over the years. I was interested in learning how quickly new earth developed in such a place, so I pulled on the chain, and dug at it, and gradually tore it from the ground. I reached the chain end and, at the end, discovered the dog's own skull.

❖ ❖ ❖

Drownings, other deaths, abrupt and defeated departures, disasters narrowly averted: this history is context for the return of our predecessor, Langley—who, we've always believed, left the fishing life before life got another chance to leave him. We're curious to find out what kind of person Langley is and what he thinks now, looking back on his adventurous and possibly perilous youth.

It's late August when George finally hears from Langley and his party. The nine of them and a dog are across the inlet, ready for George to fetch them in his dory.

The water's too rough, and George doesn't cross.

But the next day, as we're eating lunch, we hear voices and look outside. For weeks we've seen only George or one of his helpers and, one night under moonlight, three passing bears, but now the beach is alive with movement and color—all nine of them and the dog, a plethora of flapping orange and yellow, raingear so new it still shows creases. I feel almost blinded by the sight.

George had crossed for them that morning, and they'd lost little time in walking down to see their old place. We visit in drizzle, and they exclaim over changes to the beach—the thick growth along the creek and up the bluffs, the eroding banks, the presence of seaweed and beached jellyfish. Barb Langley looks down the beach at Red Rock, the inside anchor for one of their old fishing sites, and exclaims, "It moved!" Surely it looks that way. The boulder used to stand very near the top of the beach, but the eroding bluff has moved back and back, adding yards of new beach. These days, any high tide rises past it; years ago, we moved our set well to one side.

Dick Langley looks much as I'd imagined him—a lean, boyish man who exudes enthusiasm. Wisps of silver hair poke from under his baseball cap, and a mustache shadows the top of his lip. Retired as an electrical engineer, he now buys, renovates, and sells houses. He and Barb, who wears a practical short haircut and tiny turquoise earrings that catch the light as she tosses her head, share an easygoing manner that I can only characterize as "Californian." Their children, too, ages fourteen and eleven, are long limbed and sun browned, fairly golden.

I learn that Barb spent six summers here and that much of that time she fished with Dick. Why did I think she'd come only one year and hadn't been an active fishing partner? George rarely mentioned her.

All eleven of us crowd into the cabin. Dick and Barb exclaim over the cabinets (from his parents' farm), the set of bowls painted with chickens (likewise), the curtain (faded but otherwise the same as when they'd hung it), the pair of mud-colored, formerly black-and-white rugs (from Dick's boyhood bedroom). The Langley children are astonished to see their name written on every rafter. We give permission for everyone to take a turn up the ladder for a look upstairs, and we hand around eagerly received strips of smoked salmon.

We talk fish. They want to know how many fish we catch, where we put our nets for sites, how much fishing time we get, and to whom we deliver. We want to know how many fish they caught and how they ever managed to fish out of the tipsy little wooden boat Langley had built from a design of George's. We replaced that boat with a pair of fiberglass skiffs our first year; the only time we'd tried to pick fish into it we felt at risk for our lives.

We discover that they caught about as many fish in a season as we do but fished more leisurely, using just three beach nets and pushing the boat with a nine-horsepower motor, taking forever to ferry a boatload to a scow anchored off the north end of George's beach. They can't believe how hard we work for our fish—the number of sets we make in a day—and that for all but a couple of years we fished without a scow, holding our catch in our boats and waiting up half the night for a tender.

There's so much to talk about—the beach, the lake, neighbors now gone, bears, George, boats and motors, fish. It's as though we're long-lost relatives with a generation of catching up to do, but instead of family what we have in common is this place and its constant yet ever-changing life.

It becomes clear that Dick and Barb loved the beach and that both of them are nostalgic for the life they had here. And then it becomes clear that they're maybe half serious about taking up the fishing life again. When they learn that the eight camps north of George weren't fished this summer, they're at once very interested and suddenly skeptical. Perhaps it's a buyer's market, or perhaps only romantics and fools can make a case for fishing here in the 1990s.

I try to reconcile these clear-thinking, capable people with my goofball image of a Langley who required George's full-time effort to keep alive. And I can't quite see Barb, this former schoolteacher, as hysterical, running to George's instead of grabbing a line and a float and following the current that carried her husband away.

The next day, walking with Barb on the windy, wave-beaten beach, I ask her about the time Dick fell overboard.

She doesn't suck in her breath or avert her eyes. She tells the story, matter-of-factly. Just as George had said, she'd watched Dick row out to the mooring, and then she saw the overturned rowboat floating away. While she ran to George's, Dick's helper followed the current along the edge of the shore and watched for him, and Dick's mother, who was visiting, prayed. When Barb returned with George in the *Running W,* Dick was ashore. He'd kept—as she put it—"a cool head" and let the current carry him toward the point before trying to swim in. She and George went on and recovered the rowboat.

I adjust myself to the appearance of these two new characters in the drama and say something about how frightening it must have been and how I've always feared what might happen if either Ken or I ended up in the water. "And that," I ask, "was why you quit fishing?"

It's not so much a question as a statement looking for confirmation, and I don't expect her to answer so immediately and dismissively, "Oh, no. That was several years earlier. We hadn't been fishing long then."

For a minute I'm taken aback, at a loss for what to think. "Then why did you quit?"

Barb squints at the inlet, at waves tossing foam. It's not a day for either fishing or crossing, but I don't think that's what she's seeing. The Langley party seems to have vague plans to leave the next morning; Barb and Dick both act as though they're either unaware or unconcerned that typical fall weather could keep them here for days. "The reason we gave up fishing," she says, "is that we weren't making ends meet. We needed year-round work." She goes on to tell me how the money from the sale had bought them a duplex.

I think about this new information, my mind rearranging facts and adjusting years of misunderstanding, faulty beliefs, and assumed fears. In the end, it was only money that drove them away.

After a while Barb says, "I'm surprised George told you about that."

I look at her, surprised that she's surprised. George is full of stories, and surely there's relevance to one about our prede-cessor nearly drowning. The tale has guided my life here all these years, all my steps from rowboat to skiff and from skiff to rowboat, all my choices in clothes and knives, all my nagging at Ken to wear a life vest. I don't say this; it sounds too melo-dramatic. I do catch something in her face, though: a neces-sary toughness.

"You know," Barb says, sounding defensive, "George has been in the water a few times himself. I remember once when he was in for a long time. I remember being up there in their kitchen, rubbing his feet to help warm him." She pauses be-fore continuing, more kindly. "I suppose no one likes to talk about those times of their own."

"No," I offer. "I don't suppose so." I recall now, very vaguely, once hearing something about a time when George swam to shore. It's not a story George tells or one I want to ask him about. How much easier it is to think instead that these close calls happen only to someone else—to the accident-prone, the ditz, the klutz, the user of rotten, old line. Perhaps we need that much reach, a separation between experience and lesson, or we would tremble at every possibility. Our mythmaking begins with demons, gods, and strangers.

Barb spots the belugas before I do. At first I think she's only seeing whitecaps, but then I recognize the sleekly surfacing backs. It's a small pod heading south, females and young ones, the blue-gray babies tight against their mothers' sides; they all rise and dive together in a slow, connected rhythm. I've never seen belugas traveling in such rough water and have often wondered what they and the seals do at such times, how they manage to surface and breathe among such tall and wildly pitching waves. Do they never get knocked by an unexpected breaker, never inhale water by mistake?

We watch the whales until they're out of sight, and then I notice Ken and Dick standing together farther down the beach. I can tell from their serious demeanor and their gestures that they're talking fish, sets, and technology. Ken picks up a stick and begins to draw something in the sand. He's showing Dick where we fish, or maybe how he sometimes ties the leadlines to keep the net bunched when the current's running. The others, the Langley friends and all the kids, are back at George's—baking bread, listening to stories, driving the tired, old jitney around like a beach buggy.

It feels good to have these people on the beach with us, all of us very much alive and well in this hard and beautiful place, this marvelous world. Barb and I, knowing what we know, walk toward the men.

PART III

Living by Fish,
Surrounded by Water

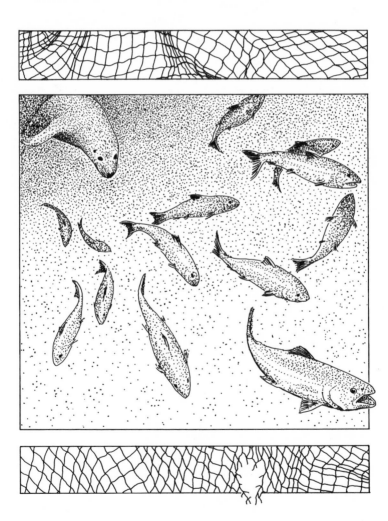

First Fish

Very carefully, avoiding its teeth, I slip my gloved hands into the salmon's gills and hoist it onto our fish-cleaning table. Thirty pounds, perhaps—a stout, barrel-sided king salmon— our first fish of the year. I hose sand from its side, admiring the silver-gray scales that overlay one another in perfect, shining symmetry. This king is fresh from the far and wide ocean, mirror bright, with flaring, nick-free fins. The moist, ringed eye in its enormous head seems to regard the entire sky. I slide my fingers along its spotted back just to touch, to feel, perfection, power.

Then I take my serrated knife and cut the fish's throat, gill to gill. Bright blood pulses out to drip like thickening jelly into the sand.

Later, I pull back wet burlap from around the fish, rinse it again, and scrape a dull knife over its sides until all the phlegmy, bacteria-filled slime is drawn out of the skin and washed away. Ken sharpens the long fillet knife and cuts close behind the head, removing one fillet and then the other with practiced sweeps of the knife. The pinbones yield with small, brittle snaps. He cuts the belly strips off separately and the scraps along the bones, not wasting even the tiniest bit. The meat is red and firm, with thick layers of fat.

I carry the bucket down to the water and toss the carcass into the sea. Small swells roll the head to the surface a couple of times and pink, spaghettilike innards stretch toward the beach; then the current pulls it all under and away.

❖ ❖ ❖

We eat king salmon fried in butter and garlic, with a pot of brown rice and a salad of beach greens and fireweed shoots. There's no meal I like better, unless I could add a hot blue-berry pie made with tart wild berries. King salmon and ripe blueberries arrive weeks apart, though; some things, maybe, are simply too good to come together in this life.

But we eat. We eat. We sit at our table on wooden kegs once used as buoys, and Ken and I fork fat, flaking chunks of am-brosia into our mouths. We loosen our belts and drawstrings and eat more, and we agree we are very close to heaven. There's nothing better than this food, this life. The fish is rich and oily. We have been craving it, and we need it. It's not just the taste we have to have; it's the protein and, particularly, the fat that fits this place and the calorie-burning work to be done here.

Each year when we gorge ourselves like this and throw the salmon carcass back to the sea, we live out a ritual that ex-tends as far back as people and salmon have lived together. Long, long before white people brought their nets to these shores, long before most of the world even knew there was such a creature as a Pacific salmon, Native Americans from Alaska to California's Monterey Bay developed ceremonies— often very elaborate—to celebrate the return of each year's first salmon.

The traditional Dena'ina of Cook Inlet marked the spring return of the king salmon with a precisely acted-out first fish ceremony, recorded by ethnographer Cornelius Osgood in the early 1930s. When the first king salmon of the year were landed, the Dena'ina carefully laid them on an outdoor mat of fresh grass. They took sweat baths, dressed in their best clothes, and burned a certain "lucky" plant, the identity of which is now apparently lost. They cleaned and cooked the fish, taking great care not to break the backbones, which, with the entrails, were thrown back into the water. This was done, Osgood's unnamed informant said, because "the salmon want their clothes." The entire ritual was underlaid with a complex mythology and accompanied by stories from the time when people and animals talked together. The first fish were treated with the utmost respect, like honored guests, to ensure that they would return again and continue to feed the people. Finally, the Dena'ina, who had—like the fish—completed another circle, feasted.

Our own ritual is without real ceremony, only a thankfulness for salmon and for those things—clean water, free-running streams, regulated fisheries—that make salmon, and salmon continuance, possible. I like the idea that the salmon carcass I threw to the sea with head, tail, and unbroken back—with its "clothes"—has taken its salmon soul to the Dena'ina place where animals wait for rebirth, and that it'll swim this way again. It gave itself that we might eat and that we might give back so it can return, on and on: a fine balance forever. This belief expresses as well as anything I know the connectedness of all things, and it is certainly more poetic than what I learned in ecology class. I think of the salmon's empty clothes flapping as they drift away, and then I switch traditions and think about a new generation of salmon fry and smolt already finning and flushing down the inlet, picking at whatever tiny pieces of nutrient they can find. These two understandings seem, really, not so far apart.

✧ ✧ ✧

I know these things about salmon—how they live and die, how people have honored them forever—and so much less about how I myself came to them, or to any fish. Several years ago my mother sent me an old, forgotten photograph in which I was holding up a fish. We were vacationing somewhere; I was about ten, and I had found—not caught—a dead fish of some undetermined species. The photograph could be the prototype for another, taken in Alaska many years later, in which I'm holding up my first Alaskan salmon. I'd caught it—an exhausted and discolored chum—on a rod and reel in a spawning creek, and I couldn't have looked more pleased. In both pictures my posture and stretch of arm holding the fish forward are exactly the same, and the look in my eye is devout.

For the most part, though, when I was growing up in Manchester, New Hampshire, I didn't know much about fish—no more than what I learned by observing the neon tetras and black mollies in my tropical fish tank. I couldn't have told you what was in the frozen fish sticks I was fed, and I can't remember if anyone caught anything the time my parents took me on a deep-sea charter in the Atlantic—when I spent the whole time hanging over the side, green with seasickness. I couldn't have had much sense of what a salmon was. I don't remember eating any and I certainly never saw a live one until I moved to Alaska. I wouldn't have recognized the long-departed Atlantic salmon, which once had been so plentiful and cheap that Massachusetts colonists were forbidden to feed it to their servants more than once a week.

In the 1950s and 1960s the clothing and shoe factories were still operating in Manchester, and the Merrimack, once a great salmon river, was a dead toilet bowl of caustic chemicals and colored dyes. When I was a teenager I watched archaeologists uncover an Indian fishing camp beside the dammed Amoskeag Falls, and the connections between the Indian names, the river and falls, fish, and the lives of a people finally came together for me with a sudden emotional clarity, a grieving sense of loss.

Today, Manchester's historic brick mill buildings have been turned into upscale restaurants and boutiques, and the river running past no longer foams and stinks. Some small stocking efforts in part of the Merrimack and a few other New England rivers have even brought back token numbers of salmon, but they are more a curiosity than a food. The reality of living by fish in that land fades further into the distant past.

✧ ✧ ✧

Here at camp, when we've eaten all we can of new salmon, the rest of our first fish goes into an overnight salt brine. The next day, after freshening them in a change of water, Ken cuts the fillets into thin strips and I tie the strips to strings. I hang them over poles in the breeze and an in-and-out sun until they glaze and then carry them to the smokehouse and rehang them, leaving the door open to more sunlight and drying air. The scraps I spread on a screen at the bottom of the smokehouse.

Everywhere birds are spilling over with song, calling out their lust, establishing territory. Two fox sparrows crash into the dust behind me; they go at each other with open beaks and slashing wings, as vicious as alley cats. They never even see me, and when the victor drives out the vanquished the grass and willow branches are left shaking. Swallows, meanwhile, are copulating on the cabin rooftop. Their fluttering wings ring the aluminum like metal brushes on cymbals. Yellow warblers as bright as canaries are all through the willows, mad for their buds. A Wilson's warbler flashes its wing tips. Other bird bullets shooting past me are so quick and gone I can only give them the name my father reserves for all of their kind—LBBs, for "little brown birds."

When I return to collect my hanging twine and knives, my eye catches a small, beach-colored bird wandering on stilt-legs near our cleaning table. Its head dips up and down like that of the balanced toy bird you set on the edge of a water glass. Shorebirds are very unusual here, and this lone spotted sandpiper looks truly lost. I would expect it to be feeding on mudflats teeming with tiny clams and worms, not hanging out where the mud is like gray grease and the spurt of a clam unknown. I watch the pitiable bird for a moment and see that, in fact, it's not tripping about in confusion but is intent on a stalk. It takes carefully stretched steps and then spears its bill toward the sand with an amazing quickness. It's stalking and stabbing flies drawn to our fish cleaning.

We all make do with what we have. Improvise, improvise.

Only when I double-check my bird book do I discover that the spotted sandpiper, in contrast to its many sandpiper cousins, typically feeds on insects as well as mud creatures. This one's behavior is not, after all, so unorthodox. I also learn of its polyandry; this mild bird belongs to the less than one percent of bird species in which females breed with multiple males and leave separate clutches of eggs to the care of their mates.

❖ ❖ ❖

Late in the day I build a small green-alder fire in the barrel attached to the smokehouse and put the first touch of smoke on the fish. As the smoke floats up through the smokehouse and out its open door and blackened screens, I admire the clean cuts and gleam of the hanging strips, the grain of the flesh. Fish in the smokehouse is like a full pantry or like a mountain of dry wood stacked beside the stove—better than money in the bank because it will truly sustain us. In a couple of days, we'll begin nipping off the thinnest dry ends; in a week, most of the rest will be dried to dark, amber translucency. Ah! The best belly strips, dripping with oil . . . the golden grease that will run down my chin and over my hands . . . the melting taste, the touch of salt. Already my teeth ache for it.

Smoked salmon is a standard of our summers, the food we reach for when hungriest, hurriedest, most in need of solid nourishment. As the summer progresses, we add to and subtract from the smokehouse—strips of hard-smoked fish, fillets smoked to lox strength for eating on crackers with cream cheese and capers, thin slices soaked in soy sauce and turned to jerky, more fillets smoked lightly before canning. The strips take the longest to finish, but once dried they will keep all summer—or all year—without further preservation. They are, after all, the same staple the Dena'ina so thoroughly depended on when they lived their traditional lives along this shore.

Our methods of cutting, hanging, and smoking fish are probably not very different from those of even the earliest Cook Inlet Dena'ina, though on a markedly smaller scale. Those first fishermen must have spent all summer preserving the salmon that would feed them through fall, winter, and spring, until the salmon came again. Day and night their fires would have smoldered, drying pounds and pounds and bales and bundles of salmon to a feather lightness. As Peter Kalifornsky wrote, in the days before the Russians came "it was the rule that one [winter] day's allowance of food was a piece of dry fish as big as from the meaty part of your palm at the base of your thumb to the tip of your middle finger."

The smoke smell drifting from my barrel and smokehouse is sweet, reminiscent of childhood days when I gladly raked piles of maple and elm leaves—yellow and orange and blood-red—to the curb and set them afire. It was a welcomed sweet smell, those bright-burning leaves into which we sometimes buried foil-wrapped apples stuffed with raisins and cinnamon. Today leaf fires are banned nearly everywhere—they produce too much air pollution, and composting is more earth-friendly. We're a smarter people now and more careful with our health, but I don't regret those days when we filled our lungs with fall's fiery smell. Nor would I eliminate smoked food from my diet, even though I know it's less than healthful. After the *Exxon Valdez* oil spill, researchers checking the safety of seafoods that had been coated with oil found nothing in the polluted waters that contained as many aromatic hydrocarbons—carcinogenic and mutagenic—as a sampling of unoiled but well-smoked salmon from a smokehouse.

✧ ✧ ✧

For us, smoking salmon is a side activity, a sort of gastronomic luxury of our beach lives, a puny dependence, a mere remnant compared with the critical activity it was for traditional Dena'ina. We lack the same absolute need, and so we lack as well a set of developed rituals and beliefs that underlie necessity. Still, what we do with our first fish seems legitimate and meaningful for us, consistent with ideals of respect and responsibility, and with sharing. Just as our initial welcome to the beach involved a package of smoked salmon, we, too, always bring out smoked salmon for visitors.

There does exist another tradition among some fishermen for greeting the season's first fish, a simple one of kissing it and throwing it back. This act is supposed to bring good luck and good fishing. Although in common practice it seems like mere superstition or playfulness, I assume this tradition originated within some cultural context—brought here by fishermen from elsewhere—as genuine thankfulness. Nonetheless, it contrasts sharply with Dena'ina and other Native American beliefs that fish and animals give themselves to be eaten and shouldn't be wasted, lest they be offended and not offer themselves again. (For this same reason, many Native Americans have difficulty with the concept of catch-and-release sport fishing; why should anyone torment any creature frivolously, without the need to eat it?)

I close the smokehouse door on our first, most valued and well-attended fish. Most other fish I touch in the weeks ahead will be handled quickly and efficiently, fleetingly, but I want to remember that every one will be eaten by somebody, somewhere, and deserves to be treated with care.

Salmon are food, and they are so much more than food. These wild creatures that come to us from far and mysterious wanderings connect all who recognize and welcome them with the open ocean and cool mountain streams, and with all their fellow travelers—whales and parasites, fishing boats and stars among them. Salmon, indeed, belong to time itself, linking us forward and back, to the cycles within years and from one year to the next, to the next, to the next.

Creek Culture

A trout lies in the creek bed at the top of the beach, flat on its side among the angular stepping-stone rocks with rusty water slipping under and past it. It's long and skinny, spotted and big headed, and its exposed side is dried to sandpaper wrinkles. Rainbows that go to sea metamorphose into sturdier steelhead, but this one looks like a fish that spent an unhappy and very hungry time in the salt. It may have reached the creek in a last, desperate effort to ascend to freshwater spawning grounds only to find the water level impossibly low. Its resting place above recent tide lines means it must have pushed and banged and slithered over several yards of less-than-belly-depth creek before giving up and turning its eye to the sky.

Our creek does not belong to anadromous fish. That is, fish don't normally travel it from sea to lake or from lake to sea. There's not enough water to it, and there are too many obstructions. Even so, now and then we find a small trout skittering through a pool—a fish that somehow washed out through the series of beaver dams from the lake above and will make its way to the unlocked sea. Perhaps this skinny specimen is one of those come back to try to spawn, only to beat out its light instead, alone, in scummy water.

When we first came to the beach, we thought of the creek as a fixture of the place. It ran alongside the cabin, chill and chattery, and we assumed it had always run so—and always would, more or less. Every spring it was my job to put in our water system, cutting loose the coils of stiff, black hose from where I'd stashed them in the fall and weaving them along the creek's course, around rocks and snags and through the deep shade of arching alders, until I was well above the cabin's height. I connected the lengths with hose clamps and set a weighted wooden barrel in place under a lip of rock. Cascading water filled the barrel and the pipe and ran to our sink. Before reaching the cabin, it could be diverted to a creekside shower house, where we heated it in a pressure tank over a Coleman stove.

In those days we'd never heard of giardia and we drank the water straight, as we still do. Apparently the beavers and other possible hosts here don't carry the parasite that causes "beaver fever," an intestinal ill that the afflicted say is so miserable it makes a person want to die.

Some summers the creek ran high and some summers it ran a little lower, and within a summer it would be up and down. In the hard rains of August we'd sometimes hear rocks rolling down it, banging into one another, and the silver salmon, sniffing their way toward home streams, seemed to nose into the muddy mix where the outflow met the inlet. The beach net there was the best net for silvers.

It was years before George mentioned that he remembered the precise day when our creek trickled into existence. Before then, water from the lake above had flowed down a draw—a cut in the bluff—closer to his camp, but one day he'd watched it seep down the bank at our place and be born as a new creek.

I couldn't fathom it. I could picture the area without our cabin easily enough, but I simply couldn't imagine the absence of the deep cut into the bluff with the creek running through alders in its middle. How could the geography of a place change so much within just a portion of one person's lifetime?

Over the years, we added to our camp. We jacked up the cabin and put new pilings under it, and we covered its leaky tar paper with metal roofing. We brought in a new woodstove, a propane stove with an oven, and a hammock. We built decks all around the cabin and put up flagpoles that, with booms and winches, doubled as systems for lifting outboards and nets from the beach to the decks. We built more deck on pilings back along the creek and erected on that deck a new building that tripled as a gear shed, workshop, and guest house.

In October 1986, when we were back in town, it rained and rained and rained, torrentially, for days. Rivers throughout the region flooded; roads and bridges washed out; mud slides knocked houses off their foundations. It was, the experts said, a "hundred years' flood," worse than any in memory and not to be expected again for another century or so.

When the rain stopped, Ken flew off to check on our camp. Fishcamps all along the way lay crumpled on beaches with tides washing through them; the saturated bluffs they'd perched on had slid from beneath them.

At our camp our cabin still stood, a little bit of tilted deck attached to one side, the whole of it an insignificant white dot against a vast mud-colored landscape. The creek ran furious and free, no longer tumbling down an alder-filled draw but instead creasing the bottom of an immense, bare canyon. Floodwaters had dumped from the lake in such volume and with such force that they'd cut walls a quarter mile wide and carried thousands of tons of earth to the inlet. Aside from our tiny cabin perched at the canyon's bottom edge, nothing was the same. The remains of our gear shed and other outbuildings lay mostly buried under sand and rocks, one glinty edge of gear shed roof pointing like the hand of a drowning person. The huge beach boulders that had stood well over our heads were gone—buried under alluvial deposits. Ken took pictures from the plane and flew home again. We still had a cabin. And our boats, beached in another draw, were fine.

In the spring, we salvaged what we could. Four outboards were smashed and filled with mud, but we dug them out and traded them away. We excavated most of our bundled nets, one cork and one tangle of web at a time. We lost our generator, our chain saw, and all our tools. Years later we still find the odd rusted screwdriver jammed among rocks on the beach or a disintegrating rubber gasket that looks vaguely familiar.

We bought all new water pipe. In its remodeling the creek fell less precipitously, so I needed additional hose lengths to reach the same height and achieve the same water pressure. It was simple, however, to string it along the creek, wide open under the sky, absent a maze of alders. On a sunny day, the water in the black pipe grew so hot it was ideal for bathing or doing laundry, although to get a cool drink we had to let the water run until the sun-baked pipe was emptied.

In those days the canyon felt to me like the moon or a volcanic island that had just shoved up from under the sea. It was new, a strange and barren place made of sand and clay and rock, of grays and browns and the occasional clot of dark coal. Even as I watched, pebbles dribbled down its sides. Here and there on its slopes, shattered trees lay where they'd fallen from the rim above, and a few struggling spruces and birches tipped dizzily from earthy root balls that had likewise been tumbled as the flood carved the canyon. Around my feet, the first colonizing fireweed and wormwood cracked the hard-packed clay and sand.

Today, when I look up the alder-chocked creek from the beach, I think of how unchanging and unchangeable it would appear if I didn't know better. The remains of our gear shed and other outbuildings are still there, still pointing hard-to-salvage rafters and splintered corners of plywood, but they're lost now behind dense alder thickets and spreading willows, some of them twenty feet tall. It takes a knowing eye to detect the demarcation line between the trees on either side of the draw and the slightly shorter and thinner ones that fill in between them. I have to look much farther up to see anything but greenery—the sand and clay walls that are too vertical for any new growth. On a windy day, sand swirls off them in mini-cyclones; rain brings them down in new slides, ever widening the canyon, ever rounding its floor.

A walk up the creek takes me past patches of wormwood, waving fireweed, horsetail and ferns, grasses and the new shoots of monkey flower. Nothing grows right in the creek, though, which just behind the camp is fed by orange-brown seeps from the hillside. The color is like iron rust, and my guess is that the seeps—which appear all up and down the beach—are a pressing out of coal seams. They're mixed sometimes with an oily iridescence—plant oils, maybe, or hydrocarbons. We are, we know, in oil country; some of the first oil to be discovered in Alaska was in natural seeps just down the coast from here, and a major field has been producing for thirty years to our north.

In any case, the orange water stains the rocks it washes over and lays down gooey deposits in the creek, like butterscotch pudding but less appetizing. In places the scum is so thick it floats in mats, capturing air bubbles that look like masses of frog eggs. It's slippery to step in, and it smells foul. With little water coming down over the bluff, this "bad" water, which seems to flow evenly regardless of drought or rain, makes up more of the lower creek than usual and lays down more un-flushed deposit.

Last year, for the first time since we've lived here, the creek's fresh water dried up completely. George had warned us for years to "do something" about the beavers that were impounding more and more water along the upper creek. One day, George said, the ponds would spill over the bluff, and that would be the end of our water. That was just the way it had happened when the water first came to our place—not through the actions of beavers, necessarily, but the creek wound close to the bluff and eventually cut a new path to the beach.

We preferred to take our chances. With the number of beavers around, we doubted that breaking up their dams or killing a few would have given us any greater control over the water situation.

Instead, as the water dried up, I kept returning to the barrel in the creek and making new ways for what moving water there was to get into it. Normally, the barrel simply sat in a pool below a natural dam—a jumble of rocks and logs and a huge shelf of coal—and collected its fill from the steady crash of water that shot out over the dam. I added pipes and hoses, and when the flow slowed to a trickle, I even stooped to installing a sheet of plastic behind the dam. Eventually, though, the water stopped running altogether and the creek bed lay bare and cobbled under desert light, in a silence I'd never imagined. The beaver ponds dropped well below their own dams until the lower one was down to caked mud on a messy bottom of decaying tree limbs and exposed stumps.

We located a spring a short way down the beach from our camp, planted a pipe, and hauled water in our kitchen kettles for several weeks. Although we called it a spring, it may have been simply leakage from the beaver ponds, working its way down through layers of sand and clay and running out among the yellow monkey flowers, clear and ice-cold.

✧ ✧ ✧

On my way up the creek to adjust the barrel and hoses again, I stop to look at weeks-old bear tracks. The bear had walked through the orange scum and then stepped across a series of dry, exposed rocks, leaving prints so perfect they might have been painted. The little rain we've had has done nothing to blur them.

I pause under the steep hillside, where streams of clay washed down in earlier rains. The clay is like lava; I can see how it flowed down and piled up over itself before it dried to a crumbly concrete. A huge chunk of earth and clay, swarming with roots, lies in the creek at my feet. I look up to see if I can tell where it fell from and whether another of its kind is about to fall on my head. Near the top, the clay and sand give way to a distinct layer of gravel and rock. As I watch, a kingfisher shoots out of its hole below an overhang and rattles off toward the inlet.

I leave the clotted water behind and walk instead through pools and rivulets streaked with green and brown algae. I look for but can't find any caddis fly larvae. Other years they've been thick in the stream—these half-inch creatures camouflaged and weighted with sticks and stones. I love to watch them skittering around with heads and front legs stuck out of the constructs they build around their pale caterpillar bodies, the masonry of found objects held together with an adhesive silk. The larvae here favor bits of bark and woody materials over sand grains and spruce needles; they generally look like ambulatory twigs.

As if it's not enough for caddis fly larvae simply to exist among nature's most intriguing design practitioners, they also strike me as perfect candidates for "bug art"—that art form in which human artists manipulate the work of insects. I saw such a show in Seattle once in which bees had hung honeycomb around frameworks both abstract and meant to suggest human forms, and I read of another artist who has silkworms spin their balls inside partitioned wooden boxes. Annie Dillard wrote that entomologists have amused themselves by placing naked caddis fly larvae in an aquarium with one color of sand and then moving them to an aquarium with another color of sand, and so on, until the larvae end up surrounding themselves in colored bands, but whether anyone has applied any more aesthetic than that to these creatures, I don't know.

This year, there are no larvae to be found. Perhaps temperatures or water levels have affected their survival, or perhaps their absence is part of a cyclical pattern. I haven't noticed any adult caddis flies around, either, but these mothy beaters with the long antennae don't usually present themselves in daylight. Caddis flies, which are important around rivers as fish food, are perhaps best known as being models for artificial trout flies.

The creek is low enough that instead of being simply noisy—producing a crash of running water—it separates into distinct riffles of sound. I listen to one run of water that gurgles through several high-pitched whole notes and then to a second slower and deeper swash and a third that slips lightly over a series of rounded rocks to pound to a final crescendo. I make a game of picking out one and then another, as if sorting out the instruments in an orchestra.

Trees that slid down the hillside during and after the flood are beginning to right themselves. They'd landed in all sorts of toppled positions, and they've adjusted over the years to new pulls of sunlight and gravity, twisting their trunks, arching into realignment. I come upon new birches with shimmery, sun-flecked leaves and remember something a friend told me about an Athabaskan friend of hers who, every year, went into the woods and tied birch branches in knots. Several seasons later, he'd return to cut the branches, now grown into lovely knotted twists, and he'd sell them, varnished, to tourists. I take a branch to knot, but it splits and breaks before I can even begin to tighten it. I try another and get the same result. There must be a better time to practice this cruelty. Perhaps when the sap runs more strongly, the branches have more flexibility.

Much of the hillside I'm standing below is still barren under and around the patches of hardy colonizers. The ground is hard-packed clay, cracked, still shifting. Tiny wormwood plants and horsetails grab a hold where they can. A flowering elderberry appears to be flourishing in a damp hollow. A clump of sod that fell from the rim lies like an oasis, loaded with mosses and fireweed, grasses and starflowers.

At the water barrel I adjust my network of collecting pipes and hoses while a dark cloud spits rain, patterning the dry rocks around me with solid round dots. I think of the same cloud passing inland and unloading more of its single drops to bounce against the surface of the lake before mixing into the water that will later find its way down this creek. An old schoolbook illustration floats back to me: the one everyone knows, showing the cycle of evaporation, clouds, rain, and water running to the sea, with various side trips through the roots of trees or storage as glacial ice. The wonder of such a system, as with so much in nature, has never left me.

Drops spatter on my head, and I indulge in a conceit, imagining a singular raindrop falling into the lake. I imagine that it doesn't evaporate back into a cloud, isn't absorbed by the surrounding land and thirsty roots, but one day—still holding to its droplet form—rides up against the beaver dam at the lake's end. It slips through, part of a melodious trickle between alder sticks and mud packing, into a shallow, weed-filled creek. For a time, the drop circles in a back-eddy behind a marsh marigold root; then it is caught in the push of other drops behind it and moves into the sluggish current, where it bounces like a slow-motion pinball from bank to bank, from stick to slippery moss, rising as it warms in a sunny pool and sinking again as other, warmer drops flow over it. It works its way over smooth stones, past the treading action of thousands of mosquito larvae. It escapes the thirst of a varied thrush that pauses from its drinking long enough to sing a burry note. It runs quickly through a narrow course and disappears under an overhang of turf only to swirl back and be carried along once again, past alder thickets, around stands of prickly devil's club, under fallen spruces. It floats into a glassy pond and then through another dam, around a second pond, and over a spill-way, into more meandering creek. It rubs over stones and past a flailing aphid. Finally it falls over the bluff's lip into sunlight and starts its faster run down the draw.

In a leap through time, I imagine this chimerical drop slithering over algae, bumping one more boulder, becoming part of the gurgling I hear up ahead, and coming my way over gravel and flakes of coal. It heads pell-mell into a tunnel of smooth black pipe and free-falls into a frothy mix of water and air held within the woody, slick barrel sides. It smacks a rock in the barrel's bottom and then rises with the rest of the water toward the overflow at the barrel's rim. On the way to the rim, surprisingly enough, the drop is sucked into another pipe, this one a narrow black hose. For the next eight hundred feet it zips through the pitch-dark stream, through a series of narrower couplings, down, down, and finally into a thin green hose, spurting at last through a spray nozzle into a large black tub on a plank deck at the edge of the sea.

This is our hot tub: a cattle watering trough of hard black plastic, the Rubbermaid name emblazoned on the side. It fits two friendly people who will recline with backs to curved ends and chins at water level. My fanciful water drop has beat me down the hill to be part of a tub filling. Ken is making a fire under copper coils, turning the pump to its lowest speed. The cold drop sinks, leaves the tub through yet another hose, passes through pump and hot coils, and returns to the tub, one hot drop.

And here I am. I don't wait for the tub to steam, as I do on cold days. The sky has cleared into full sunshine and, although residual storm swells pound the beach, the wind has stilled. As soon as the tub water is bathwater warm, I strip off my clothes and get in. Ken pushes a piece of coal and another stick of driftwood into the fire.

The sun, warm on my face, diffuses through the water to light my whole white body. The clear water magnifies my body's contours, and I suddenly have hips. Just out from the deck, breakers angle in over the flats, crashing into ribbons of foam. The boat rears and plunges on the mooring. I lie back in the tub, stretched out, floating. The water is silk-smooth against my skin, and I'm supremely content. I cannot imagine a finer place in the world, nor a finer moment.

A huge, green-headed moose fly—Alaska's version of a horsefly—lands on the edge of the tub and walks the couple inches down to water level, where it tests the edge of the water with its hairy feelers, like a potential wader checking temperature; then it sticks its tubular mouth into the water and sucks up a stream so urgently that it leaves a ripple like a wake. It backs up, turns around, climbs to the rim, cleans its whiskers with a few wipes of its front legs, and flies off. I think that must be the warmest water it's ever had reason to sip, although the females of their kind feed on blood, delivering the nastiest insect bite known in these parts.

The water heats up. I make room for Ken. Displaced water overflows the tub and splashes to the deck, draining into the sand. Underwater surges bounce between ends of the tub. I am up to my ears, and all the muscles of my back turn loose and ropy.

Beside us, three white totes, scavenged at sea for net storage, take up most of the deck. They are four feet square and nearly as deep, with lids; on top of the lids are set smaller totes—the red and gray ones we use for hauling and brining fish and for doing laundry. There's a hunk of scavenged plywood with rounded corners that we've been using as a fish-cleaning table since we lost our actual table to storm tides. There's a huge piece of ball-and-socket hardware Ken had made to attach a boom to our latest flagpole. The pole itself lies flat beside the deck and back along the creek, another victim of storm tides; its enormous root end—a cluster of big rocks and cement around the tarred wood base—now offers us a way to climb to the far side of the deck and gives us something sturdy to which we can tie our running line. Also on the deck with us is a bent cooking pot that holds a bar of sandy soap and a shampoo jar that's secured inside a plastic bag because its lid was reassigned to a gas can. An old net lies in a lump at my end of the tub, partially covered with a blue tarp; some of its corks dangle over the edge of the deck. A five-gallon bucket, a piece of fishy burlap, a scrub brush, a short length of board, the end of a pole that fell on the deck when an earlier boom pole collapsed—these are the familiar things that share our immediate tubbing area, the stuff of our fishing lives.

I soak and gaze fondly upon all this: a kingdom of sorts, not the cluttered mess another person might think it—no, not at all—but each object an element of our lives, a necessary part, a story. I need look only a few feet past the deck to see Ken's stainless steel sink; a set of rusted bedsprings that forms part of our breakwater; our old, decrepit cart; the cabin, with its own surround of important parts. John McPhee wrote in his classic book about Alaska, *Coming into the Country*, that those places you pass on back roads in various parts of the United States, with old car parts and washing machines piled in the yard, belong to Alaskans who just haven't left yet. He captured in one line so much of Alaska's truth: in remote areas, and particularly at working places like mining claims or fishcamps, it's unwise to get rid of something you will very likely need, at least in part, at a later date. Old, deflated buoys; scraps of line; an empty mayonnaise jar—you will need these things. You will treasure the splintered square of plywood, the foot-length piece of hose, the handle of a wheelbarrow even older than the cart. What you see is not a trashy mess; given the lack of indoor space, each item is actually more or less in its place, waiting for its next use.

Insects seem to be attracted to the heat of the tub, or perhaps I just notice them more because I'm bare skinned and engaged in nothing but looking around me. A very tiny, dark beetle, not much bigger than a grain of sand, has joined us in the tub, legs kicking. I rescue it and deposit it on the rim. Somehow, though, it's all wrapped up in a drop of water, with most of the droplet under its belly like an overstuffed beanbag chair it's straddling. I watch as it rolls one way and another, unable to break the surface adhesion. In the sunlight on the tub's black surface, the water droplet begins immediately to shrink, and the beetle begins to tilt lower and lower like a car being brought down by a jack. Then the water's gone and the beetle fans out its double wings to dry, reminding me of the way cormorants spread their wings to dry in the sun. I look away, and when I look back the beetle is gone.

Dandelions in the yard behind us have just in the past few days burst into flower, and bees have appeared out of nowhere to work them over. A rather large butterfly—a copper, I believe—lands on one for a long moment. Its wings are chestnut brown with a cream-colored stripe, then a wider orange stripe, and then a very ragged outer edge of brown. I know almost nothing about butterflies except that I always take pleasure in watching them and that there are only a few dozen species to be found in all of Alaska, mostly in the state's warm, dry interior. Butterflies are limited not by the cold of winter but by the coolness of summer, and they're experts at collecting heat from the environment. Alaska's tend to be small and dark, the better to absorb heat, and they know how to position themselves in southern exposures, sometimes laying their wings out flat against warm rocks. This individual looks as if it's had a long or a hard life or both, and I wonder if it traveled far to get here or spent the winter buried deep under insulating layers of snow, as some northern butterflies do.

Ken jerks. A swallow, coming in from over the water, has very nearly flown into his face before veering off at a sharp angle, as startled as he is. Only this morning I found a perfect half of a white swallow egg on the ground below the birdhouse. It was so fragile I was afraid I'd crush it when I picked it up. In one of nature's well-timed moves, the swallow hatch came just days after the first mosquito hatch, and the birds now are all over the sky, filling themselves and, assumably, loading up for their voracious dependents back in the nest.

I hold my hand in front of my face and look through the water drops that swell and dangle on the ends of my fingers. This is one of my favorite tub pastimes—to watch the world through a drop of water. I locate a view of my opposite arm and regard the shimmer of skin color; then I find a wooden post and do the same thing with its brown stripe. I look through a drop at Ken, bringing my hand closer to my face and then moving it farther away until I capture him most completely, upside down and backward, refracted. His beard is sylvan and silver tipped, his wet hair slicked back from a heightened forehead. The outline of the droplet forms a silver-edged frame around him. I look for the skiff on the mooring but can't find it through my lens, can't negotiate the distortions and angles to bring it into my sight. I find only a deep, deep blue, bluer than either sky or water—a concentrate of color, as though the drop is absorbing color into itself. Each drop is a prism, a magnifier, a jewel. The drops fall, one by one, from my fingertips, and I dip into the water for another handful of riches.

Ken asks his rhetorical question: "Who has the best life?"

I answer as if I were reciting a catechism. "You do."

We both have, in fact, the exact lives we want. We envy no one. I am, however, not as quick as Ken to boast of happiness. We've been tremendously lucky in our lives, and luck is just that—good fortune that's come to us through no particular virtue of our own. We're blessed with good health and good brains. I suspect, too, the fragility of such fortune. The old Dena'ina never spoke of their hunting skill or luck or even of their expectations—an attitude that strikes me as being more than mere superstition. It is born of humility, an acceptance that something besides ourselves is in control.

Still, who wouldn't be delighted to live with a man who claims the best life in the world and who attends with enthusiasm to a variety of challenges? Ken's life doesn't translate well to a paper résumé, doesn't fit on a line calling for "occupation," doesn't, in fact, separate into work and nonwork or have an earnings schedule tied to it. He is a man who takes his satisfaction in fashioning a door handle from a curved root, drafting language for fisheries or forest practices law, and coaching young *Nutcracker* dancers, as well as catching fish, driving small and large boats, flying an airplane, and cooking up huge panfuls of greasy potatoes—a man who wants his epitaph to read, *He was competent in many things*.

The tub water gets too hot and we stand in the breeze to cool ourselves. We turn on the cold-water hose and aim it at the tops of our heads, watching the blood fill each other's faces. We leave the hose in the tub and let it massage us like a Jacuzzi jet. When the sun begins to flicker behind the alder trees and, superheated, we feel as though our bones have turned to cooked pasta, we stir ourselves to fill and hang the shower bag, and then we wash and shampoo on the deck.

I think again of that one drop of water that might have fallen as rain and come down the creek and pipeline to our tub. Where is it now? It might have been swallowed by the moose fly, or it might have evaporated from under the tiny beetle. It might have overflowed from the tub or served as one of my lenses on the world. I imagine it, though, inside the shower bag and now streaming down over my hair and my hot, soapy shoulders, now falling to the sand and draining to the edge of the sea, now being taken back by the next wave.

A Day in the Life

I wake before the alarm, as I always do on fishing mornings. Nights before fishing, I'm never really asleep but only waiting, monitoring the wind and water. For hours already, I've listened to the creek trickle and the songbirds warble. Now I sit up and look outside. The skiff—which I always check first—is still on the mooring, slack on its line and milk-cow tame. In the northeast sky, behind layers of low clouds, the sun glows with an oyster-shell light. The water lies as flat and dull as a pewter plate, its edge solid against the shore. It's my kind of fishing day. It might also be a very good one. We're in the third week of July, and the sockeye run should be close to its peak.

Ken stirs. "Wicked surf," he teases. He knows I've worried all night that the weather might change. He's never in his life worried about something he couldn't affect, and he prides himself on his ability to fall asleep the second he puts his head down and to sleep through the ragingest storm.

I get up and dress, then make myself a bowl of instant oatmeal. I learned a long time ago that if I didn't eat before going out to fish, something would happen that would keep me from eating until way past the point of low-blood-sugar grouchiness. It's one of the laws of fishing, like another I generally obey: take raingear or it'll be sure to rain. Ken, however, doesn't need to eat. He waits until the last minute to get out of bed and throw his clothes on.

Chestwaders, flotation vest, raingear, hat, glasses, gloves, lunch box. I run down my mental checklist. Make sure Ken has his knife. We go out the door.

The tide is still coming in—an easy tide to set on. It's a good day of tides, all in all—large enough to move fish but not so large that the water will suck out as we watch or leave our low-water sets in rock piles. We carry our nets to the water's edge; then we carry the rowboat down, and Ken rows for the skiff.

Ken motors in and we load the nets. He does leads and I do corks, piling them into the center and port bins so they'll set out neatly over the stern, in order. We work quickly and silently, except when I ask "This one?" before grabbing a new end and Ken grunts in response. Most inlet setnetters divide their allowed gear into three thirty-five-fathom nets—indeed, that's the rule for most areas—but we fish more nets of shorter lengths, as short as ten fathoms. Throughout the day we move, switch, replace, and tie these together, depending on location, stage of tide, height of tide, wind, waves, current, time in the season, and how things are going. Ken's the master at devising these fishing plans, and I'm the crew that follows directions and just sometimes suggests we move a net sooner or let one soak a little longer.

No fishing day is the same as any other, and we always think we can be a little smarter about how we fish, work harder, and catch more salmon.

❖ ❖ ❖

Ken ties one end of the corkline to the setline at the high-tide mark and climbs back into the boat; I pull us out along the setline; Ken lowers and starts the motor; and at exactly 7:00 A.M.

we set our first net. Leads and corks tumble out over the stern as I watch for snarls, and then, when we reach the end of the net, I wrap a bite around the setline and tie the net off.

We both turn expectantly to see what's happening behind us—whether fish are hitting the net, whether this will be a fishy day. I continue to watch behind us for splashes as we speed to the next set, but the corkline lies in a perfect gentle crescent against the current.

Our first sets go like clockwork, right down the beach. I love fishing when it's like this—the smooth, voiceless teamwork, the echoing clank of orderly corks over the stern, the practiced feel in my hands. I don't think so much as I *am*. The body knows; the memory is in my fingers, my shoulders, the knees that brace me. My physical self knows the grip of line, the quick tightening, the double hitch pulled over itself. If I stopped to think about what I do, I would surely fumble.

The nets are out, and I stoop to scrape seaweed and sand from the bare boat bottom. I'm sweating inside neoprene; the sun, breaking through the clouds, has lit the fireweed and monkey flowers on the hillside into a blaze. *The red salmon come when the fireweed blooms.* So they say; so the old-timers said about the sockeyes, the money fish. We are ever hopeful.

To a fisherman, every fishing day is like Christmas, every net like presents to be opened. We never know what surprises we might find, only that there'll be something there and that it just might be, this time, the stuff of our dreams. That's why we fish on days when we catch just ten fish, and in storms, and on those days when nothing seems to go right—because the only thing predictable about fishing is that we won't catch anything if we don't have web in the water.

This morning our nets are not, however, loading up with fish. Ken blames the weather. It's too good; we need a storm to move fish up the inlet and in against our shore.

We start back through the nets, pulling leads and corks between us across the boat. Ken snaps loose a silver, worth just half a sockeye. The next fish is a silver, too. I slip a finger under one gill to peel away web and then shake the other side free. Every fish is its own puzzle to pull through, spin out of a twist, unbag, ungill, shake off. After years of practice the hands know, but my brain still clicks through its calculations, seeing the patterns.

Ken looks glum, but at least we've got fish in the boat. This is another maxim among fishermen: we have to have one fish before we can have ten, and we have to have ten before we can have one hundred. We pull more net and Ken grabs for our first sockeye. "Now *that's* a beauty," he says.

The fish, still fighting fresh, leaps around the center bin as though it would throw itself from the boat. It smacks against the aluminum, splashes water, dances on its tail, and comes to rest against one of the still-twitching silvers. It is, in fact, a very good looking fish, with a rounded body and a dainty-featured face, marred only by the gillnet's score across its head. It's the color of distant water, a soft gray-blue that deepens over its back into a metallic, nearly cobalt shine. Mirrory scales divide into contour lines like shifting plates of antique, tarnished mail.

The fish flops again, spattering blood that's hemorrhaging in thick, tomato-bright clots from its gills.

Wherever this ocean fish was headed, it was a long way from beginning its transformation to spawner. In another week or so we'll begin to catch an occasional wasted-looking sockeye, as flat as if it had been driven over by a truck and rose-colored, with a monstrous green head and hooked snout, all the better to scare its competitors once it reaches its spawning grounds. One will spill eggs like jewels into the boat, and we'll wonder if it lost its way home.

The fish makes a last flop and then lies quietly, its mouth working open and shut as though it's gasping for breath.

I'm well aware that some people think this crue—killing fish like this, killing anything. They forget—or they never understood—that killing is part of how we live, the fish as well as the fisherman, the fish eater as well as the most committed vegan. Something dies that another may live. To me, the morality lies somewhere else—in what happens after the killing. When salmon are caught as "bycatch" in other fisheries and discarded overboard, or when someone takes a fish but leaves it on the bank or in his freezer to get freezer burned, that's when behavior must be faulted.

These days, I frequently find myself examining that most basic of Dena'ina beliefs—that all things have wills and give or withhold themselves by choice, depending on whether a person shows respect or is insulting and wasteful. Among Peter Kalifornsky's Dena'ina belief stories is one about a young man who didn't listen to his elders about the proper treatment of animals. He left bones lying all around, and he killed mice cruelly and threw their bodies away. Other mice spoiled his meat, chewed up what was in his traps, and scampered over him in his sleep. At last he dreamed of going to the place where the animals wait to be reborn, and there he saw the ones whose bones had been walked over. They were horribly disfigured by his mistreatment and unable to return to human space.

Such lesson stories clearly helped enforce what the Dena'ina considered proper behavior and served the culture well in the long run. Would that our own laws and practices worked so well to feed people within a conservation framework.

What's a better end for a salmon—being chewed on by a seal, rotting to a slow death after spawning, or flopping into a fishing boat? From a salmon's point of view, the question has no meaning. The salmon's brain can't consider the options. The salmon doesn't think; it reacts. Nor does it feel pain as we know pain, not with its simple nervous system. The sockeye in the boat isn't gasping. It only looks that way to people, who know what it feels like *to them* to struggle for breath.

In the belief that a quick death is a humane one, sport fishermen often club their catch on the head. We knock only the lively kings with the back of the gaff, to keep them from bruising themselves—or us—as they thrash. The smaller fish are difficult to club without damaging their flesh, and they fade away quickly as it is. In any case, most fish we bring into the boat are already dead; once they're in the net, the web caught in their gills prevents them from working water through properly to extract oxygen. In fishermen's language, the fish "drown."

The best way to handle a fish—to be quick and to ensure good quality for whoever's going to eat it—is immediately to slit it gill to gill and drain out the blood and then place it on ice. Some commercial fisheries have moved in this direction, and the better care brings a higher price. Change is slow, though, in those fisheries that have traditionally dealt more in volume than in quality. Our processors still want salmon untouched by a knife, and they won't bring us ice.

We do the best we can. We don't step on our fish. We don't let them go dry on the beach or get beaten into noodles in the surf. We keep them out of the sun.

Our count now is up to eight—four sockeyes, four silvers. There's the sockeye with the metallic shine and another that's smaller and greener, the silver with a thick tail and two lankier ones that look like twins. These are the fish in a "mixed-stock fishery," where salmon headed for a variety of large and small, glacial and clear, fast and slow-running rivers and lake systems mingle before turning right or left and separating out. Bluebacks belong to one river, bullet shapes to another. That's the beauty and the essential genius of salmon: the custom design that matches each separate stock to color and stream flow, the natural conditions in their different home waters. As the big kings evolved to dig spawning beds below the scoured depths of powerful rivers, the sleekest sockeyes perfected their ability to move through shallows; the strongest, to throw themselves up falls; and the greenest, to blend into mossy depths.

I soak a piece of burlap over the side and cover the fish, a little brown mound in the center of the boat. Across the inlet, the sky is streaked with rain. The time is 7:40.

✧ ✧ ✧

"How many?" Ken shouts as he cuts the motor. This is one of our games—to guess the number of fish in a net. Ken has not only much better eyesight than I do but also an uncanny ability to predict what lies under the surface of the thick, flourroux water.

I always make a conservative guess. That way, when there are more, I feel lucky to have them. "Three," I say, leaning from the bow to grab the corkline. I already see two heads.

Ken guesses six.

There's a silver along the leadline right away, and then the next pull of net brings in a big, headless sockeye, all gnashed red meat and dripping eggs. Ken curses and we both look around.

The seal's right there, just fifty feet off the outside buoy, bobbing up to get a better look at us. The way it stretches from the water makes it look as though it's standing on something solid, on tiptoe. Ken and I both yell, and I grab an aluminum post and bang it three times against the boat. I always think this should sound to a seal like gunfire, but it never seems to have much effect. This seal—a harbor seal, the most plentiful of Alaska's seals—merely ducks under and reappears seconds later a little farther downstream. "Go away," I yell as I might at a dog loitering around a picnic table.

The seal lowers itself to whisker level and stays where it is, watching us. It has a bowling-ball head, dark and shiny, and saucer eyes. Most people think seals are cute; they would have a completely different opinion if seals had hard, little eyes and ferocious fangs—if a seal looked, for example, anything like a bat. Seals, in our modern classification system, are closely related to Bambi, and everybody loves Bambi. As a culture we Americans have Bambified ourselves away from any real understanding of individual species and their importance in the ecological picture.

Sometimes, grudgingly, I, too, will admit to being taken with fawns, bunnies, puppies, the baby seal that once swam to our boat wailing and still wearing its umbilicus—all soft and cuddly animals, cartoon creatures with fluttering eyelashes. *Bambi* was the very first movie I was taken to as a child, and I was struck to the soul with empathy. It was many years before I came to understand that there could be cultural systems—even within my own country—with beliefs different from and as strong as any I grew up with. This understanding came to me with pinprick clarity the day a Native woman told me about the time *Bambi* played in her village: when Bambi and Bambi's mother came on the screen, all the boys in the audience raised their arms as if to shoot.

At least cartoons were recognized as cartoons then. A more recent movie, about a seal named Andre, stars as Andre not a seal at all but a young sea lion. Every few years we spot a sea lion in the inlet, and even from a distance—with most of the animal underwater—it's easy enough to distinguish it from a seal. Much larger, more brown than gray, a sea lion swims and rolls along the surface, tossing its flippers. It has a pointed, doglike face and visible ears. Out of the water, it has longer limbs and an altogether different, more upright shape. Perhaps it was the sea lion's superior posture that attracted Hollywood, or perhaps they're easier than seals to train or have some other cinematic advantage; I don't know. Hollywood didn't care about correctly depicting a marine mammal, and most viewers, more familiar with E. T. and the Little Mermaid than with either seals or sea lions, didn't have a clue.

Ken keeps an eye on the seal as he works to free the mangled fish. With the head gone, there's no good way to grip it, and the web is tight in the flesh and tangled with bones.

It's not that we begrudge the seals having a meal; it's just that we think they ought to get it on their own. We can only guess how many gilled fish they steal from us. Often there's little evidence—just an empty or near-empty net. Their usual technique is to grab fish by the heads and pull them cleanly through, though sometimes they tear the heads off salmon that are too fat to slide through the web, and rarely, like vandals or epicurean wastrels, they swim along a net and bite out just the sweet bellies.

Ken finally frees the fish and it drops into the boat with a lifeless thud, like a sack of wet sugar. Since we can't sell it, we'll take it home for ourselves. The seal has ducked out of sight—on its way, we imagine, to our next net. We rush to beat it there, though we know our slapping around in a tin boat is no competition to a creature born to the water and shaped like a torpedo. At most, we can try to keep our nets picked clean, to avoid leaving fish dangling like so many buffet items.

Seals—though in recent years they've grown both more numerous and bolder along our beach—have, of course, been a part of the life here for as long as anyone knows. The traditional Dena'ina relied on them for their skins, meat, oil, bladders—all their various parts, down to their whiskers. It took twenty seals to make one large skin boat.

After Americans brought the canned salmon industry to Alaska, seals—despised for eating fish that could otherwise be caught by fishermen—were systematically slaughtered. For most of the past hundred years the government paid a bounty on their noses and even, for a time in the 1950s, dynamited seals at the mouths of salmon rivers. At the peak of bounty hunting in the 1960s, 70,000 seals were taken in a single year. Not until 1972 were seals protected; the federal Marine Mammal Protection Act prohibits the hunting of seals and other marine mammals except by Natives for subsistence purposes.

Today, although seals are notoriously hard to count, biologists estimate there are about 250,000 harbor seals statewide, a population considered healthy. Alarm has arisen only recently over apparent sharp declines in the Gulf of Alaska and the Bering Sea. Those two areas are—perhaps not coincidentally—the locations of aggressive harvesting of bottomfish by factory trawlers.

When we began fishing, we rarely had problems with seals raiding our nets. Most seals in the area kept to the south of us, to the clearer water of the river sloughs and the easy hauling out along the bars. Whether population growth has pushed them north or they've simply learned how to find an easy meal, I don't know. I imagine the sound of our outboard calls seals to our nets in the same way the grind of an electric can opener calls a hungry dog to a kitchen.

Not too many years ago, Alfred and Ann Topkok, Natives originally from the coast near Nome, fished a few miles north of us. We sometimes saw Alfred boat past our camp as he went to hunt seals, and when we visited them at their camp Ann showed us baby booties she sewed from the spotted silver pup skins.

Alfred and Ann are gone now, and the local seals are probably less hunted today than since before the Dena'ina first arrived on these beaches. Perhaps they are also as fearless as any seals, ever.

✧ ✧ ✧

When the tide's high, it's time to move nets.

We tear over the flat water at full throttle, the shore along-side us a narrow band, the water everywhere high and capa-cious, swirling in muddy boils. Darkening clouds make a patchwork of the wide sky. I lift my chin and breathe deeply of the rushing air, lick my lips clean of salt and splashed gurry. We pass under a low-flying flock of gulls, and for a time we neither gain nor lose on them but keep their exact pace, float-ing with them in the same ethereal dimension. We stare at each other, the birds and I. Their wings sweep up and down. I could be a feather, a barb of a feather, one of the one million fluted and hooked barbules of a single feather. I could be the floating lightness of down.

This, too, is a part of fishing.

✧ ✧ ✧

We take a break and go ashore, clipping our bowline to a net. The sun has broken through and beams down warm on the sand, rumpled with old bear prints above the tide line. I shed my gloves and vest, peel neoprene to the waist, open the lunch box, and take a long drink of water. I make myself com-fortable against a rock and unwrap a Fluffernutter sandwich, an obscenely high-fat, high-sugar, sticky concoction of peanut butter and marshmallow cream. Ken and I both ate these as children and somehow came back to them for fishing food, though even the thought of eating one in any other circum-stance makes me gag.

I've taken just two bites before Ken spots a seal at one of our nets and we rush back out.

We pick fish, and then we sit on one net and then another, waiting for more fish, watching for seals. The water's so still we can both see and hear salmon moving past—jumpers behind us, a finner leaving a ripple, small fish squirting through our nets. The jumpers leap elegantly into the light; like dancers or basketball players, they defy gravity to hang in the air, stop-time. We watch one launch itself several times, closer, closer, closer to a net, and then we don't see it again. Another, instead of slipping back tail first or landing on its side, traces a high arc, like a diver springing from a board to make a clean, headfirst entry into a pool.

Why fish jump is one of those questions that may forever entertain us with possible answers. Surely one good reason is to escape predators—in this case, the seals that continue to pop up around us. Some biologists, noting more comely females than hump-backed males among pink salmon jumpers, believe that at least some jumping has to do with females trying to loosen their eggs. I think it's entirely possible that fish may appreciate, on some level, the sensation of leaving the water, of feeling air ruffling through their gills and the blast of all that white light on their eyeballs.

Off to the south, a skiff at Kustatan glides out toward the rising bar.

As we pick one fish, two more hit the net, kicking up splashes of water. Ken shouts, "They're really poppin' now." This is what our former neighbor Lou used to say before he quit fishing and we bought his sites, and it's become part of both our lexicon and our folklore, our ritualistic good-luck chant.

✧ ✧ ✧

The tide goes out. We pull nets from the beach and reset them between offshore anchors. When we return to pick the first of

them, I've only just lifted the corkline and begun to gather
web when a huge, purple face floats up out of the murk.

"King!" The word squeaks through my teeth. We rarely see
king salmon after the beginning of July. Ken squeezes into the
bow, and I let my side of the net go as he studies the way the
fish lies against the net and begins to bunch web around it.
Kings are too large to gill, and when they don't simply bounce
off a net they often only rest up against it or are snagged by a
single tooth. They can be gone in a flash.

Ken loves nothing in fishing more than catching king
salmon, and he is at his most intense at this moment. This is
his art. He works quickly, delicately, wrapping web around the
passive fish and then grabbing for the bundle.

The fish comes alive. It thrashes with violent, tortuous
twists of its body, spraying water ten feet high, which falls on
us in sheets. But Ken has hoisted it over the side, and it dumps
into the boat to finish beating itself out among the little fish.
It's not as large as its shapely head made it out to be—perhaps
thirty-five pounds—but it's a fresh ocean fish, still gleaming,
its spotted tail unfrayed. It's rounded like an old-fashioned
pickle barrel. Near its tail, a couple of scaleless circles the size
of nickels mark where lamprey eels caught a ride through a far
sea.

On average, our kings are smaller than this, but they can
reach Bunyanesque proportions. Earlier this summer, a sport
fisherman across the inlet caught an eighty-nine-pounder. A
catch like that on rod and reel must surely be a thrill, but the
burgeoning sport fishery that's developed around kings threat-
ens those who fish commercially. Across the inlet more than
here, commercial seasons have been shortened—targeted to
sockeyes and timed to avoid the early- and late-running kings.
In addition, fishermen there have begun their own campaign
of releasing live kings from their nets; they hope this altruism

will keep them from losing more fishing time. I try not to be overly pessimistic, but if history is any indicator, the battle over fish won't be won by the commercial side. There are many more of them than there are of us. Already the "sports" get the main allocation of silvers as well as the kings, and now they're casting into the political system for more sockeyes, our money fish.

❖ ❖ ❖

We head for the scow to make a delivery and lighten the boat. As we motor past George and his crew, bent over a net, I slip my hands into our king's gills and hoist it high for them to admire—and envy. George pushes the air with his hands and yells across the water, "Throw it back! Throw it back!"

After we've tied up alongside the scow, Ken and I pitch our salmon. We grip them by their heads, tossing sockeyes into one tote, silvers into another. We keep our own silent counts. The fish drip slime; stiff and discolored now, they handle like sticks of firewood. Ken lifts the king last, steps up onto the scow, and drops it in on top of the sockeyes.

To our north, Mount Spurr towers whitely over the land. A volcano as raw as the beginning of time, Spurr belched ash and steam and nearly brought down a passenger jet just a couple of years back. Its Dena'ina name, which translates to One That Is Burning Inside, attests to its eruptive fame; of the four volcanoes in the region that have been active in my time, it's the only one whose traditional name refers specifically to its status as a volcano.

Today, as we chase fish in its shadow, scientists are poised on Spurr's rim with a NASA robot—the world's most sophisticated, designed for exploring Mars. The spiderlike machine, named *Dante II*, will descend into the crater on its computer-programmed legs and then beam up video and geochemical data to a satellite. I take a minute to marvel at the juxtaposition—fishermen on water as perilous as it's ever been, engaged in the same basic hunt for food that people have pursued since day one, and space technology on the mountain, as state of the art as it gets. What a world we live in, that can accommodate both in the same here and now.

The reason we chose setnetting over other fisheries in the beginning was largely for its simplicity: its basic, low-tech nature. All we really needed was a skiff, a net, and a couple of pairs of hands. When the world's oil was drained, we told ourselves, we would row our boat with oars; we would work with the tides. And yet, I'm surely no Luddite. I follow the space program with a keen interest in all its inventions and discoveries. I want to know about the farthest stars just as I want to know about the bottom of the ocean and the inside of a salmon's brain. If the "crater critter" designed for Mars can also totter down into an active volcano and add to our collective understanding about rocks and gases, that's gravy.

Rachel Carson wrote that the picture of the sea that existed at mid-century was "like a huge canvas on which the artist has indicated the general scheme of his grand design but on which large blank areas await the clarifying touch of his brush." That picture, surely, still has plenty of blank space. Why *do* fish jump? Where do the belugas go when they leave the inlet? What's the reason for the sudden sharp decline in the numbers of seals and sea lions in the Gulf of Alaska? Only recently have marine biologists discovered that the deep ocean floor, long thought to be a biological desert, is in fact home to a diversity of species rivaling those thought to exist on the planet's land surface—somewhere between ten and one hundred million different species. Imagine the possibilities for undersea discoveries in light of the fact that an entire species of large terrestrial mammal—the goatlike *sao la* of Vietnam—escaped scientific notice until 1992.

Although I don't doubt that someday humans and their machines will reside away from the earth's surface, I also believe with absolute certainty that no artificial creation or substitute world will ever be as infinitely interesting and lovely—not to mention munificent—as this one and only earth.

We motor past George again, and this time *he* holds up a fish. It's a pink salmon, we can tell even at a distance—skinny as a knife blade, weighing less than two pounds. If we were closer I'd hear George saying, "I caught one of them spotted-tail fishes, too."

✧ ✧ ✧

At low water we move nets again, back around the point. These offshore sets we make with regular anchors, whose buoys have popped to the surface now that the tide's out and the current has eased. It takes my whole body to lift each anchor while Ken motors into the current; from the soles of my feet to my aching shoulders, every muscle pulls. For each set, I hook the anchor on the gunnel and tie off the outside end of the net to its buoy. We motor to shore; I hop out and fetch the onshore buoy and tie the inside end of the net to it. Then we motor out again, spilling net behind us. When the net is straight and tight, I drop the anchor over.

This time, though, we screw up. One of the nets catches on itself, and a lump of corks and web flies out of the boat all at once. Ken slows and tugs on it, but it doesn't come free, and then the current swings us into rocks, where we bang the prop. We pull back on the net to try again, but as we back up with the motor in gear the net flags, and suddenly there's that abrupt clothy sound that's always like a kick to my gut. The prop has caught web and ground to a stop. Ken swears and slams his hand against the boat, then climbs onto the seat and balances over the transom to begin twisting and untwisting and peeling the tightly wound web from the prop. I'm grateful for the calm weather—that we're not caught in surf and having to hack away with a knife while the boat pitches.

✧ ✧ ✧

All afternoon, seals continue to plague us. We pick nets and find only viscera or telltale catches in the web, and one very large new seal-shaped hole. We break sticks, throw back flounders, and shake out the aptly named jellyfish that roll in the net and fall to pieces like Jell-O taken too soon from a mold. We pause to eat again from our lunch box. I peel an orange with hands that smell as foul as the insides of my leaky rubber gloves. A seal surfaces well outside the net with a flopping fish in its mouth. It bobs high and looks as though it's juggling the fish as part of a circus act, though it must only be trying for a better grip. We continue to pick fish—one by one by one. We're catching more sockeyes than silvers and are glad of that.

Ken chants, "One fish, two fish, red fish, blue fish." I try to remember the words to a Russian peasant rhyme that counts dresses and sacks of flour and magpies. Gulls squabble over something in the rocks and are silenced when an eagle lands in their midst. Eagles are, above all, scavengers, which is one reason Ben Franklin didn't think they were particularly suited to represent our country. "He is a bird of bad moral character," Franklin wrote of the eagle after it was selected as our national symbol over his own favorite, the turkey. "Like those among men who live by sharping and robbing, he is generally poor, and often very lousy." In places with clearer water, eagles are known to dive for fish, but here they rarely even circle the water when salmon are finning or jumping. We've never seen one catch its own fish, though we did once see one carry off a wiggling one.

When the tide comes in, we move our nets back up the beach.

✧ ✧ ✧

At 6:30 we begin to pick up nets, and at 7:00 P.M. on the dot we pull the last piece of web from the water and head in to dump the whole pile on the beach. We deliver again to the scow, tossing our afternoon fish into our totes while George and his crew do the same into theirs. The tender will be by later, sometime during the night; we have only to leave our permit card and some outgoing mail in the "mailbox" tacked to one end of the scow.

While Ken fills our gas tanks from a barrel we keep on the scow, I pour water over the fish and fit the covers back on the totes. I summon a last spurt of energy to wash down the boat, coil lines, rinse the burlap and stretch it to dry. My legs are bruised and my shoulder creaks. The muscles in my hands are tight, and my little finger got squashed between an anchor and the skiff's rail. My chest aches from being pressed into the bow every time I lifted a corkline. I hurt with the hurt of a full day's work, hard work done well.

Before we leave the scow, I take a look into George's totes. We highboated him again, just barely. We have two hundred sixty-two fish for the day.

✧ ✧ ✧

Back at the cabin, I strip off my fishing clothes and wash my face and arms. I scrub aluminum stain from my forearms until they're pink, and then I pick off fish scales with a fingernail. Each scale pops off like a brittle flake, leaving a circle on my skin like a slightly gathered pockmark. There's something satisfying in this picking of scales, even in finding a last, crisp scale days later on the back of my arm. Better than gold stars, they're the medals that remind us how we live with fish.

"We work hard for our fish," I say to Ken. "We work harder for two hundred than we do for a thousand." It's been a long time since we caught anything near a thousand fish in one day, but it's true that when there are more fish to pick, we pick more and work our gear less. It's trying to maximize possibility that's so hard.

Ken yanks off his hip boots and drops them with heavy clunks in the center of the floor. He has mud on his cheeks and fish slime glistening in his beard, and his hair is so matted his scalp shows through. The back of his neck has darkened one more shade. He smiles a tired smile and says, "You can expect to find a little extra in your paycheck this week."

The leftover pizza warming in the oven has begun to fill the cabin with its burnt-cheese and tomato smell. Ken asks, "How many sets do you think we made?"

The individual pieces of the day are becoming a blur to me, but I know Ken recalls every set, every circumstance of every set, every pick of every set. He has a memory that can recall the play of a bridge hand six months earlier, and he carries a map in his head for every city he's ever visited and every road he's driven, just as he knows every contour of our beach and its every rock.

"How many?"

Ken lists our sets in order, holding up a finger for each. "Cove, Point, Emmet's, South Point, Eddyset with a short net, Eddyset with a full net, 12K, short net at Point, Eddyset deep, Lou's, Emmet's deep, Point deep, short net at Slide, full net at Slide, Rock, Campset, Emmet's, Cove."

Eighteen. The recitation is like poetry to me, but it's poetry I want only to wash over me at the bottom of deepest, absolutely motionless sleep. Eat, then sleep. The next fishing day is four days away.

Food Fish and the Fairness Question

Late in July, our friends Tom and Emily come from town to visit and catch salmon in a subsistence fishery, separate from the commercial fishing we do.

Tom is one of our oldest friends, from college days, before any of us came to Alaska. Emily, his daughter, is four—a woodland sprite as tough and resilient as her rubber boots. They've been here before, and Emily's mother, too—though this year, eight months pregnant, she's elected to stay behind.

The day they arrive, Tom and Emily fish in the lake, and Emily reels in her first-ever rainbow trout. She's excited, but not nearly so excited as her father. At the cabin, I find our tape measure and stretch it out beside the fish, lovely in its roundness, its rosy blush. Emily counts the tape's inch marks—thirteen from nose to caudal tip. This one delicately fleshed fish feeds us all.

In the evening, we tune in the radio for statewide news. There's been yet another subsistence lawsuit, and the next day's opening may or may not actually happen—depending on whether a judge allows it to go forward or agrees that the newest set of regulations was improperly adopted and issues a last-minute injunction to shut the fishery down.

Twenty years after Alaskans decided that "subsistence" use should have priority over other resource uses, including commercial and sport, the battle of interpretation goes on. About the only thing most people can agree on is a general definition. *Subsistence: the customary and traditional harvest of fish and wildlife for food and cultural enrichment.*

While we wait for the go/no go word, Tom tells us with obvious pleasure that when he notified his bosses in Anchorage that he would be at fishcamp for a few days, they didn't react in the slightest; it was as though even they understood the rituals of summer. In rural Alaska it goes without saying that people will miss work or school when it's time to fish, to hunt, to gather berries. Even in Anchorage, "going to fishcamp" suggests that intense family time at the peak of summer amid racks of split and drying salmon. It's not just the food that's important, everyone seems to know, but the act of gathering it in. Sustenance comes in more than nutritional forms.

As a reporter, Tom has visited other fishcamps—more traditional ones than ours, Native and generational. In southwest Alaska, where the Yup'ik Eskimo people aren't long removed from a way of life based on seasonal migrations, families routinely pack up in spring and move from town or village to ancestral camps spread along the coast or rivers. Tom has gone along, camping on the tundra and helping in the boats, playing with the kids, and he knows fishcamps as those places where people reconnect to rhythms and values that the rest of the year might be all but lost in the noise of modern life. In Yup'ik camps, the women cut fish with the round-bladed knives called *uluqq*, each in her own style, one learned from her mother and her mother before her for the precise weather conditions and drying methods of the area. Traditional life continues even as fishcamp fishing there has expanded from providing food for the table in the most literal sense to also providing cash incomes.

By contrast, that changeover from subsistence to commercial use occurred a long time ago here in Cook Inlet, where
European and American business presences entered so much
earlier and more forcefully and destroyed earlier cultural patterns. Still, the concept has not been lost. Fishcamps here as
elsewhere carry with them all the sense of seasonal, family-
centered living, of providing the many forms of sustenance.

And, of course, one of those forms of sustenance is what
we're now calling subsistence. It was the honoring of tradition—recognizing the nutritional and cultural needs of
Alaskans, primarily Natives—that led to state and federal subsistence laws. The only problem is that no one has yet figured
out how to implement such laws fairly. Every attempt has divided rural and urban Alaskans, whites and Natives, friends,
neighbors, and relatives. Interpretation and decision making
have fallen to the courts—often to judges in far-off San Francisco.

Although most people may agree that for traditional Native
people, subsistence is an actual economy—a way of providing
food and materials for which, in a cash economy, people would
exchange money—there has been no agreement on where to
draw the lines in this modern state. Can't white people in the
bush share the same harvest dependence as Natives? Doesn't
the cultural need still exist for Natives now living in cities?
Should subsistence be a sort of welfare, reserved for those who
meet certain income guidelines? And what about Alaska's
constitution, which guarantees equal opportunity to all
Alaskans?

Tom and Emily's subsistence obviously isn't the purest form
of resource dependence. Tom has taken time off from his
job—vacation time—to come here, and the grocery store
back home is far closer than this shore, a long trek by car and
plane. Their cultural ties are, like ours, on the thin side—connecting back not through generations of family tradition but

to what we value and have shared together. We're a people who've folded together our pasts and our futures, who've formed our own social and family units and sought meaning within our own rituals. Emily calls Ken "Uncle Kenny." She knows the Dena'ina name for raven—*ggugguyni*—and likes to collect what she calls "beach combs." She's growing up without television reception but with computers and videos, without a flush toilet but with moose in her yard and stew pot, with winter camping trips and Spanish lessons.

I'm glad Tom feels his welcome here, glad that he can speak of this visit and the pattern of which it's a part as his and his daughter's own "going to fishcamp." And yet—in this world of diminishing resources and growing demand, I'm not ready to say that everyone should enjoy this same "right." I want my friends to have fish, but must these fisheries always be directed by the courts, in crisis, with winners and losers, and commercial fishermen usually the ones to give that others may receive? I'm uneasy in my stomach, not even knowing what *I* want.

At the moment, after much thrashing around in the courts and legislature, current law applies subsistence rights very broadly. Every citizen of Alaska—regardless of length of time in the state, place of residency, race, dependence, prior experience, or economic need—is considered by the state to be a subsistence user for the purposes of harvesting fish. On certain days throughout the summer all Alaskans have exactly equal rights to lay a net on this beach, or on any of the other open beaches that extend most of the way around the inlet, and to take "their" twenty-five salmon per household head, ten more for each additional family member. Across the inlet, they can catch even more salmon in a subsistence dipnet fishery. Additionally, anyone with a sport fishing license—resident and nonresident alike—can take "sport" fish with rod and reel, within season and bag limits.

Tom asks about the morning tide and where he should put the net. We assure him we'll be up before the water starts to climb the beach and will help lay out the net. I'm still wrestling, though, with that other question. Wherever will we draw the line, the one to separate those who *must* subsistence fish from those who only want to? Or is that even the right line? Am I trying to draw the line—the circle—too small, too exclusively? Whose culture is it? Whose traditions? Whose fish? What future will there be for those of us who earn a living from catching fish, for those whose living *is* catching fish, for the fish themselves? Alaskans are always accused of wanting to close the door behind them. I stand accused.

But—if every person in the state is a subsistence fisherman and subsistence has priority over all other uses, what then? If everyone now living just in the Cook Inlet basin were to take just ten salmon each year, those three million salmon would come pretty close to the long-term average of the commercial catch in the region. What happens then, not just to Ken and me but also to the thousands of others employed as fishermen, and to the cannery workers, net menders, boatbuilders, outboard repairers, hardware store stockers—all the people who directly and indirectly depend on the commercial industry? What happens to the Native village up the coast, where what cash economy the people have comes from commercial fishing?

Part of me recognizes an agreeable logic in feeding the people who are here, all of them, before we export fish to Tokyo or Chicago, before anyone makes money. It's a bioregional solution: eat what's here. Alaskans should eat salmon from local waters, not Gulf of Mexico shrimp or fish sticks from the North Atlantic's dwindling populations of groundfish. It's what the Dena'ina did, what all peoples did before the invention of cans and freezer vans. Let people feed themselves from what's already theirs, at home.

While the subsistence debate rages on—conspicuously absent any political leadership that might steer us to a kindlier understanding or reasoned solution—the rifts among Alaskans grow wider and deeper. As each "user group" scrambles after its own allocation, we lose sight of what it means to live together with at least tolerance, if not mutual respect. While we argue over moose and salmon, what's really at stake are ways of life. Alaska's urban people, much the majority in the state, very often are of short residence and usually have little understanding of village or bush life. Increasingly, in their attitudes and deeds, these urban people act as though they think there's only one way to live—as they do. They don't understand that subsistence elsewhere might be the work people do, the currency in which they deal, and that commercial fishermen also belong to a tradition and do useful, responsible work. They don't accept that different ways of life and cultural traditions have values that we—as a people, state, and nation—may want to preserve and perpetuate. Cloaking themselves in the language of democracy, they say they want only to assure everyone of equal rights.

The fact is, we don't all live—or believe, dream, eat, earn money, or walk our walks—alike. That diversity is our strength, the strength of Alaskans and of people everywhere. But instead of letting it be so, we're using it to tear ourselves apart.

And me—do I have a right to subsistence resources? As a commercial fisherman, I have another way of getting salmon, to be sure. I also have the opportunity to do other work in winter for money, back in town. On the other hand, beach fishermen have always taken fish to eat; before subsistence fishing was formalized, most camps I know kept a scrap of net, hung without corks so it wasn't obvious, for grabbing a fish for dinner or the smokehouse. It's "customary and traditional"

along our beach to take fish to eat and share, and it's a practice that defines the place as surely as do picking berries and
cutting beach logs for firewood. I suppose I feel I have a *right*
to the fish, just as I assume I have a right to the berries and
firewood and the trails through the woods. I do, and so do you
if you live or even visit here, and all is well until too many
come here and there are no longer berries, wood, space, or fish
to go around.

✧ ✧ ✧

On Tom's day of fishing, there's no injunction. Ken and I help
him tie our ten-fathom net to the running line at low water;
then we watch the tide come in with a lumpy swell that does
not, however, bring many fish. We let the net soak all the way
to high water and partly into the ebb before pulling it in.

As the net drags onto the beach with its catch, Tom pumps
up his enthusiasm. He cries, "Look, Em! Look what we
caught! Here comes another!" while Emily dances over the
beach, twirling like a ballerina. He wants her to like fishing,
to see the salmon as creatures to be admired, to make the connections between fishing and eating. He wants her to remember this moment when, deep in winter, another block of frozen
salmon comes out of the freezer. To be absolutely sure the moment is saved, Tom gets out his camera. He positions Emily
with her hands on the running line, pulling, and then
crouched over a pile of web and gleaming fish. Emily poses
with a finger on a fish's heaving side.

We pick out ten fish—nine silvers and a sockeye—and show
Emily the difference between the two species, the glinty radi-
als in the silver salmon tails. Tom bends awkwardly over the
net, wrestling with the fish, holding them up instead of letting
their weight work toward their own ungilling. He cradles a
fish in the crook of his arm and twists its head. Ken and I snap

fish free more quickly, though it's always harder to pick fish on the beach than over the boat, where the net's stretched open and the fish hang at an easy height. We reset the net for what's left of the tide, and Tom bleeds his fish and takes a photograph of them spread on plywood.

Later, Ken and Emily and I sit in the cabin and look out at Tom, subsisting in what has become a cold rain. In borrowed raingear, he's sliming the fish the way we taught him, running a dull knife over their sides until the dark, bacteria-rich ooze stops working off the skin. He's earnest and slow, taking more time, more care, than we do. When we look again later he's begun to fillet, the easier to pack and transport the fish home. He's slow and looks bedraggled. Ken goes out to help while I discourage Emily from eating all the bacon she's helping to lay on a pizza.

Emily doesn't remember being here two years ago, when she was two. I'm surprised at first, but then I decide that no one remembers much of being two. There's so much to take in at that age that it must all become a blur, like speeding along in a car and trying to watch things out the side window.

I don't remember what age I was when my family began to spend two weeks every summer at a rented camp on a New Hampshire lake or for how many years we did this, but surely I was four one of those summers. I remember a large, dark, mildewy house and a screened-in porch with an ancient gramophone. Sweet wild strawberries grew in the side yard, and snails the size of chestnuts left slime trails in the woods. I remember visits to the nearby country store, which sold penny candy, and hiking up a hill where we inevitably attracted ticks, which my father burned off us with matches. My clearest memories are, however, of the camp's dock and boathouse, where I must have spent many hours bent over a fishing line, hooking tiny sunfish, never anything big enough to eat.

Perhaps I was four—more likely a year or two older—on the day that stands brightest in my memory, when I dangled my line inside the boathouse and watched a turtle swim up out of the green depths to take the bait. It was a large turtle by my standards—not one of those little things that came from pet shops and were kept in plastic bowls made to look like toy swimming pools, but an actual wild turtle with a shell seven or eight inches across. With mixed wonder and horror and perhaps some assistance—I don't remember—I hauled the creature in. My grandfather, visiting at the time, freed its lip from my hook and drilled a small hole along the front edge of its shell so I could put it on a leash. It went home with us at the end of vacation and eventually, before freeze-up, was relocated to a neighborhood pond.

As long as I live, I'll never forget the image of that magnified turtle floating up through green water as if through some mysterious deep sea, its feet like small hands paddling, its rubbery, pimpled neck straining, its cool eye set on my wiggling red worm. I can feel even now the tug of line, the moment I connected to the exquisite beauty of the animal, the possibilities this world might bring. It was I who was caught that day.

I have no idea what species that long-ago turtle was or whether any of the adults properly identified it or instructed me in any of its habits. That wasn't what mattered, any more than the inappropriateness of putting a turtle on a leash. In *A Sense of Wonder,* her book about introducing children to nature, Rachel Carson wrote that it's "not half so important to *know* as to *feel*." Once a person's emotions are engaged, the rest will follow. The child or the adult will find out whatever he or she needs to know in order to continue to satisfy that emotional hunger. How many wildlife biologists started out collecting frogs' eggs and caterpillars? How many philosophers by looking inside a flower or counting stars? How many fishermen began by playing with rubber rafts and snorkels or chasing minnows in a ditch or catching something unexpected with a homemade pole?

I wonder, as we put the much-poked-at pizza in the oven, if Emily will take forward with her any memories from fishcamp that might equate to my turtle. Did the trout she caught make an indelible impression as it swirled up through the lake, its side flashing an unearthly orange light? The salmon today—will she remember the cool touch of silver scale under her finger, the gaping of gill? Or will her childhood be so full of this kind of experience that no one moment will grip her with a sense of powerful discovery and awe, of meeting the unknown? I think of Nathan, a slightly older boy who visited us once. He'd grown up on fishing boats and was perfectly comfortable on the beach and water—climbing all over the rocks, handling fish, steering the skiff. When Ken returned him to his mother, the immediate and exciting thing he had to tell her about was Fluffernutter sandwiches.

Very likely, if anything here strikes Emily with turtle-force, it will be something entirely unanticipated, even unnoticed, by me and other adults. It may be the capture of a common piece of quartz or something I would consider utterly trivial, like a "beach comb" of a plastic doll shoe. It may be something I'm too large or too old to the world to see or appreciate, some mystery that will forever escape me.

Prepare the soil, Rachel Carson said. In early childhood, prepare the soil for the seeds of knowledge and wisdom that will grow there.

✧ ✧ ✧

In the end, Tom and Emily have fifteen salmon to take home.

Driven by the still-ticking clock of townside lives, they leave in a steady rain. Ken and Tom go ahead to the lake, and Emily and I follow more slowly. The wet brush that only swipes at my pant legs and waist engulfs Emily like a jungle, and the deepest mud holes would swallow her if I didn't boost her across them. She complains of the difficulty the whole way, but the one thing she doesn't seem to mind is the rain it-self. Streamlets roll off her duckling-yellow slicker and drip from the end of her nose. She is, after all, an Alaskan child ac-customed to unlovely rain. She knows and accepts it as one el-ement in which she exists.

Meanwhile, I'm left as uncertain as ever about where I think the subsistence line should be drawn, who should get the fish that pass our shore or any shore, and what the future can be for commercial fishermen. I trust Carson—about emotional attachment leading to knowledge and wisdom—and in this I place my hope. Aldo Leopold wrote very much the same thing: "We can be ethical only in relation to something we can see, feel, understand, love, or otherwise have faith in." I want to believe that all fishermen—commercial, sport, and subsistence—make these attachments, concern themselves with salmon in ways that put their care and continuance first, well beyond the arguments about how they'll be divided.

To be sure, ethical behavior was easier when people lived in tribes or bands or small communities, when the rules of right living were incorporated into customs and traditions in ways our modern laws and regulations and court decisions—aimed at large numbers of people scattered across territory to which they might or might not feel responsible—can never sup-plant.

I want, however, even more than this. I want fish forever, and then I want people who live with fish to be able to catch and eat them, and then I want there to still be room in this world of ours for fishcamps. I don't mean vacation camps vis-ited by people temporarily absenting themselves from their "real," working lives. I mean places not of escape but of full and satisfying lives, where fisherfolk continue the traditional work of feeding themselves and others, living their lives in re-spectful relationship to their environment and all those with whom they share it. In such places children may learn that beaches and bodies of water are necessary and true homes, sources of food and of life worth living, places meriting their love and protection.

On up the trail, I swing Emily over yet another mud hole. For the moment I've distracted her from her complaints with the thought of the hot dog her father will buy her once they reach the other side of the inlet. She is only four, and she doesn't know that not every child in the world goes to fish-camp; catches trout and salmon; is expected to slosh over nar-row, drowned trails; and flies in a bush plane. She has yet to learn what she stands to inherit—fish, I hope, and the plea-sures that come with all varieties of fishing, if not a fishcamp life, then at least some connection to that life. By the time she's grown, the world will probably have a very different look to it, but I suspect we won't be done fighting for fish and over fish and about what it means to be nourished, in spirit as well as body. That will be her inheritance, too—a part in the strug-gle to understand what it is we're all doing here, to define what's right and fair.

PART IV
That Which Grows

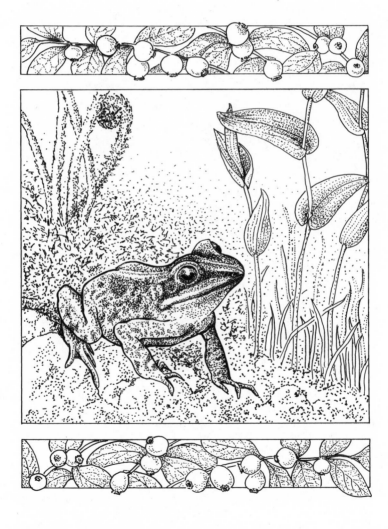

Naming the Green

Our backyard is a rather steep hillside that we've gradually opened from close alder thickets to a sort of meadow. Green alder—that is, alder freshly cut and full of moisture—is our preferred fish-smoking wood, and we take just enough of a stand each year for our smoking needs. This gradual pushing back of the long-limbed, fast-growing trees has also opened the cabin to afternoon sunlight and, we hope, helped stabilize the slope, which, Ken argues, is made more likely to slide down on us by the leaning weight of tilting alders than by a good anchoring mat of grasses and low vegetation.

This creation of open space also suggested to us that we might grow something there, and over the years we've transplanted strawberry and mint plants from a neighbor's camp, raspberry canes from our yard in town, and a single rhubarb plant from a town neighbor's yard. These are hardy things that can dig in their perennial roots, survive the long winters in earth that's more clay and stones than soil, and grow fast enough to give us results before the summer's over. We've terraced and contoured these into the hillside, fertilized them with moose nuggets and nettle tea, and, occasionally, watered them and pulled away horsetails. On this day in early June, the rhubarb plant lifts hand-sized fronds over pencil-thin stalks; the raspberry canes are well leafed; and the leading strawberry plants are budded nearly to bursting. The tallest mint is three-quarters of an inch above ground level, but the plants have multiplied themselves widely well outside the old bed. The latest addition—chives bought at the supermarket—is holding its own, leaves like tender grass.

In truth, though, I'm not a gardener but a hunter-gatherer. I've never taken particular pleasure in nurturing plants or in trying to arrange nature to please a sense of orderly aesthetics, preferring instead to value what exists on its own, in its own time and place. Even in our yard in town, I've seen no need to replace with a trim and chemicalized bluegrass lawn the wild plants that make it their well-adapted business to live in such a spot. People wonder if our house is abandoned, but each spring, moose brush the windows as they browse the first sprouts of fireweed and cow parsnip and flocks of migrating songbirds fill the alders.

The domestic plants at camp are a hobby, a diversion, an acknowledged aberration to the life of this place. What interests me this day, as I gather greens for a salad, are not the transplants but the native plants that inhabit our hillside. They belong here; they are perfectly adapted for this soil, this light, and this amount of moisture, for doing their best in this place. They require no watering, fertilizing, or weeding. At the first sign of spring they leaped from the earth, and now they're thriving.

I graze up the hillside—picking, tasting, forming the right mix for a salad. There's not a single plant present I don't know, not only in name but also in at least a few of its characteristics.

✧ ✧ ✧

These go into the salad bowl:

Fireweed. The fireweed's red shoots appear like magic, absent one day and three inches tall the next, with feathery heads. They're many and tender, and for a long time they play a major part in our salads, though they can also be steamed, stir-fried, or prepared in any way you might prepare asparagus. (Another name for fireweed in its spring form is wild asparagus.) As the stalks grow taller and greener, I pick just the clusters of top leaves. The plants compensate for this amputation, redirecting and even speeding their growth into side shoots that will each eventually create a new top, and by summer's end the yard will look like a field of mutant forms, candelabras of flaming flowers.

The first blooms come in mid-July, when the plants are head-high and so thick they shadow most of the rest of what grows on the hillside. "The salmon are coming," we say as we watch them unfold. From that point on, fireweed serves as the summer's calendar; the pink blossoms open from the bottom and climb the stalks as the days pass, an ever-present reminder of where we stand in time. When the leaves toughen, the petals instead go into our salad.

Beach lovage. A lover of sandy soil, beach lovage is the smallest of three members of the parsley family that grow in the yard and the only one I eat. The leaves, which are arranged in three groups of three, similar to the strawberry's, have a sharp, almost spicy taste that intensifies as the plant matures. Lovage eventually flowers into crowns of tiny white blossoms.

Dandelion. An old familiar, dandelion sends forth its toothy leaves very early and is exceptionally high in A, B, and C vitamins as well as a whole host of minerals. Older leaves can be steamed, the buds pickled, the flowers rolled in flour and fried in butter, and the roots boiled, baked, or added to soups. Early to rise and to bloom, it's also early to seed and is then a favorite of the pine siskins and common redpolls, which bend the stalks with their weight as they pick seeds one by one and send the fluff flying. In late summer the dandelion again sprouts new sets of tender leaves.

Bitter cress. Despite its name, bitter cress, a small member of the many-membered mustard family, isn't bitter, only a bit peppery. I rarely pass it without a nibble. Like the dandelion, it's very high in vitamins A, B, and C as well as in iron, potassium, and other minerals. Aside from its edibility, the most interesting aspect of this plant is the shape of its leaves; the heart-shaped ones around its base are distinctly different from the narrow leaves higher on the stalk, as though they belonged to unrelated plants. The small white flowers have four petals, as do the flowers of all the mustards, whose family name, Cruciferae, means exactly that—flowers shaped like crosses.

Twisted stalk. Also known as wild cucumber and watermelon berry, twisted stalk is true to each name. Its stalk indeed twists, taking a new angle at each leaf juncture so that it looks as if it were somehow assembled from parts by someone of little skill. When peeled for my salad, the stalk tastes very much like cucumber. The berries, which hang heavy and dark red in the fall, resembling little footballs, are less tasty than simply wet, something like watermelon. There is one particular plant, growing among my raspberries, that I leave alone each year to grow and flower and seed; once I watched a black bear do the harvesting, stripping the berries with its facile lips, more quickly and delicately than I might have done by hand. Twisted stalk wasn't known to be much of a food source for the

Dena'ina of this area. Their two names for it translate to "dog's penis berry" and "brown bear's berry."

These other plants inhabit the hillside as well; although they don't go into my salad bowl, each has its uses and delights:

Wormwood. Wormwood's name is unattractive, but less so than its regional name—stinkweed. "Wormwood" comes from its use as a wormer of both people and pets; two cups of wormwood tea per day for two weeks is supposed to take care of roundworms and pinworms. "Stinkweed" refers to the plant's distinctive odor, which is actually quite pleasant. The leaves, which appear very early in spring at the base of the previous year's seedy stalks, are deeply toothed and somewhat lacy looking, with silvery undersides.

In Alaska, wormwood might be considered the "magic bullet" of traditional medicines; it's the plant most often turned to by Natives for a very wide range of ailments—for colds, sore throats, sore muscles, athlete's foot, toothaches, earaches, tumors, any kind of infection, arthritis, sore eyes, and boils; as a help for pregnant women; and more. The Dena'ina still use it for a steambath switch and also rub fresh wormwood leaves over themselves in the steambath "to help get rid of any sickness," according to Priscilla Russell's ethnobotany, *Tanaina Plantlore*. Once I tried it as a hot tub switch, to see if, as Peter Kalifornsky claimed, I could taste wormwood in my mouth right after slapping it on my skin. (I couldn't.) Wormwood is a major ingredient in a commercial liniment used by fishermen to treat sore, beat-up hands and prevent infection, and it is also commonly used as both an insect repellent and a relief to bug-bite itching. When I pass a plant, I like to pinch off a leaf and roll it my hands, just for its scent and goodwill.

Horsetail. Horsetail, survivor of three hundred million years of ice ages and other inhospitalities, is one of the earth's old-

est and most tenacious plants. It has two forms, both of which
have jointed stalks, the characteristic responsible for its other
common name—jointed grass. The early spring form is brown
and leafless, with a cone head containing spores. The green
form, which is sterile, looks like a miniature fir tree or a bottle brush. Both forms can be eaten, and the Dena'ina especially value the berrylike tubers that grow on the spring roots.
When prepared as a tea or tincture, horsetail is also said to be
useful in treating kidney, lung, and other disorders. My favorite use is as a scourer; the green plants are rich in silica, and
I had better success in cleaning rust off an old barbecue rack
with handfuls of horsetail than I did with a wire brush.

Yarrow. Yarrow in spring looks like little ferns, which can be
eaten if you don't mind the feathery texture and the strong,
peppery taste. I prefer to use the leaves externally as a mosquito repellent and to enjoy the bursts of white flowers in their
time. Medicinally, yarrow reportedly works well as a blood-
clotting agent (other common names include nosebleed, soldier's woundwort, and staunchwort) and infection killer.

Angelica. Angelica is in the same parsley family as beach lovage, cow parsnip, and the extremely poisonous water hemlock, all of which bear their flowers in umbrella-like clusters
supported by many spokes. The Dena'ina consider angelica
one of their strongest medicines and use the root externally to
treat cuts, sores, and various infections. Fresh angelica root
was reportedly eaten by Canadian Indians to commit suicide.
I leave the plant alone except for weeding it from around the
strawberries to give them more light; the bulbous root pulls
easily from the ground, as though one of its additional attri-
butes lies in loosening and aerating the soil.

Willow. New growth is sprouting from the roots of a willow
tree we cut years ago. The willow's catkins, young leaves,

spring shoots, and inner bark are all edible though not necessarily palatable. I forgo their high vitamin C content (ten times that of an orange) but will occasionally chew a willow twig for its salicin, sometimes known as "nature's aspirin."

Grass. I don't know the names of any of the several grasses and sedges that grow here, only that it all goes to seed about the middle of July and sends Ken into paroxysms of sneezing. Just before it seeds, I attack the yard and knock off the grassheads with a manual version of a Weed Eater—a stick with a wavy metal edge that, when whipped into the grass, bends and sometimes breaks the stems. Where the grass mixes with the blooming fireweed, I select by hand, yanking stalks in my gloved fists. Right now, the first bold shoots are only just rising from the yellowed mat of previous years' growth—the mulch that has warmed, like straw, the side of hill.

Moss. Where we've cleared and benched areas for our strawberries and mint, short-napped mosses have moved in, creating a groundcover around our plants like the felt on a pool table. It seems our interventions have created microenvironments that are wetter and less well drained than the rest of the hillside. This same moss covers some of the rocks. I touch some and it lifts off its rock like a loose toupee; the underside is attached not to the rock but to a weave of old grasses that overlie the rock. The grasses and the underside of the moss have made a warm, moist place for several small beetles with brown-fluted wing covers and one fat grub. I replace the toupee carefully, patting it lightly back into place.

Starflower. They're only short, starchy-green plants now, but very soon the starflowers will pop open their delightful, seven-pointed flowers. When I walk among them when they're in flower, their flat-open faces seem to follow me and I feel as though I exist in a kind of middle earth, between the starry fir-

mament and this mimicking lower world of equal complexity
and mystery.

Cow parsnip. Cow parsnip, the third and largest of our parsley
family members, is a plant I prefer to call by its regional name,
pushki (or *pootschki* or *buchgi*), a loanword from the Russians.
It's also sometimes known as wild celery or Indian celery, and
its stalk is indeed celery-like, a bounteous vegetable that once
peeled can be eaten raw or cooked. It was and remains a significant food source for Natives, who also use the root for
medicinal purposes.

My interest in *pushki* is primarily in noting that it's one of
the earliest plants to lift its head in spring. I've collected leaf
clusters from the bases of the previous year's dead stalks and
eaten them as boiled greens. They were edible, certainly,
though I was in more of an experimental than gastronomical
mode; I wanted to assure myself that if the supermarket
shelves were suddenly bare, I could still find something fresh
and green to eat in April.

Pushki, however, very quickly overshoots everything around
it, stretching to eight or nine feet, with leaves as wide as dinner napkins and stems as big around as napkin rings. The
stems are hairy and contain a sap that, especially in sunlight,
can be extremely irritating to the skin. I generally leave *pushki*
alone to tower and crown into parasols of white flowers and
then to fade away into hollow stalks of many potential new
uses. I once used one in a pinch to carry water, but wherever
there are children the stalks are most often made into sword-
fight weaponry.

Currant. The currant, sporting symmetrical, maple-shaped
leaves, is already in bloom with pink flowers that later will
turn to sour red berries. It drapes itself over the hillside now
but will soon be hidden behind fireweed and grass.

Elder. The elder bush is sometimes known as Alaska's lilac, for the clusters of white flowers it will soon bear. The flowers later mature into red berries with seeds that are toxic to people and thoroughly enjoyed by birds. The strong-smelling leaves are said to repel mosquitoes but are less pleasant to the human wearer than the alternatives of wormwood and yarrow.

Lady fern. A week ago I could still find tightly curled lady fern fiddleheads to sauté. With enough butter and garlic, even vegetable-phobic Ken exclaimed over them. But now the ladies have all stretched and unfurled into lacy loveliness. If I really wanted to, I could continue to harvest fiddleheads all summer by cutting back a patch of ferns and forcing them to start again and again with fiddleheads from the roots.

Devil's club. The devil's club is so nutritious that it must guard itself—every bit of its thick stem and flappy leaves—with hellish spines that a person need only brush against to find deeply embedded in hand or bare knee. Although the very early leaf clusters may be eaten and the root is medicinal (devil's club belongs to the ginseng family), I generally keep my distance. The red berries of fall, which grow in a tight fist on the end of the "club," are a favorite of bears; the black bear that ate our backyard watermelon berries also swiped a mouthful of these as it continued up the hill.

Devil's club, elder, currant, twisted stalk—it's no accident that the berries of all these are red. Red is a beacon color for birds and many mammals, and it's to a plant's advantage to be noticed in a way that will lead to seed dispersal. Red is not, however, visible to insects, which might infest berries with their larvae.

Alder. The alder trees begin, tall and shady, at the terminus of our cut. They're catkined now, though many of last year's

brown cones are still hanging on. Alders love disturbed places
and are the first trees to grow into the retreat paths of glaciers,
mud-slid gullies, and abandoned roads. They are nitrogen fix-
ers—that is, their roots are inhabited by bacteria able to take
in gaseous nitrogen from air spaces in the soil and convert it
into soluble nitrogen compounds that the alders can absorb.
When the trees die and decompose, the nitrogen is released to
fertilize other plants.

✧ ✧ ✧

To think that we used to buy iceberg lettuce in town and carry
it to this green place—the effort was as silly as it would have
been to bring canned tuna to a shore awash in fresh salmon.
As the store-bought lettuce grew brown-spotted and slimy in
our box under the cabin, we now and then peeled off the
tasteless and watery leaves for salads and sandwiches. We not
only didn't use what we lived among, we didn't even see it; we
were as blind to it as a person with only the dimmest, blurri-
est sight. Except for blueberries, which Ken and I have picked
with a passion from the beginning—perhaps because we knew
them from childhood—the rest was just green background.
When I wanted to, I could identify the obvious—the alders
and devil's club, the grass and dandelions—but I didn't "see"
the plants I didn't know, not even as species and certainly not
as individuals. We didn't have a relationship; there were no
names, no context of knowing.

  In the same way a person might begin to notice every passing car of a certain model after buying one herself, it was only
when I began to learn their names and appearances and
smells—some from field guides, some from other people or my
own novice attentiveness—that the plants among which we
lived became visible. Suddenly, everywhere I looked I saw
wormwood sprigs coming through the earth and then the waving fronds, the leaves lifting their silver sides into cover for

buds, the connections between the living plants and the seedy skeletons among which they grew. Similarly, those leafy, white-crowned plants of the parsley family eventually sorted themselves into *pushki*, angelica, and lovage, and I learned to recognize both their similarities and their differences. I came to notice not just the obvious watermelon berries of late summer but also that plant's first spring appearance, to monitor the twisting and thickening as I waited to harvest the stalks. One day I finally studied those odd brown, prehistoric-looking shoots that grew among the horsetails and discovered something new about plant reproduction.

It took time and attention, but just as in a human community I might finally have learned which person was sister or child of another, which I could count on for help, and which I'd best stay away from, I reached a certain knowing intimacy with the local representatives of that category of living things the Dena'ina call That Which Grows. Each summer, the plants and I grow together, our lives interwoven into the texture of the place.

In his book *Wintergreen*, Robert Michael Pyle wrote about the reasons why he, a butterfly expert, chose to live in a place—Washington's Willipa Hills—that has few butterflies. Chief among them was that, as he put it, "a modest assortment of species is a palpable, tenable array that an average intellect can grasp." In addition, "a simple fauna allows one to concentrate on the individual animal." He went on to describe his observations of a single butterfly, the only one he might see in a day, and the pleasure he took in giving its behavior his full attention. Change "fauna" to "flora" and this is precisely how I feel about the plants in my yard. Another place—with, say, the diversity of a South American rain forest—and my average intellect would not be able to identify even a fraction of the species, never mind be able to take in their relationships to one another and the larger community.

People commonly think of Alaska as having a great deal of "nature." In fact, the diversity and very often the numbers of living creatures in the north are much smaller than those in temperate or tropical areas, and the popular impression of Alaska's wildlife wealth exists only because the state has yet to remodel most of its land for agriculture, cities, and other human purposes or to exterminate its big predators. But the north is a hard place—in climate, food availability, and geographic barriers. Moreover, the ice has been gone for such a short time that the number of species of anything have had little time to evolve, adapt, or move in from elsewhere. Circumnavigate the north and you will find the same caribou or reindeer, the same tundra lichens, the same clouds of mosquitoes all the way around.

In our backyard, as in the waters we fish, we're able to get to know a few things well. I now know every species of plant in view of my door and most others that I can find along the beach, up the creek, and in the woods. I know where to go to find nettles, a single bush of pink chiming bells among the blues, the lovely chocolate lily. I have relationships with individual plants. Here's the one twisted stalk that grows among the raspberries, its buds dangling on crimped threads so thin they're almost invisible. Here's the fireweed whose top I ate two days ago. Here sprouts a tiny new wormwood plant where yesterday there was only a patch of tough earth.

I climb my backyard hill to where several twisted stalks are reaching harvest stage at the edge of the alders. I think of the earlier Dena'ina eating alder catkins and digging horsetail tubers, trying to get through a lean spring to the first runs of salmon. When they gathered plants they left whatever parts they didn't use in neat piles that animals might easily find, and they often replanted pieces of root or seeds. But they also did not hesitate to use what they needed. Among the rules they lived by then and still honor now is this, recorded in Russell's

Tanaina Plantlore: if edible plants are not gathered and used, there will be fewer the following year. If they aren't gathered over a number of years, they will all disappear.

I kneel and cut a twisted stalk neatly through its reddish stem at ground level and then trim the leaves and upper stems into a small pile. I'm wary of the romanticization of Native American cultures and of their appropriation by others, but simple laws of respectful use fit my own cosmology. I like the idea of a vole coming upon my clippings and being able to reach the tender tips. I like to think about the leaves adding cover and warmth to what will grow beneath them and the fact that their decomposition will eventually add to the thin soil.

A varied thrush flits between ferns and lands on the out-stretched limb of an alder. Startled to find me just a few feet away, it tips its tail and defecates—more nutrients for the plants, more recycling among residents. I play a small role even in this: as the surprise that caused the bird to defecate in that particular spot and that kept the bird, perhaps, from nab-bing a spider it otherwise might have pursued among the ferns.

Before I toss my salad, I add one more local edible—a hand-ful of beach greens I gathered earlier, farther along the beach. These cloaked, somewhat waxy greens, once known by sailors as scurvy grass for their good doses of vitamin C, grow in thick mats right at tide line and are tender enough to eat raw all summer long. We used to pick from a generous patch in front of our camp that has since been lost to storm tides. I only hope the plants rode the waves to another shore for someone else's—perhaps a bear's—harvest. With their shallow, runner-style roots, they're clearly designed for such a trip.

Let me be clear: I'm neither a purist nor a traditionalist. The last ingredients I add to my salad are sliced red onion, Greek olives, raw sunflower seeds, and garlic-flavored croutons. I douse the whole with an oil-and-vinegar dressing and then eat of sunlight and rain, the nitrogen fixed by long-dead alders, taste and texture and foreign influences.

✧ ✧ ✧

When I go out to toss olive pits into the compost, a wood frog a couple inches long jumps from a few spoiled grapes I'd thrown there earlier. I wonder if it's been eating the grapes or merely using them as bait for the insects they must attract. In any case, some voracious creature has hollowed each of the grapes from the top, so they appear like Lilliputian green-glass punch bowls.

Impulsively, I grab the frog and hold it so we stare into each other's faces. Its outlaw mask makes it look slightly ornery, and a line of gold, as brilliant as freshly applied gold leaf, edges its upper eyelids. Its heart pulses hard and fast, stretching the skin on its pale chest like the thinnest rubber, pumping pure energy into my hand. I set it down and watch it leap away, skinny legs and all.

Identifying this frog as a wood frog was no feat, as Alaska has a mere two species of frog and one of toad, and the wood frog is the only one of the three to be found this far north. Its range extends well into the Arctic, which makes it the far-thest-north amphibian in the world. The secret to its north-ernness lies in a couple of unique adaptations. Its development is very fast; eggs laid in early spring quickly become tadpoles and then frogs, ensuring complete maturation before freeze-up. The frogs then hibernate, making pockets for themselves in the duff and letting the loose earth and the snow serve as insulation. As further survival assurance, they produce a sort of antifreeze. Wood frogs can, in fact, appear to freeze as solidly as rocks and then thaw back to life.

Frogs take a measure of the earth's health, like the prover-bial canary in the mine shaft, and overall they're presently re-porting, "Not so good." Worldwide they're in rapid decline, thanks to the loss of wetlands and the prevalence of pesticides and other chemicals in their food and water. Some scientists also conjecture that their sensitive skin is being scorched by the ultraviolet light that passes with increasing intensity through the earth's thinning ozone.

I leave my kitchen midden, my little pile of weedings and organic refuse. By adding olive pits and green grapes I suppose I'm disrupting the local ecology in a minor way, though neither, at least, will take root or, I trust, introduce any disease. This is not a paradise like Hawaii, where introduced species flourish at the expense of native ones. Not even a rat would survive here. There are few places left in the world that aren't, however, global in the sense that they participate in some sort of long-distance commerce. The bones of the salmon we catch must end up in Japanese landfills or gardens or be run through Japanese kitchen disposals and sent back to a different corner of the sea. The dollars I earn for one red salmon buy me one jar of tasty olives from a Mediterranean shore. So the modern world goes 'round.

❖ ❖ ❖

An hour later the sky opens and rain showers down for a brief moment. When I step out again, the day is the kind Thoreau used to call a "washing" day, when everything looks freshly washed and polished. The air is thick with mingled scents of damp earth and oily plant breaths. I move along the hillside path, admiring the freshly quickened life. Every leaf of every plant looks shapely and entirely unblemished, as though it wears a fresh coat of paint, and the pink currant flowers swell under water droplets that act as magnifying lenses. I pick a sprig of bitter cress and savor its clean bite, stroke a rain-jeweled wormwood frond, inhale deeply. Warbler song bursts from the creek willows. When I come to the strawberry patch, the first white blossom has sprung.

The Prettiest Tree

One June morning when I push open the cabin door and step onto the porch, the unmistakable sticky-sweet smell of cottonwood assails me. I sniff the air greedily like a dog searching out the scent of meat, but I can't imagine where the cottonwood smell can be coming from. The nearest cottonwoods I know are a cluster of four stately giants in a draw more than a mile up the beach. For years I assumed the location we know as Hightowers was named after those high, towering trees, but then I learned there had been people of that name—a family that once fished for George—who had tucked their camp into the bottom of the draw. I continue to spell the place-name without a possessive apostrophe and to associate it primarily with its trees.

The light breeze out of the north has picked up an almost balmy early morning warmth from the beach, exposed at a zero tide and baking under the sun. It stirs the alders and willows along the creek, but their subtler scents aren't what I'm smelling.

It's possible that somewhere close along the beach there's a cottonwood drift log still partly alive, sprouting new stems from its old, broken trunk. These trees—as wide as sofas and more than a hundred feet long—often wash down northern rivers during floods and ride up along our beach, where they roll and grind against rocks until they wear their root systems to stone-tied knots and shed their thickly furrowed bark in slabs like long serving plates. But sometimes these broken and battered trees come to perch onshore with their life intact, shiny new leaf bunches erupting from crevices in their bark. Undetected, such a tree may have burrowed into our beach.

The other possibility is that cottonwood, its capsuled seed carried by a bird or another animal, has made its way to our own creek bed. Cottonwoods like alluvial places, which is why they so often find themselves being washed out of river valleys and floodplains. One might well have found a receptive home in our draw, which has recovered from its flood enough to have hearty colonizers holding the banks together and adding nutrients to the sandy soil. I haven't seen round, shiny leaves among the thickening alders and willows, but they could certainly be there, wafting out their scent.

✧ ✧ ✧

Of all the trees I know, the cottonwood is my favorite, though I also love birches and aspens for their smooth lines and rattling leaves and the soft yellows of their fall foliage. Birches I grew up with in New Hampshire—the home, after all, of Robert Frost, whose poem "Birches" I once recited in a school talent show. Since then, I've never seen a birch tree without thinking of Frost's lines about ice storms and bending trees and boys swinging them, though the paper birches we have here are a different make—stout and gnarly instead of long and elegant. Aspens I discovered in the Colorado mountains, where sheepherders carved their names into the trees' smooth bark and the western light shone through their leaves like sprayed sulfur.

Cottonwoods I didn't meet until I came to Alaska. During our first years, Ken and I lived in a homestead house that looked out on a grove of trees I thought of as long-armed dancers. In spring their "cotton" lofted past our windows, and in fall the leaves turned a soft yellow that I found more arresting than all the hues of the flaming maples I'd grown up with. Mostly, though, I remember those cottonwoods in winter, bare and gray, trimmed with curvaceous layers of snow. There were others along the road to town, and all of them seemed like works of art, most graceful among the stunted spruce, reaching high over fields and a winding river.

Why the cottonwood appeals to me so much I don't know. The reasons must be aesthetic rather than associative, though sometimes I like to think my memory may reach beyond childhood, past my birth and back into my genes. People who study such things say that those who like to surround their homes with lawns and cover their living spaces with carpets are exhibiting a deep, innate preference for grass landscapes, possibly attributable to human origins on the East African savannas. Lawns and carpets don't do much for me, but wild places and trees do; maybe I go back to ancestors that weren't yet committed to running around on two feet.

Other than that, I'm willing to think that somewhere in my genetic past, between my human origins and my New England forebears, there were cottonwoods or cottonwood-like trees and that when I react to the sight and smell of them, there's something more at work than simple aesthetics. *Populus* is well represented in the world a long way back; in Genesis, Jacob reportedly wove its branches into a striped pattern to encourage his goats and sheep to produce striped offspring. More significantly, people have for a very long time settled in the company of cottonwoods, since the thirsty trees are a sure sign of available water. Even in rain-rich Alaska, the old homestead cabins are very often set beside cottonwood groves. It makes perfect sense for our deep instincts still to recognize cotton-woods as signifying "home."

Aldo Leopold wrote, "To me an ancient cottonwood is the greatest of trees because in his youth he shaded the buffalo and wore a halo of pigeons, and I like a young cottonwood because he may some day become ancient." I can only say, *Amen.*

✧ ✧ ✧

Later in the day I set off on a cottonwood hunt, hoping to find the source of the morning scent and knowing I'll at least find bark for my smokehouse fire. I walk leisurely along the top of the beach, sniffing, stopping to look at a particularly well-endowed male willow tree, its show of catkins spiky with golden pollen. Of the three hundred willow species worldwide, about fifty grow in Alaska, half of those in this region; these hybridize with one another so that even experts have trouble telling them apart. I don't begin to know one from the next, only that some, like these, are more substantial than the bushy wetland varieties favored by moose—and that a willow is either male or female, with the female's catkins made up of ovaries that develop seeds.

Along the banks, where sunlight has reached, I find starflowers in bloom and the first purple lupine flowers to have popped loose. Elderberry shrubs, too, tucked in among the alders and willows, wear lilaclike clusters of white. Bear tracks of at least three different sizes are thick but indistinct along the top of the beach; we haven't had an obliterating high tide in nearly two weeks. Scattered among the drift I find a couple lengths of birch we cut last summer and threw up on a bank to haul home on a nice day that never came. Beached birch trees are uncommon, and we prize as stove wood whatever we find.

I come before long to a cottonwood log, rubbed bare of all its bark. Even so, I examine it for possible sprouts, for signs of life, a scent that might carry on the air. There are only stones embedded in its knots and caught among its broken roots and claw marks along its smooth side, where a bear has walked across it. The root end is partly hollowed; the tree has rotted from the inside out, and I see how soft it is there, with the wood splitting into curved pieces. The Dena'ina used to seek out precisely such logs to use for roofing; the curved pieces, overlaid much like Spanish roofing tiles, were just as efficient in shedding rain.

I find another, thinner cottonwood. This one is still patchy with bark, and where the outer bark has been ripped free, tresses of finely shredded cambium hang loose like manes of hair. Cottonwood cambium, like that of its willow cousin, is edible, especially in spring; it often served the traditional Dena'ina in times of famine, even being ground into flour. This tree, though, is well dead and scentless.

✧ ✧ ✧

Farther on, I reach my destination—a berm of drift logs behind which piles of cottonwood bark have washed up since last season. I stuff my gunnysack. Some hunks are as long as my arm, some as small as my hand. All are dry and light, a half-inch to an inch thick, and their inner surfaces are smooth except where they're still stuck with strands of cambium. That smooth side makes a good painting surface, and I'm reminded of how much bark ends up in tourist shops decorated with wildflower designs. Cottonwood bark is, as well, easily carved; the Dena'ina used to shape pieces into spoons, toys, snow goggles, and floats for their fishing nets, and now souvenir hunters can buy little animal or totem pole carvings.

It was Native neighbors who taught us to add cottonwood bark to our alder fires for fish smoking; the bark gets a fire going easily, smolders well when wet, and imparts a nice flavor to the fish. From a traditional, pre-chain saw point of view, it was also easy, needing only scavenging. Other people use hunks of split cottonwood for smoking, though we prefer the slow burn of green alder. Cottonwood burns without much heat, so it's good for smoking but not for other kinds of fires.

Cottonwood, in fact, is generally not well appreciated in economic terms. In some places, it's processed for paper. As lumber, the wood has a pretty yellow color and a nice grain, but because so much of the tree is water, the wood shrinks badly. Ken likes to say, "A twelve-inch cottonwood board will shrink an inch a year for thirteen years."

Even the traditional Dena'ina criticized the cottonwood's usefulness. Peter Kalifornsky, in describing the Dena'ina belief about the pairing of plants when the world was first created, passed on the understanding that "cottonwood, which is the prettiest tree, is the most worthless." For all its worthlessness compared with birches, spruces, and so many other plants of greater purpose, the Dena'ina still did value its looks. In a study of Dena'ina place-names, cottonwood appeared more than any other plant name; clearly it was something the first people paid attention to, something they noticed as they marked locations. And though the Dena'ina treated all plants with respect, the cottonwood seemed to demand a little extra. Old Dena'ina from the river valleys north of here tell a story of someone who camped near a cottonwood and died because he didn't treat the tree with proper respect.

I haul my sack of bark home without having found the source of the cottonwood scent. It may be only that a sprigging tree rode past on the waves.

✧ ✧ ✧

Another day, on the way to George's to borrow a pipe fitting, I suggest to Ken that we stop at Hightowers. For years I've been watching the big cottonwoods high on the bluff and letting my eyes wander through the tall-grass meadow around them. The spot draws me with a sort of magnetism, some ideal combination of pastoral softness and wild beauty, much like the sunny slope beside the beaver pond where I saw the expected bear. I can imagine picnicking there, or camping under the swoosh of big leaves, or just being for a few minutes a small presence between two heights—the beach below and the high, sculpted limbs overhead. I regret that in all the times of all the summers I've walked by, I've never yielded to the pull, never climbed the hill. In another week, the vegetation will be too dense for me to make my way through, and I'll have lost another year's chance.

A steep, sweaty climb through prickly and stinging plants is not a chance Ken minds missing. He won't come with me, but he's happy enough to add to his agate count while he waits on the beach. It strikes me that this is our yin and yang: Ken, on the beach, faces the ocean, conscious always of jumping fish, the rising back of a whale, or a piece of possibly interesting flotsam passing on the tide. He is a true mariner. On the same beach, I'm as likely to have my back to the sea, instead watching swallows dart in and out of holes in the bluff or peering through the alders at a spot of color. I don't cleave to the ocean as I do to the land, don't find the same comfort in its slippery movements and bottomless cold.

I clamber through willows and over rotten planks that must once have been part of a stairway along the creek, which rolls through rocks in a crease down the center of the precipitous draw. Rose brambles claw at me, and I try to avoid patches of stinging nettles. My passage disturbs mosquitoes resting in the weeds, and they fly up in buzzy clouds. Dwarf dogwood is in bloom, in sets of four white bracts designed to look like showy petals and bring pollinators to the dark, tiny, easily overlooked flowers at their centers. Chiming bells also are full in flower, casting a cool blue light over the hillside. Twisted stalk elbows into odd angles, its lines of droplet-shaped buds dangling on thready stems. *Pushki* spreads wide, furred leaves that will soon overshadow nearly everything else on the hillside. I place my feet with difficulty, crossing and recrossing the steep-sided creek.

The trees, when I reach them, are thick bodied and athletic, their bark so deeply grooved I feel I can almost slide inside through its cracks. It would take two of me to reach my arms around any one of the trunks. The fresh leaves are perfectly shaped, spangling in the sun, and new growth sprouts all the way to ground level. I pull off a leafy twig at a nodule, where stem connects to branch. I'm looking for stars.

This is a bit of cottonwood lore I learned from Robert Michael Pyle, the butterfly man, who wrote that the cottonwood twig breaks off in a star shape. The Arapaho people of the Colorado plains believed that this was how the stars came to populate the heavens—straight out of cottonwood trees. The stars were born in the earth and flowed through the roots of cottonwoods and up their trunks to wait at the tips of the branches. When the night spirit wanted more stars, it would ask the wind spirit to break them out of the trees. After storms, the Arapaho said, you always find these star-ended twigs on the ground under the trees, as sure as proof.

It's true. Inside my broken twig I find a dark center in yellow wood with points radiating outward, a single star as lovely and mysterious as the heavens. The juncture is still sappy, the sweet smell intoxicating.

Below me, an inverted triangle of beach shines white in the sun, opening out to water as smooth and glaring as chrome. Cumulus clouds are building over the far shore. Mosquitoes fly into my eyes and attack the bare backs of my hands and neck, and there's no question, even if Ken weren't waiting, of lingering in pastoral splendor, lolling on the hill. Nor do I feel driven to pass beyond the trees to climb another couple hundred feet to the top of the bluff, where dark spruces prick the sky.

I swat mosquitoes and notice a cluster of paper wasp nests on one cottonwood and, on the next, a downy gray bird feather fluffing in a tiny hammock formed by two leaves. Two of the trees grow like twins, their bottom trunks pressed together, and the farthest tree leans uphill at a sharp angle, as though its weight is slowly pulling it to the ground. All four trees are arranged in a straight line, and I see that in fact they have all grown from the same nurse log, ancient now but still exposing its crumbling corpse in the grasses at their feet. I circle the trees again and wonder whether the Hightower family paid much attention to the trees thirty years ago or whether they kept to their tent platform in the lower draw, fishing and looking out. Back then, with fishing a full-time business, there probably wasn't time to look at trees. The grass under my feet might hide a rusted can or an old bottle, but I see no stumps, no axe marks, no nails or old lines, no sign of human use or occupancy.

The Dena'ina knew of what they spoke: the cottonwood is simply prettiest. That's enough, finally, and it doesn't matter if my own attraction lacks a cultural or associative basis or even a genetic one. I think again about Dena'ina respect as I take a last look up into the leafy crowns and then open my pocketknife and carefully trim three short branches from the bushy growth around the base of the twin trees. Back down the hill, I set them in creek water at the top of the beach and then run in circles until I lose my tag-along mosquitoes.

Ken asks, "What are those for?"

"I'm going to plant them along our creek." I tell him that cottonwood branches are supposed to root and transplant easily. I tell him, too, that in some places where water is scarce, people have cut down lovely old stream-bank cottonwoods because they thought they sucked up too much water. They do drink a lot, perhaps as much as a thousand gallons per day per mature tree, according to Pyle, but they also act as reservoirs, storing water and releasing it through their leaves.

"Plant one beside the smokehouse," Ken says. "I'd like to see it dry out the mucky seep there."

I laugh. "It won't happen right away."

"Fifty years?" He seems content to wait.

When we get home, I set the branches in a tall jar of water. Their scent fills the cabin. My plant-lore book tells me that cottonwood buds are burned to clear the psyche for dreaming and that dried buds can be added to balms and pillows. I sleep in the scent of cottonwood and, that night, dream wildly. On waking, the only dream I recall in detail involves taking a lengthy and elaborate bath in the house where I lived as a child; it's a dream full of water, all of it rushing, pouring, and spraying, all of it clean and sweet smelling.

Thinking Like a Berry Bush

There are other berries — salmonberries, watermelon berries, cloudberries, highbush cranberries, bog cranberries, lingonberries, crowberries, currants, a few wild raspberries — but blueberries are the berries that count with us. It's blueberries we've picked from the beginning, blueberries as much as fish that mark the passage of our summers.

Although we eat them by the bowlful with milk, in cobbler and buckle, in muffins and pancakes, sprinkled over waffles or stewed to a sauce, we prefer above all else a hot blueberry pie or two. I'll eat half a pie hot and soupy from the oven, and then two hours later I'll reheat and eat the rest. When it comes to blueberry pie, I outeat even Ken.

We log the date of each year's first blueberry pie in the book where we record the numbers and species of fish we catch, tide and weather and best-net details, and announcements from the Department of Fish and Game. Pie dates are the only non-fishing information in the book.

We make multiple pies and spread them like cheer. With Ken's Rube Goldberg invention of inverted pie tins and Styrofoam cutouts, string, and a bucket, we carry hot pies along the beach. We deliver pie to George and to the crew on the tender. Our pies are decorated with crude fork-puncture designs meant to represent fish.

This is not, however, a blueberry year. We wait, and a few ripen along the trail. We eat them and wait for more. All our dates of previous pies pass.

✧ ✧ ✧

One day while Ken's setting posts for a new breakwater, I scour the blueberry patches above our camp. The woods are dappled with sunlight and sweet with a muddy decay. The roses are gone, but wild geraniums hold up their pale, summer-sky petals. Chickadees work over a dead snag, tweezing insects from around and between scabs of bark; I watch one pluck a broad-winged moth from a branch and hold it sideways in its bill like a large bow.

I pick berries one and two at a time, moving from bush to bush. Sometimes I walk ten or twenty feet between berries, hoping always that around the next bend I'll find the mother lode. Like fishing, berry picking can be an act of faith, an acting out of fondest wish and dream, the desperation of incurable optimism.

In other years, these bushes have been a sea of blue where I could crouch in one place for half an hour and still not have picked all the berries within my reach. It's a mystery to me why there are so few berries this year, why the bushes seem instead to have devoted the season to growing fine displays of well-appointed leaves. It's been a dry summer but not as dry as the previous one, and last year we had all the pies we wanted and still took home twelve quarts of berries for the winter. Spring this year was a little late, but summer caught up soon enough and temperatures have been normal. There's been sun, and the sunlight finds its way into openings around the bent spruces and the awning-sized devil's club leaves.

The only other year I can remember witnessing such a berry failure was the summer it stormed nearly every day. Our Kustatan neighbor told us, with what seemed the confidence of long experience, that the problem was too much salt spray in the air. We had, in fact, noticed that even in the woods we couldn't escape the earth-shaking pounds of the surf, and the air all around felt misty and cool.

I pick the berries I can find, and they ring one at a time into the bottom of my bucket. The picking itself—however slow, however little I'll have to show for it at the end of the day— has its own sacred-time value. I listen to music not of the spheres but of the earth close at hand—the background buzzing of millions of mosquitoes, the dee-deeing of the chickadees, the squeak of wood as an alder branch grows the one micromillimeter more that forces it against another limb.

Of all the things we do at fishcamp, blueberry picking takes me closest to familiarity—to connections with my childhood. My family made late-summer blueberrying excursions, just as we went apple picking in the fall and traipsed through December's snow to cut a Christmas tree each year. Perhaps it's only because I was smaller then, but I remember the berry bushes towering over my head, dangling their dark fruit like grapes. I liked being in a thick, unruly growing place where— if I could believe one of my favorite books—it might be possible to come face to face with a fellow berry-picking bear. I wanted to be the little girl in *Blueberries for Sal;* I wanted to meet a bear. But there were few bears in the New Hampshire woods then, and the places where my family picked berries and apples and cut Christmas trees weren't wild at all but pick-your-own farms where we paid as we left, by the pint and the bushel and the foot. The woods and fields were tame and organized, compromised by ownership and careful pruning. In those days I was too young to put a name on my discontent, but I know I felt it—a wish and a dream for something more.

These days, of course, I don't *really* want to meet a bear face-to-face in the berry patch. It's wiser and safer for us to keep clear of each other in the woods, but I do like to see—there—flattened bushes where a large animal recently walked and—there—a disintegrating pile of furry scat. I know I'm not really alone here. Every now and then, as I move to a new picking area, I add a few toots to the woods' chorus: a couple of bars of untuned whistling or a "Ho-ho-bear," just enough to make myself known.

After a time I wander along a game trail to an opening in the woods, the edge of a bog. I pick the few berries that grow around the edge and then walk into sunlight. The trail crosses the bog like a trench, packed by the weight of regular moose and bear traffic into a hard-bottomed depression about a foot lower than the surrounding ground. When I leave the trail, the surface is spongy and uneven, and I tip and stumble like a drunk.

The wild irises, which must have been glorious purple flags a week ago, are folded up like dirty socks, leaving rattly seed pods. But the cloudberries! The cloudberries are everywhere on the surface like gobs of orange salmon eggs, like riches dumped from the heavens by a Jack-in-the-Beanstalk character. I eat several; they're soft and delicate but not really to my taste. The feast for me is simply in the looking.

I walk farther along the trail, into the middle of the bog. I sniff at Labrador tea, note the cranberries and crowberries, the low bog willow and tiny spruce trees, the white-tipped cotton grass. After the woods, this landscape feels comfortably exposed, a place where I can look both close and far and tread unannounced. There are no bears to surprise here.

A sudden crash throws me off-step, and then I seem to be in the center of a whirlwind, with wings beating every which way around me. I grip my berry bucket hard in front of me, holding it like a shield, but the tempest is already receding. It's

only *ełyin*, the old spruce grouse. White people call them "fool
hens" and think them unwitting. Native people are more generous, grateful to the birds for the agreeableness with which
they offer themselves to the hungry. The traditional Dena'ina
way of hunting them was with sticks—by first tossing rocks
over their heads to make them think a hawk was attacking
and then walking right up and striking them while they cow-
ered. This one has a brood of at least a dozen chicks, scattered
now and settled like spray into the margins of the woods. The
hen, which at first had launched herself straight up into the
sky, struts along the bare-bone limb of a spruce snag, well out
in the open. She clucks brusquely until I'm back into the berry
bushes from which I came.

I pick and pick, and I finally go home with enough blueberries for muffins.

❖ ❖ ❖

Two weeks later, we're desperate. Ken announces an expedition. He knows the berry hot spots. He will lead us, and we
will surely find enough for a pie.

Richard, one of George's helpers, comes along. Armed with
bug spray and buckets and Ken's metal berry picker for raking
the really loaded bushes, we climb the hill and enter the
woods. Mushrooms have popped up all over; we pass inky caps
dissolving to black goo and warty red amanitas, deadly poisonous or transcendentally hallucinogenic, depending on one's
point of view. Although the amanita has a long history in Native cultures as a ritual hallucinogen that allowed shamans to
communicate directly with their spirit guides, I don't know
anyone who's been brave enough, foolish enough, or sure
enough of his or her spiritual power to try a taste. We sweep
past ripe watermelon berries and near-ripe highbush cranberries, and Ken leads us off the trail into blueberry bushes as

empty as the ones I'd picked earlier. We pick and wander, and after a long time our sounds are still of single berries hitting the bare bottoms of our buckets. Ken forges ahead and returns, disgusted. There's only one thing to do: try the hottest of all our hot spots, our special reserve at the end of the lake.

We continue on the trail, stopping only to show Richard a magnificent false hellebore, as high as our heads and drooping thick clusters of greenish flowers, and to sniff around the edge of the beaver pond. When we make a turn in the trail there we're always assailed with a sweet, heathery smell, but we've never been able, despite all our sniffing and leaf pinching, to find its source.

We hike past a spruce tree that stands out like a burning bush or infrared imagery, its needles from top to bottom the color of orange rust. I pause long enough to touch its rough bark and observe the typography of pencil-point-size holes, the riddling of an army of spruce bark beetles. The tree drips with pitch like candle wax, layers upon layers—its last and unsuccessful defense against the invading beetles. Under the bark I know I'd find galleries etched into the wood, empty now of both eggs and the fat white larvae that grew there into beetlehood.

Few spruces in these woods are so bright an orange, but many more stand at either side of this death—either still green and pitchy, their tops drooping with the weight of the seed cones they've given themselves over to, or a plain, washed-out gray. The dead trees grow stiff and brittle and will eventually break apart and blow down. They're not, however, "just" dead trees, "wasted"—as some would have us believe. As they stand dead and as they fall and rot, they're filled with a voracious insect life that supports, in its turn, much of the rest of life in the woods. Even now, a woodpecker drums. From death, as usual, comes new life.

Bark beetles, however much a part of the natural order, are currently at levels considered epidemic in the region, and biologists are predicting significant habitat changes. Across the inlet, where the beetle's spread has been aided by homestead and right-of-way clearing and by poor logging practices that leave downed trees, hundreds of thousands of acres of spruce forest are already entirely dead and dying. Large-scale timber operations are under way to capture economic value from the trees while there's some to be had, though logging won't halt the beetle's spread or reduce the danger of forest fires. The latter argument is a red herring repeated at every opportunity by many in the logging industry and their political allies; the truth is that a live spruce, soaked in highly flammable sap, burns more readily than a dead spruce.

Either way—whether trees are removed by logging or allowed to follow their own course into rot, insect food, and new soil—many now-forested areas, perhaps even here above our camp, are likely to be replaced for a time by a vegetative regime closer to grasslands. The ecological consequences could be significant. Black bears, for example, rely heavily in early fall on devil's club berries, and devil's club plants depend on shady, damp places; both will find it hard living here without spruce forest. So will red squirrels. The one chittering and shaking its tail from the back of the next tree is doing very well at the moment, feasting on seedy endowment. There seems to be some cruel—or at least awkward—irony here: that squirrels are made wealthy and encouraged to eat, breed, and otherwise prosper at the very time their source of wealth is collapsing.

In any case, while the current beetle epidemic continues to be debated in terms of "control" and "salvage," the latest research indicates that even such a large-scale event is perfectly natural and, in fact, that bark beetles may be the key factor in forest succession for this coastal ecosystem, as forest fires are elsewhere. Ever since white people came here, this fact of life has been masked by human activities—principally by purposely or accidentally set fires—but recent tree-ring and lake sediment studies suggest that bark beetles may have caused major spruce die-offs on a fairly regular long-term cycle.

Old trees are most vulnerable to beetle attacks, but I note as I walk that there are young trees in this forest, too, and elfin seedlings just getting started. As the old beetle-killed trees fall and open the canopy, these resistant others will "release," as foresters say—will grow more quickly in the greater space and light.

We start now up the hill to the lake, parting the grass before us and calling out to bears. I slip and come very close to grabbing at a thorny devil's club branch, and then I stop to see what it is I've stepped in. It's bear scat, new since our last trip to the lake, and very seedy. I can't tell what kind of seeds they are—but I take it as a sign we may be headed for blueberrying success.

Slipping in scat flashes me to a story common to a number of Alaskan Native cultures regarding a woman who marries a bear. Hauntingly similar stories appear, in fact, in a wide variety of indigenous cultures around the globe, wherever people have lived among bears. The version I know best is a Tlingit one from southeast Alaska.

The story begins with a young woman slipping in bear scat. She's on her way home from berry picking, and when she slips she spills some of her berries. She curses the bear and then stops to scoop up the dropped berries. A bear, disguised as a man, comes along and takes her for his wife. She lives with the bear and has his children. Eventually her brothers discover the den. The woman is torn in her loyalties between blood and marriage, but the brothers kill the bear and return their sister and her children to the village. There, she drapes herself in the skin of her dead husband and becomes a successful hunter until her jealous brothers attack her. They fight, and in the end the woman, her children, and all but one of the brothers are dead.

Cultural interpretations of the story point out the significance of its beginning—the slipping and swearing. The bear took the woman from her people because she insulted him. She showed disrespect for a fellow creature—in this case a particularly powerful one—and for this it was her fate to be parted from her people to live with bears, to become herself like a bear, to have children who were bears. In the end, when so many have been killed, the story again emphasizes the consequences of breaking taboo and the fragility of relationships between people and animals. It's as fearsome and cautionary as anything in Aesop or the Brothers Grimm, and wholly appropriate to where I stand.

At the lake, the three of us arrange ourselves in the rowboat. Since Ken is the heaviest, he gets to sit in the middle and row, while Richard and I accept the work of balancing each other in the stern and bow.

The yellow pond lilies have given up their petals for another year, but the elderberry bushes around the edge of the lake, so recently snowy with blossoms, are now set with bunched red berries that double themselves in the water's reflection. We row very close by the lake's resident loon—*dujemi* in Dena'ina—which is floating high like a well-painted decoy. The bird calls out, and it's hard not to hear loneliness in its always mournful cry, one that repeats and repeats and gets back only a soft echo from the hillside. For years a pair of loons lived on the lake, and then, about three years ago, Ken found one of them dead, floating bedraggled among the reeds. Even though loons, like swans and various other birds, are said to mate for

life—and such behavior must have evolved for a practical advantage—I wonder aloud why this bird hasn't found a new
mate. Surely it mixes with others of its kind wherever it
spends its ice-free winters, and surely survival of the species is
better ensured by re-pairings after mates are lost.

The three of us float down the lake in company with the
one loon, and Richard tells us something about himself and a
woman who died. We talk about death and healing and the
lives we live and want to live, and though only three of us
speak of these weighty personal issues, *dujemi* is very much a
fourth participant in the dialogue. We would not be having
such a conversation if the loon were not among us and if we
didn't know something both of its general habits and its particular history.

I come back again to thinking about the Dena'ina—how
logical it was for the people of this place to know and report
so much about animals and to return again and again to the
stories from "the time when animals could talk." When Peter
Kalifornsky began to teach the Dena'ina language to others,
his first vocabulary lists were largely the names of animals. He
didn't teach Berlitz-style phrases like "I would like" and "how
much" and "a cup of coffee, please" but began with what was
important—the names by which we can know our fellow creatures.

So many people today live apart from animals and know
nothing of their habits, or what they do know comes not from
firsthand observation but with the gloss and entertainment
value of television. This "extinction of experience" troubles
me—not just because experience is different from viewing but
also because when we don't live with birds or weather or
waves we lose the opportunity to think hard about ourselves,
to discover from nature important facts about *human* nature.
I'm convinced we need something *other than ourselves* in order

to recognize the truths of our existence and make sense of what we do. More than talk shows, advice columns, and psychiatrists, our lives need metaphors.

At the end of the lake we disembark and rove from bush to bush, picking berries one at a time, no more fruitfully than we did in the other woods. Every now and then we call to one another to find out where we are and to hope someone has stumbled into a blue heaven. A beaver patrols the shoreline, slapping its tail.

Away from the others, I climb over fallen trees and brush past blue-caped monkshood blossoms, chasing those single berries, savoring the very few I allow my appetite. In the west, cumulus clouds ascend like castle turrets over the mountains.

Once, in a plant-lore class, the instructor asked each of us to choose a favorite plant and write for ten minutes as though we *were* that plant. I imagined myself as a blueberry bush, bare branched and bent under winter's protective snows, then lifting into light, leafing, popping out all over with pink bellflowers. I wrote about developing hard, green berries that swelled and softened as they turned purple and then satiny blue and how it was when worms burrowed into those berries, and when birds and bears and people picked me over, stripping my leaves, missing the berries that hung low and hidden. I realized as I wrote how little I knew the blueberry plant *except* for its berries. Now I look at the one I'm picking through—not just spotting berries but also studying the way the leaves affix to the stem, their lippy edges and points, the patterns of yellow and brown decay. I draw my hand over the bush and feel it, stiff and prickly, avoiding the taut, glinty thread a spider has strung between branches like a high wire. I trace down the plant to its hoary root and find a very few dropped and withered berries in the moss.

I try for a moment to think like a blueberry bush, and what I think is how good it feels to be in fresh air and sunlight, having a purpose in some larger scheme that's not at all clear except in a few of its connections. A bush takes in light and sucks up water and minerals, becomes what it is, is always becoming, always changing, transforming, giving back, going back. A botanist would describe what a plant does differently, but for the moment I'm thinking as the plant, and it's enough to consider the pleasures of rattly leaves and a few plump berries; a rootedness in thin, acidic soil; a sense of belonging.

Berry-bush perspective is long in time and far in space, and it doesn't include money, fame, power, or any number of other preoccupations of the human species. A berry bush is not obliged to shop for new clothes or to vote for the least-bad candidate. A berry bush is not alarmed by bark beetles and beetle-killed spruce trees; it spreads into sunlight, succeeds, and is succeeded. It knows the patterns because it lives them, and it knows the players because it lives among them. It does not need to be in control.

Ken and I meet back near the rowboat and compare buckets and purple teeth. As usual, I picked—or at least saved—more and cleaner berries than he did; it's one thing at which I have greater talent. He pours my berries in with his own and goes off to show Richard. *Here's what I've picked. Oh, is that all you have?* This is one of Ken's oldest tricks, and Richard is taken in. He's so impressed and then so discouraged with his own effort that I have to yell across the bushes and let him know the truth. The beaver slaps its tail on the water.

✧ ✧ ✧

When I measure out the berries, we have very close to four cups. That night, we eat hot pie.

PART V
Animal Dreams

On Not Being Alone

The swells rolling in over the flats crack against boulders with a sound like distant thunder. Spray hangs as stop-time silver mist before falling onto the gleaming rocks and mingling with the shore foam. When I lie back on the deck, my vision fills with high cirrus clouds stretching into banners and the dozen or so tree swallows that stitch the spaces between them.

Even over the crashing waves, I hear vigorous chirping from behind the camp each time a swallow delivers another mouthful of mosquitoes to the birdhouse there. They seem never to quit—the feeding flights of the parents, the hungry clamor of the young ones. The instincts that drive them must be powerful indeed. I'm not sure I understand how what's good for a species is reconciled with what's good for an individual. If birds think, do these parent swallows ever wonder why they're so driven to do unto others? Certainly no baby bird is ever going to thank them or care for them in their old age.

I haven't seen another person in a week, which doesn't bother me in the least. The fishing season is slow now, between the early run and the main sockeye run that begins in mid-July—not worth the gas and the wear and tear on our gear and ourselves—so Ken has left to run a fish tender in another, fishier part of the state. Before he left he referred to the tender job as his "day job." It does, in fact, provide more of a paycheck than does this life, which is perhaps becoming more art than livelihood. We pulled our boat out of the water, and I'm using the time Ken's away to prepare all our gear, to do camp chores, to think.

People ask me, "Why don't you get someone to stay with you? Aren't you afraid to be alone? Don't you get lonely?"

Alone. Lone. Lonely. Lonesome. Solitary. How negatively our culture defines these words, as though they're all undesirable conditions. "I like to be alone," I say defensively, and I mean, in this context, *without other people*. It is not at all the same as lonely. I'm not lonely when alone; I don't wish not to be alone. And yet, I need only look in the dictionary to see what our cultural biases are.

Alone: without company; solitary; excluding all others. That sounds grim, even to me. *Lone* is even worse: without companions; solitary; isolated; lonesome. *Lonely:* sad from lack of companionship or sympathy; lonesome. But *lonely* has a second definition: having no companions or associates; habitually or frequently alone; solitary. Thus, one need not regret her solitary state—might even be quite happy with it—to be judged lonely. *Lonesome:* depressed or uneasy because of being alone; forlorn. And yet we say "all by one's lonesome" to mean simply "alone."

I'm not, I think, a genuine misanthrope. I like people, and I love and enjoy being with certain individuals, but I also like—often—to be away from other people. Days at a time or a week or so without seeing anyone, a month without my sweetie—these are comfortable, even desirable, to me.

Loren Eiseley wrote in the 1960s, " 'Wisdom,' the Eskimo say, 'can be found only far from man, out in the great loneli-

ness.' These people speak from silences we will not know
again until we set foot upon the moon." Perhaps, but I think
the men who walked on the moon were so well wired to the
earth that they experienced neither silence nor loneliness.
Even the various Eskimo peoples, through the wonders of
modern technology and communication, seldom visit the
great loneliness anymore. It's the rare individual of any nation
who finds or puts himself in far places where the human voice
is not the dominant one, where there's even the chance to
hear another voice in the pauses.

In our 1990s American lives, there are few enough opportu-
nities to be alone. Prisons and mental hospitals are two; solitary confinement and isolation rooms are where we put people for punishment or because they're dangerous to others.
People are alone in their cars even as they're surrounded by
other cars and drivers. Certain people opt for structured ways
of being alone, specifically in the outdoors. Among these
structured ways is the Outward Bound model, which I think of
as a cross between a Marine Corps boot camp and a vision
quest. These guided adventures generally culminate with a
three-day "solo" in which each person is left alone in the
woods or desert with only a prescribed minimum of tools. I've
never done this myself, but people who have done it describe
it to me as "spiritual," a confrontation with self perhaps aided
by going for a time without food. It's artificial, of course, the
entire arrangement, but judging by the number of people who
participate each year, such artifice clearly addresses a need
that's no longer met for most people in the course of their
daily living.

In general, though, our American culture doesn't value or
respect a need for solitude. We don't encourage children to
play alone, instead arranging for them constant social activities. A quiet child is suspect; he must be "up to something,"

just as a lone adult is not to be trusted. We're raised—girls and women especially—to fear being alone. The things that could happen! You might be attacked by someone. (The missed irony, of course, is that the presence of another person means you're not alone, and it's common knowledge that most violence today is of the domestic sort.) You could hurt yourself and not be able to call for help. You could fall off the roof; a bear could eat you; your appendix might burst; you might cut yourself with a knife; you will certainly be lonely. Won't you be bored? What will you do with yourself?

Even after all these years, I don't escape my mother's voice sounding in my head, warning me of the dangers of being alone. I walk miles on the beach to prepare our fishing sites, and a pain in my leg sets me to wondering what would happen if, like Debra Winger in the movie *Shadowlands*, I had a cancerous bone that was about to snap in two and send me sprawling. A bee buzzes past me and I wonder what would happen if it stung me and I had an allergic reaction. I don't actually worry about these possibilities; it's just the voice I hear in my head—my mother's concern, which is the expression of our culture's disapproval. It doesn't matter that statistically I would be in much more danger riding in a car back in town or walking on a street almost anywhere at night. I do, of course, take normal precautions, such as watching the beach ahead of me for bears and staying off high ladders. I'm cautious by nature; I've never broken a bone, needed stitching, or been stung by a bee.

Part of the fear business is not simply of being alone but of being alone in nature, an environment thought by so many people to be threatening. Even people who think they like nature don't necessarily want to be *in* it. After all, a majority of Americans say they get their "nature" from television, where the camera angles are better and there are no mosquitoes or wet feet. When Ken's nephews came to visit us, his mother wrote that she hoped the boys would *not* see any bears.

✧ ✧ ✧

When I step behind the cabin, the two adult swallows streak toward the birdhouse at the same moment. Only at the last second does one veer away, like an airplane overshooting a runway, and circle for a new approach. The other—steely blue from the eyes up and all along its back, with white chin and throat and belly—clings vertically to the shaking house just long enough to deliver its load to the largest, widest mouth. There are at least three young birds of various sizes, and the largest of them takes up most of the doorway; the others shoulder around it with competitive cheeps and breathy grunts. The largest looks bigger—or at least fluffier—than either parent and is grayer in the head, which marks it as female. The way the swallows' head plumage divides dark from white, all three appear to be wearing helmets that are a size or two too large and have slipped down to their eyes. Their lips are rimmed with school-bus yellow, the same color as the vast interiors of their mouths, which fly open to become impossible-to-miss food targets.

It's been three weeks since I found the broken eggshell that just fit over the end of my little finger. That these bright-eyed, fully fledged, shake-the-house-down creatures have come from such a beginning surely testifies to the numbers of insects removed from the sky, an awesome transfer of material and energy.

A few more steps up the hill and I'm on a level with the birds. The air is full of potential swallow food today—a white moth, a bee, flies, a spider on a thread—and I watch the young birds as they watch the insects pass. They stretch their necks and lean, sharp-eyed, toward the objects of their passion. It cannot be very long before their eagerness will launch them all the way out the door.

My own less-sharp eye catches a spot of color beside the path, and I bend to examine it. I hadn't counted veronica among my backyard plants, but here it is, six inches high and already bearing a single purple flower. It had grown in the same spot last year, and I'd forgotten. I'd neglected to look for it and didn't see it among the fireweed until this moment. Its name—from *vera iconica* ("true image") refers to Saint Veronica, who captured Christ's image on a cloth. It is, as well, the true picture of its own self.

✧ ✧ ✧

The traditional Dena'ina and other Native Americans didn't share my dictionary's anthropocentric concept of aloneness. They knew they were never alone. They lived in a community that included animals and plants, rocks, spirits, and weather— all things with which they had intimate relationships. These relationships always worked both ways: a person responded to the weather and the weather responded to the person. Such a belief system has no room for separation and isolation, no possibility for anyone to feel lacking in companionship. A Dena'ina would never wish away another part of the community; aside from the disrespect implied, it would be unthinkable to consider one's own life without bears or devil's club or hot sun. These "others" had as much right to exist as any person and would certainly continue to be themselves.

The Dena'ina culture is not my own, of course, and its relevance for me lies chiefly in the knowledge that a now-dispersed people lived very successfully on this shore, drawing their entire material and spiritual culture from a place, largely unchanged, that I now call my home. It would be foolish not to acknowledge this, not to learn what I can from their generations of experience. In an earlier time they didn't build birdhouses, just as they didn't use outboard motors on their boats, but they surely watched and knew with some intimacy the swallows that lived in various holes and crevices around them.

My background connects me perhaps more solidly to another tradition of relating to nature—that of Henry David Thoreau. *Walden* was formative for me as it was for so many other young people, helping me think about value systems. In college, one of my classes reenacted Thoreau's exploration of the Concord River, comparing his scenic wonderments with our scenes of urban blight; as we canoed we took water samples to document pollution levels.

Thoreau went to the woods to live deliberately, "to front only the essential facts of life, and see if I could not learn what it had to teach." Although his writings often labor under a narrow dogma of what is essential and good, and although I was disappointed to learn that his adventures at the pond were less self-sufficient than advertised—that, for example, he regularly carried his laundry back to Concord and filled up on free meals and social discourse when he did so—he was surely right about being able to learn much from close observation of nature. Moreover, he never could have paid such attention to his pea patch and his journal if he'd too often had other people with him at Walden. At this late date I also forgive him for taking his laundry to Concord; although I do what laundry I must in a fish tote with a scrub board, I'm always happy to save up dirty clothes at the end of summer to haul home to a machine. Virtue doesn't necessarily fall to those who do things the hard and pure way, even if clothes dried in the sun do smell sweetest.

It was Thoreau, too, who, when asked if he was lonely at Walden, was tempted to reply (though he only wrote it in his journal), "Why should I feel lonely? Is not our planet in the Milky Way?"

Swallows, veronica, incoming tide smacking against rocks—
these share with me one corner of the greater cosmos. Even if
we don't talk, exactly, we still have relationships. I know them
for their constancy and their changes, and I have much to
learn from them. Although I'm without *human* companionship for a time, I'm surely not alone.

There's a lovely, well-grounded word—anchorite—that
comes from the Greek word for "retire" or "retreat" and refers
to a person who withdraws from the world for religious reasons. Although my belief system is informed by a variety of
traditions—the Dena'ina and the transcendental being only
two among them—I would settle for calling myself, if anything, a sporadic and atheistic anchorite. I like to retreat from
the world as most of us know it—the worldly version that's almost exclusively involved with humans and human wants and
desires—and live within one that is at once both broader in
scope and simpler, quieter. If I don't quite embrace a doctrine
of souls, I still think that the creatures, objects, and phenom-
ena of the natural world have values in themselves, completely aside from their usefulness to people, and that these
values are most closely seen by a person who has separated
herself to some degree from the din and domination of her
own kind.

The borders of my community don't end with the physical
presence of rocks and water and birds, though. My companions include not just nature but also ideas, things to think
about, and to think about best when I have command of my
own time, my own uninterrupted thought processes. My ideas
come not just from private observation and contemplation but
also from reading and listening to news and public affairs pro-
gramming on the radio. I do, after all, have other people who
share their thoughts with me, and to whom I respond, even if
they don't know it.

Around me in my cabin, books and magazines lie open or are marked with dried plants and old tide book pages. I read in one and then another, moving among them until their ideas intersect, until they're like voices in a salon of my own direction. I read about Tibet, the last ice age, why gun control won't work. I travel with Dickens into Victorian darkness, with Willa Cather through a professor's examined life, and with Tatyana Tolstaya to a Russia that's both modern and mythic. I question Loren Eiseley's broodings and borrow old newspapers from my neighbor to get a look at disaster scenes and faces.

The radio, too, brings me more sets of voices. I listen to callers on *Talk of the Nation* and to city council meetings broadcast from town, and I talk back, scold, praise. I'm brought to tears by reports from Bosnia and Rwanda and a report on an anniversary of Mississippi's Freedom Summer. Saturday mornings, I learn tact from Scott Simon. Now and then I tune to an oddball call-in program from across the inlet to hear people complain about taxes, government, and commercial fishermen. Reality check—that world still exists, too.

I write letters, continuing conversations that stretch back years, knowing I may not get a response until midwinter. I read old letters as though they just came, pick up where we left off, add a *P.S.* a day or two later. My letters will be mailed eventually; I'll trust them to the tender or to my neighbor's briefcase when he makes a trip to town. I write in my journal. I write to think, and to find out what I think.

I talk aloud to the swallows when I pass by their house. "Hey, babies," I say. "How about trying those wings? Hey, fatty. Don't eat so much you get stuck in the door." I wonder just how much they do eat, and I take my clock to the strawberry patch and check its hands each time a parent bird flies in with a load of food: 12:13, 12:14, 12:16, 12:17. The deliveries come every one to two minutes, which means each bird spends about three minutes per trip. If this same pace were kept up for the nineteen daylight hours, the young would receive seven hundred sixty feedings each day. If there are three young, that averages to two hundred fifty-three feedings each—though, at least while I watch, the largest bird gets much more than its share. Of course, the parent birds must sometimes feed themselves and rest, and stormy weather must surely keep both insects and birds from the skies for long, blustery, rain-swept hours. Nevertheless, it's a prodigious operation.

During my own, less prodigious lunch, I listen to A *Prairie Home Companion* on the radio. The show includes a radio play with a ringing telephone. The phone rings and I jump, ready to answer it. My phone's in town, and by now its message tape is full, but I am the perfect Pavlovian dog. I snort at this ridiculous conditioning, this control of my life by an annoying piece of technology. My heart no sooner stills than the radio show phone rings again. I jump again, as much as I did the first time. A third time, and I'm nearly a wreck. As much as I know that the sound of a telephone does not belong to fishcamp, as much as I'm sure I don't want to answer one for the entire summer, I can't escape my training.

The radio voices remind me of the previous night's dreams, which carried over into the mood of my day. At fishcamp my sleep fills with extravagant, vivid dreams, and when I'm without other people I dream of them—intimates and strangers, old friends, and large, anonymous crowds. I'm not someone who pays particular attention to dreams or strives to interpret them, but I do think they function in part to fill in around our waking lives, to bring a balance to our experience. My most recent dream world was a busy and well-populated one, and a whole series of faces and feelings have kept me company through the morning. In one dream, I was back in an old workplace, happy to be running up a stairway among people I hadn't seen or thought of in years, and then I was finding a place to live—a room that had to be crossed through to get to any other room in a much-shared house. It's clear to me that in that dream and a number of others crowding the same sleep, my psyche was compensating, making sure I didn't feel too much alone. And I don't. When I awoke, in a sweat, it was with gratitude to find myself alone at last; though I enjoyed most of what went on in my dreams, I feel I've had enough of other people to last me through another day.

I know that my propensity for solitude is beyond the average and that problems can come from being too self-contained, too unwilling to need or be needed. Thoreau wrote, "I cannot lean so hard on any arm as on a sunbeam," a line I find immeasurably sad. Even such friends as he had thought Thoreau an odd duck. One once asked, "Why was he so disappointed with everybody else? Why was he so interested in the river and the woods?" Another time Thoreau watched a hawk tumbling through the sky and recorded in his journal, "It appeared to have no companion in the universe and to need none but the morning. It was not lonely but it made all the earth lonely beneath it." I'm not sure in this case if he identified with the freewheeling hawk or the earthbound, but clearly he was thinking about what might define loneliness.

Perhaps I do get, if not lonely, a little "bushy" after a while. I look forward to greeting the swallows each morning, make kissing noises to a frog, spend an hour turning an agate in the sunlight to admire every bend of light and shade of line. I wear Ken's sweaters and shoes—not that they come anywhere close to fitting me. I think about what I should have replied to a slight suffered in a dream. These are probably not things I would do if I were living among other people, but they seem no less legitimate for that. I do brush and floss my teeth every day. I keep a tidier kitchen than when Ken is here and use a clean plate every day, an improvement on our usual habits.

I'm aware, certainly, that too much time in the bush can upset the checks and balances that normally come from living with other people. It's not uncommon in Alaska's remote places to find odd, unsocialized, or even antisocial behaviors, from people who talk to themselves and eat out of the same pots as their dogs to dangerous psychopaths. However, since odd and mentally unstable individuals are often drawn to the bush in the first place, it's hard to say which is cause and which result. Just last year, not far from here, a man who'd been alone for several weeks called for a plane to take him to town. When the bush plane arrived and landed, the man shot and killed the pilot. He later said he'd been confused; he'd thought he was being invaded.

I'm standing under the birdhouse and about two feet away from it when a parent swallow arrives with more food. It flutters to a vertical landing and pauses to look me over, head held away from its noisy brood, long enough for me to see the insects protruding from its bill like an arrangement of flowers— a bouquet of pellucid wings and sprawled legs, antennae and furry body parts. They are large insects, some of them—moths and dragonflies and crane flies. I wonder how it can be possible for a creature with one bill to catch so many insects, big and small, in midair and not drop the small ones as it goes for a big one, or a whole load while opening for one more fly.

✧ ✧ ✧

In the evening, I have a live visitor of the human variety. Mark, who's staying with George, appears at my door complaining of cabin fever. Mark is twenty-five years old, a Nebraskan who's known George all his life and, as one of George's granddaughters puts it, looks like an advertisement for Cabela's hunting and fishing catalog. Indeed, all his clothing and gear seem to be both new and clean. While we're talking, I pull on the sleeve of the turtleneck I'm wearing under an oil-stained sweatshirt and the cotton rips.

Mark's eyes open wide. "Did you just rip your shirt?"

I show him the cuff, which had long ago ripped into two layers and is unraveling all along its ragged edge. I know exactly how long I've had this particular shirt, and I explain to Mark that it was already secondhand when I got it from a college friend, twenty-three years ago. Mark is disbelieving—that anything made from cotton could possibly be so old, that any person could own a piece of clothing nearly his own age.

Mark is supposed to fish with George for the summer, but he's discovered that he doesn't like sand or getting his hands wet, and he's told George he wants to leave as soon as George can find someone to replace him. He says, "I could do a job I didn't like if I were making an obscene amount of money, or I could do a job for no money if I loved doing it, but I can't do a job I hate for no money."

We talk for a while about expectations, about the fact that George isn't particularly good at explaining what fishing is all about. It's not clear to me what Mark expected except that he wanted a chance to see Alaska and he doesn't feel as if he's seeing it here. I tell him that I've always wondered about Lorraine, George's second wife—what she thought she was getting into when George brought her here from Nebraska. Lorraine is a lovely, warm, good-hearted woman, but it was clear from the minute Ken and I met her that she didn't want to be at a remote fishcamp. Since that first summer she hasn't returned except for a very few brief visits, always swearing when she leaves and in her Christmas cards to us that she'll never, ever, come back again. "Ha!" she writes. "George thinks he can get me to Alaska this summer. Ha!"

My father always says, about people having their own tastes, *"Chaque à son goût."* I don't say this to Mark, who has already told me that he lost a girlfriend to a year in France and that he positively hates everything French. Mark has strong opinions about everything, which is endearing in someone his age. He's good company, and he makes me laugh. He's disappointed that I've never heard of any of his favorite bands, but he's also been wondering how to spell *chaos* and what existentialism is, and these I can help with. When he leaves and I tell him, "Come visit again when you're crazy," he answers without a second's hesitation, "Tomorrow at eight." He's kidding, but he's quick.

After Mark disappears up the beach I hear a raucous, crowy cawing and the warning cries of the adult swallows. From the porch I watch a magpie rock an alder near the cabin and then take flight back toward the smokehouse. One of the swallows shoots toward it like an arrow and seems very nearly to strike it as it alights in another tree. I can't remember seeing another magpie this summer, although they've been around in other years.

The word *magpie* always makes me think of "maggot pie," though the bird's name apparently traces to *mag*—short for Maggie or Margaret, "a chattering female"—and *pie*—for its pied, or starkly black-and-white, plumage. The magpie's Dena'ina name, *q'ahtal'uya*, translates to "the proud one"; a traditional story explains that the magpie lives in the mountains in summer and normally comes to the lowlands only in winter because the bird doesn't want to dirty its fine clothing with fish slime.

Suddenly an entire flock of magpies sweeps through the yard as though they own it, flapping their wings and shouting out what sounds like *yak-yak-yak-yak-yak*. With their stately long tails and tuxedo-style markings, magpies normally impress me as elegant, but this group feels predatory, like a gang of overdressed thieves. Clearly the swallows see them that way and want to drive them far from the nest. The young swallows, I note, have heeded the warnings and withdrawn into their house, out of sight. Like their omnivorous cousins, crows and ravens, magpies will eat the eggs and young of other birds as readily as they'll gobble berries or pick apart a dead fish.

One magpie settles onto a pole in front of the cabin and makes croaking noises with its mouth hanging open. It's scruffy looking, with the shorter tail typical of immature birds, and I have the impression it wants to be fed. Undignified, it scratches its head with one foot. When the others flap off up the beach, this one trails after them. I imagine the gang of them mobbing swallows all along the bluff, nest hole to nest hole. Perhaps some of the holes are big enough for them to get into to grab a nestling. Or perhaps they'll find a young swallow that's already left the nest and tear it apart. I don't know how vulnerable such swallows might be or whether they quickly learn to fly off with their parents. I think, anyway, that the birds in my birdhouse are safe, at least until they leave it. The hole is regulation size—right for swallows, too small for predators.

Still, I ask myself: what would I do if I saw a magpie attacking one of "my" swallows? Would I run out and chase it away or let nature take its course? I'm quite sure I wouldn't interfere. I might grit my teeth and think about all those parent-bird trips through the sky and the weight of mosquitoes that make a swallow, but I understand that the magpie must eat, too.

I stay outside to watch the adult swallows resume their insect gathering. The beach and cabin are in shade, but the western sun is still shining over the top of the bluff; the birds, spinning against the blue sky, catch the light like fire. Their white bellies flash as though they are themselves incandescent, and the front edges of their wings slice the sky with the glint of knife blades. I think of Thoreau again and of his doubting friend, who might as well ask about me, "Why is she so interested in birds?" I don't know that I could give a very satisfying answer to someone who would ask such a question. I would probably be equally mystified by his own interests, whatever they might be.

The young swallows are still chirping madly when I make my own nest for the night. I settle into the middle of the flannel-sheeted bed, under a dome of mosquito netting, and begin reading. The book is Alexandr Solzhenitsyn's *One Day in the Life of Ivan Denisovich*, about a man who never, except perhaps in his dreams, had a moment to himself.

✧ ✧ ✧

The next day, the gray morning is weighted like a stone. The outgoing tide barely breaks on the shore, rain taps lethargically against the roof, and I have trouble bringing myself to consciousness. When I finally leave the cabin, I find bird feathers on the porch—a dozen blue-gray wing feathers spread across the wet wood, a bit of down fluffing among them. They are virginal, perfectly formed inch-long, scalpel-edged plumes, and they are dewy with rain. But they are all. They are unflown and lonely feathers.

Three more steps and I can look up to the birdhouse. The doorway is empty, and there's no sound from within. The unpainted wood is water stained and dark.

"Hey, babies. Cheep, cheep."

No one answers me. High overhead, a lone swallow sails in circles.

I remember hearing, just as I was drifting off to sleep, the sound of magpie feet on the rooftop—feet hopping along the metal cap from just over my head in the front of the cabin, back to the rear. I can imagine it now, how the magpie must have leaned off the back of the roof, getting a look at the fat young swallow that pressed itself into its doorway. The birdhouse roof extends over the doorway, so the fledgling could not have been attacked from overhead, but the magpie might have darted under it just agilely enough to knock loose its prey. The others? The smaller birds, which would not have been filling the doorway? Perhaps they're only just resting now, safe inside, waiting out the rain.

I had thought it wouldn't matter to me. Why should it—an act of nature, the kind of thing that goes on constantly, the very basis of life? Baby birds don't all survive, or we would be living in a Hitchcock movie. The magpies need to eat. I had told myself I wouldn't interfere, and I hadn't—except that I had put up the birdhouse, and I lived under a roof that magpies could walk across. Maybe it had all been a setup.

I'd thought I wouldn't care, but when I make my breakfast I inexplicably cut up my french toast without buttering it first. I have never done such a thing in my life. I'm all shook up.

All morning I listen for the swallows. I hear a golden-crowned sparrow, a redpoll, a chestnut-backed chickadee, and other birds I haven't learned to identify. A raggedy wet eagle perches on a boulder in front of the camp and shakes itself like a dog, head to tail. I go out and check the birdhouse several times. No one seems to be home. A gust of north wind flaps my rainpant straps against the side of the cabin. Once I hear the warning cry of an adult swallow and rush out in time to see a magpie wing steadily past the cabin. The swallow follows it from high overhead and then sweeps back over the creek and disappears.

I look up something I remember from Darwin. Even a no-nonsense scientist could write, "What a book a devil's chaplain might write on the clumsy, wasteful, blundering and horribly cruel works of Nature."

I do my chores in an unaccustomed chirp-free silence. I work out a possible alternative scenario. It could be that the largest and fittest young swallows had flown off with the adult birds and only the weakest was struck down. Perhaps at this moment the survivors are swooping after their own mosquitoes and exulting in all the sky-high joy their bird brains grant them.

After a time, a string of commanding caws sounds from nearby, and I look out at a magpie strutting along a willow branch and picking off old catkins. The look on its face is one of alert satisfaction, as though for the moment it's both quite content with its lot in life and on the lookout for its next opportunity. I notice for the first time that the iridescent blue along the backs of its wings, below its white shoulder epaulets, is the very same shade as the backs of tree swallows.

We are, of course, all in this together, as the Dena'ina understood so well, and as I'm just beginning to learn on a level beyond what I know in my head. The magpie is made of swallows and mosquitoes, long flights through clear and stormy skies, and even maggots, just as I'm made of the salmon I ate last night and veronica leaves, sunlight, radio news, and bone. The willow is made of yellow warblers and muddy water just as the yellow warbler is made of willow and song and the salmon is made of phosphorescence and drowned fishermen. The sky is made of chirpings, mirage, a dragonfly's flight, the scent of lupine on a wet day. Someday, when I die, I expect to become sweet salmonberry, rain, spindrift, eagle, dream, fluff on a dandelion seed, webbing between a beaver's toes, a piece of black coal.

With this kind of closeness, we creatures and others must at least nod in passing, acknowledging our mutual connections and worth, the blunders that bind. I look the strutting magpie in the eye, and I say, with more declaration than rancor, "Just you wait."

The Beauty in the Beast

At 10:45 P.M. I'm reading in bed, paging through an old *New York Times Book Review* from a stack I'm trying to catch up on. This one is two years old, and I realize with despair that many of the books I'm only just learning of will already be at the shredder's. I can't read enough, not even through the nights of the midnight sun, not even with Ken gone, when I have only my own schedule to keep with the tides and the net-mending needle.

It's a calm evening, with the outgoing water merely licking the beach, and when something bumps the porch the sound floats up to me clearly. Night noises always sound like bears to me; I immediately stiffen and listen for more. Nothing comes, and after a minute I dismiss the sound as just some element of the life that goes on around me always, even as I sleep. It's a raven landing with a thud or that scrappy little weasel that's been around, knocking something over, or it's only the wet washcloth I left out, slipping from its nail.

I skip a review of a book about the French Revolution. After two years, I tell myself, I needn't read everything, though I very often find that a little age adds an extra, heightened dimension: current events have a way of catching up in surprising ways to earlier perspectives, and life does imitate art, delivering absurd postmodern plots into the true-true news.

The porch jars again, with a force like that of a person stepping up onto it. My neighbors would never come without calling out from a distance, and never this late. I turn and look out the window. The shadowy beach is untracked below the last tide line. I get up, and the cabin creaks as I walk to the other end and look out the opposite window. There's nothing to see behind the camp—just the back hillside, the alders that run up the creek, the top of the smokehouse weighted with rocks against the wind. I can't see the porch without climbing down the ladder and opening the door, but all seems quiet again. Perhaps it was only the wind coming up, slapping my raingear against the wall. Or maybe the cabin is settling, one of its ancient pilings collapsing a bit more to earth. I go back to bed.

Five minutes later there's a shaking and rattling, and I know for sure there's a bear in camp. I rush to the back window just in time to see the top of the smokehouse pitch over into the alders. The crash is heavy and splintering, and I think of all my carefully tended smoked fish flung from its hangings, now to be wasted on a slobbery bear.

I shove open the window and shout, "Go away, bear! Git-go! G'wan! Git-go!" There's a single, quick flash of yellow-brown fur as the animal rears up on its hind legs—the better to see me? Or because it's startled by all the noise and trying to get away? I look to the alders beyond, hoping to see them shake with the bear's retreat. They're still, but so is everything around the toppled smokehouse. Quick as I can I spring down the ladder, grab a pot and serving spoon from the dish rack, and race onto the porch. I give the pot bottom a ferocious beating and yell some more. Nothing's moving back by the smokehouse, and when I pause to listen, there's only a ringing quiet all around.

For all the years we've left smoked fish hanging in the closed smokehouse, we've never had any problems with animals. Black bears frequently come into the camp, roving up or down the hill beside the smokehouse or along the creek, but they've never shown much interest in the skinny shed or what it might contain. I concluded long ago that smoked fish didn't smell to them like anything to eat and that smoky smells in general were something animals tried to avoid.

Brown bears, on the other hand, never come into camp. They walk the beaches and the woods and perhaps sometimes sneak up and down the draw when we aren't looking, but never, until tonight, has one walked right through the camp or bothered anything in it.

By shouting at the bear, speaking its bear name, I undoubtedly have broken a whole set of ancient taboos. In culture after culture all around the world, bears have traditionally been spoken of and to with a respect reserved for the sacred—usually indirectly, by polite euphemism. *Bruin* came to us this way, from the German word for brown. People in most Athabaskan cultures—especially the women—talk around the brown bear's name in a similar manner. In his study of the Koyukon Athabaskans, *Make Prayers to the Raven*, Richard Nelson described an experience with a woman who looked away from where she'd sighted a bear and mumbled to her companions that "a dark thing" was on the far riverbank.

From what I've learned, this euphemistic speech and extreme avoidance of direct eye contact don't seem to be the case among Dena'ina. Still, the brown bear is so significant in Dena'ina culture that their word for it—*ggagga*—is sometimes also used for speaking of animals in general. The Dena'ina do, as well, have respectful alternative names for the brown bear—among them "big grandfather" and "black bear's partner." They employ a wide vocabulary pertaining to different kinds of brown bears—specific to coloring, age, sex, degrees of

ferocity, and whether they leave their dens in winter—and to
details of their bear lives.

Ggagga: the double-g is pronounced deep in the back of the
throat. It's a name I like to speak just to feel and hear the
sound of it. It's primal, like the first babblings of a baby, only
with a rougher edge.

I yelled harshly and very directly at the bear and now it
seems to be gone, but I easily justify my behavior. That's *my*
food in the smokehouse, and besides, it's in a bear's own best
interest to keep it from temptation. The best human behavior,
of course, is not to put temptation in a bear's way; bears that
learn to associate food with people usually end up dead. Under
a liberally interpreted Alaskan law, anyone may shoot a bear
when he or she judges such action necessary "in defense of life
and property."

Back in bed I read about a book that discusses the hidden
lives of dogs. We used to have dogs, and when we did, we
rarely had any other animals around the camp. The dogs
would bark and take off into the brush or up the beach and
that would be all we'd ever know about *that* hidden life, unless, of course, it belonged to a porcupine; we got to be quite
proficient at pulling quills out of muzzles and tongues. Without dogs we watch, unhurried, as a weasel presses its face
against our screen door and then chases its black-tipped tail in
a wild, leaping scramble over the porch. We follow a beaver
that waddles from the inlet one day and heads up the creek,
and we freeze only inches from a mellow porcupine that looks
soft enough to pat—until it notices us and turns with a great
fanning up of all its stiff back quills. Pine siskins flit around us
as they pick apart seeding dandelions, and party-time gulls
mob the beach for dead hooligan. Bears walk past and around
and sometimes through our camp. Although I would rather
not have our smokehouse smashed and its fish ruined, keeping
a dog means dog domination, the forfeiture of sharing in the

goings-on of all those other, more secretive lives. The lives of weasels and siskins and bears are already so nearly hidden from us, I want just about any glimpse I can get.

I sleep lightly that night and wake later to the sound of footsteps on the beach. I know the sound instantly; it comes from the creek, where the braided water has washed away the fine sand and left only a fragile architecture of intricately balanced layers of gravel. There's no way to walk there quietly, with all that collapsing under one's feet. *Crunch!* It's like walking on eggshells.

Face to the window, I look right to where I know the bear will be, across the creek now and headed away. Under an overcast sky it's only a woolly dark shape, plodding on heavy feet as though it expects to travel a long way, one foot in front of the other. I have an intuitive feeling that this bear is not the same bear that knocked over the smokehouse but one just passing in the night, as they so often do. I wouldn't have heard it—would have known nothing except what its morning tracks will tell—but for the inlet's uncommon quiet. I watch *ggagga* until it rounds the corner and disappears from sight, and when I turn back to sleep I dream of being surrounded by bear highways. I'm a traffic island in a sea of freeways, overpasses, underpasses, cloverleafs, and scenic bypasses, and along every mile tramp the world's bears, as mysterious and wholly in charge as ever.

❖ ❖ ❖

In the full light of day, I take a paper bag and go out to the smokehouse. It lies on its side, split open like a cracker box. Both the door and one side are broken clear off, exposing nails and screws and splintered wood, and the uphill side is covered with muddy paw prints the width of my two hands spread one beside the other. Oddly enough, all the salmon strips are still inside, still tied to their strings and looped over sticks, all of them fallen against one sooty wall. It takes me only a minute to reach through the openings and fill my bag. Clearly, the bear didn't get even a bite. My yelling and banging, perhaps even the surprise crash of the smokehouse, scared it away. Maybe it wasn't even after something to eat but only pushed on a curious object it found in its way.

The smokehouse will need substantial rebuilding, something we'd planned to do anyway. The smoked fish needs only dusting.

Later, I look at the bear tracks on the beach. Most have been erased by the tide, but I follow a set to the front of the camp, leading to the steps. When I climb up to the cabin I find on the horsetails next to the porch—about four feet from our door—a thick wad of chewed vegetable matter, grassy and leafy and shiny with strings of dried saliva. It's a truly sloppy looking bit of business, and my mind conjures the bucket face and lippy, open mouth of an oh-so-casually grazing bear.

I look more closely. Very near the wad lies an uprooted angelica plant. The root has been chewed off, rudely, leaving part of the bulb. Angelica root is poisonous to people; perhaps it's mildly narcotic to a bear, something to loosen its inhibitions. Grasses beside it are bent, and I now see a sort of trail parted around the side of the porch and down to the creek. I can see clearly that the bear stepped on a loose board—one of the sounds I heard. Its path took it over a rock, around an old post, and along the creek to the smokehouse.

This bear that walked through our camp may or may not have been the same bear I later saw pass on the beach. I know only that it was amazingly unconcerned, for a brown bear, about holding its course through the middle of all our dunnage and unexpected sweet-and-sour scents, right past the places where we purposefully pee to set our territorial markers. What *ggagga* in its right mind, angelica or not, would even think of stopping to munch the greenery in such a place? Either my night visitor is without its wits or it possesses a remarkable sense of self and invulnerability. It's the feeble one George calls "the retard," or it's the mythic Kustatan bear.

✧ ✧ ✧

The bear George calls retarded is one that's wandered the beach the past couple of years, sickly looking and careless. Ken and I have seen it only once, last year, when it dragged by our camp in broad daylight. Its head belongs to a full-size bear, but its body is shrunken and malformed, its back legs so rickety they're bent almost double. Its fur is thin and dull, with patches that look like threadbare carpet, and its shoulder and hip bones turn sharp corners. We thought then that it looked ready to collapse and surely wouldn't last a winter, but George has observed it again several times this year. It takes the fish heads he puts out for the eagles and otherwise knocks indelicately around his camp.

We are like the bears, or the bears are like us, in this: our beach is a hard place to make a living, and the more able or determined are someplace else. The biggest and smartest bears locate themselves along one of the many salmon streams or tributaries, where they can feast to gluttonous contentment with little more effort than dropping their muzzles into the water. Only the lesser bears—the young, the weak, the injured, sows with cubs to protect—are pushed to the margins like this, reduced to prowling tide lines. Then, too, there are the passers-through—bears going from somewhere to somewhere else.

It's a sign of overall bear plenty that so many bears try to share this beach with us. In other years, when brown bear numbers are down, they'll leave here to fill in where the living's easier, and then we find ourselves surrounded by black bears. Beautiful and intriguing in their own right, the black bears also tend to be pesky. They leave teeth marks in everything they find around camp—buoys, net corks, tent nylon, raingear, motor oil jugs, toilet paper rolls—as though their way of knowing anything comes from feeling it with their mouths. The teenagers among them, like their human counterparts, have yet to learn judgment, anything about their own vincibility. They come to the cabin door and only *hrumph* and stare shamelessly when we shout and pound cooking pots.

When the brown bear numbers rise again, the black bears are driven away to some even more marginal place.

✧ ✧ ✧

The Kustatan bear, in contrast to most bears of our experience, is no minor bear. On the scale of bears, it outweighs all others; it is of mythic proportions. As I speak of it now, it's not a single bear but two different, definite and specific bears of legendary importance. One, belonging to the Dena'ina people, has deep-rooted cultural meaning. The second, belonging to Ken and me, has meaning of a more personal, but still legendary, nature. Our Kustatan bear was named for the earlier one, and so that story needs to come first.

As Peter Kalifornsky tells it in *A Dena'ina Legacy*, an aggressive brown bear appeared one winter at the village of Kustatan. Actually two shamans from an enemy village who had taken the form of a bear to seek revenge for a theft, the bear first killed the two trappers who had stolen from a cache and then came into the village. It broke into homes, and the villagers hid in the sturdiest smokehouse. For three nights running, the bear attacked and the men of the village fired at it with rifles, to no effect. Daytimes, the bear retreated to the woods to rest. After the third night, the village chief went to the church and got a cross and Bible. He and his brother opened some rifle shells and let the smoke of burning incense waft into them, and they sprinkled holy water on three of the shells. They went to where the bear was trashing one of the houses, shot it through the smokehole with the smoked and baptized bullets, and finally killed it. This is my simple summary of a story that fills many pages and runs to elaborate detail, including the individual escapes of various villagers and the shamanism and countershamanism that continued after the bear was killed.

There are traditional stories and there is history; in this case, the historical record supports, at least in part, the story of the Kustatan bear. A Russian priest who visited the village shortly after the event was told of it and placed the time as the winter of 1895–1896. He noted that the people considered such an attack highly unusual—"happens only once in their lives"—and that the bear was finally killed with a bullet dipped in holy water and marked with a cross. "It is amazing, but true," the priest wrote. The villagers, he said, told him they'd interpreted the attack as God's punishment for their sins. As members of his Russian Orthodox flock, they understandably said nothing to him of shamanism.

From my perspective—filtered through story, history, what I know of bears and the hungry or disturbed reasons why they occasionally come out of hibernation, and a distance of one hundred years—I have no doubt that an unusually aggressive and tough-hided bear once terrorized the villagers at Kustatan and would not be killed. Beyond that level of outsider's belief, I try to grasp the story's cultural significance. The story seems to say that the Kustatan people's traditional powers were insufficient to fight the bear and that only when the symbols of the church were called upon was there enough power to vanquish the evil shamans.

The changes occurring in Dena'ina culture at the time of the Kustatan bear have been referred to by anthropologist Alan Boraas as a sort of "indigenous enlightenment," similar to the European Enlightenment. The Dena'ina, for whom the ideal had always been sameness and stability, were restructuring their worldview to accommodate teachings and technology—including both Christianity and modern weaponry—brought by contact with Europeans and Americans. The term *enlightenment* recognizes the intellectual vigor with which the Dena'ina and other Native peoples considered new information and made choices regarding its interpretation and adaptation to their own lives. The Dena'ina adoption of Russian Orthodoxy, for example, wasn't a conversion that repudiated the old ways but a mixing and blending of not-incompatible rituals and beliefs. The spiritual life of the people continued. "The Kustatan Bear" in this context represents a remarkable coming together—a merging of or a transition between old and new belief.

If the Dena'ina could adapt with such innovation and aplomb to the momentous change brought them by Euro-American contact and colonialism, it seems to me that those of us who follow them can do no less than consider whether a new period of "enlightenment" might be called for. We humans have succeeded in interfering on a massive scale with the natural equilibrium of the world—the other species we're pushing to extinction, the atmosphere we've altered, the land and oceans we continue to strip and poison. Traditional Native attitudes of respect, accommodation, and linking of consequences to actions suddenly seem more than relevant. Nothing else makes sense if we're to live in reasonable harmony with our environment instead of destroying it—and ourselves.

The shape of existence known by the traditional Dena'ina was circular—the seasons, the cycles of life and death, the next generation following the path of the last. We twentieth-century Americans have tried advancing in a straight line, but now the time has come to look again to a system that once worked well and may again. We're circling back after all.

✧ ✧ ✧

Drawing some circles of my own, I turn my thoughts from "The Kustatan Bear" to another bear story—one closer to the traditions to which I was born—and the role it played in another people's transition. William Faulkner's Old Ben, immortalized in *The Bear*, was a big, old Mississippi bottomlands black bear, but like the Kustatan bear, it had a powerful hold over a people caught in changing times. Faulkner's bear, like its Kustatan counterpart, was based on a historical presence, a bear with a maimed foot that was known for killing dogs set after it and generally ravaging the countryside when Faulkner was a boy. The two real bears—in Mississippi and in Alaska—most likely both walked the earth for some overlapping years in real time.

The Bear is, of course, fiction and not meant to represent actual events. On one level it's a hunting story, and on another it's not only Faulkner's interpretation of the history of the South but also a quest to understand and comment on the nature of nature and of God. Old Ben was a bear and a representation of the end of an era, a change in the way people were to live ever after. No more would they live on a frontier where such an animal could exist and where they might measure themselves against it, and no more would they live within the old southern order of easily recognized and managed race relations. Old Ben made Faulkner's characters think about what was happening in their lives—how they lived and would live. The story continues, at least in part, to serve that same function for modern readers, to prompt us to think about community standards, moral confusion, and measures of progress and success. Someday when we take oral literature as seriously as we take that of Faulkner and others who put words into print, "The Kustatan Bear" might be as widely accepted as part of our shared heritage and as closely studied for its contributions.

Attitudes toward bears and the rest of nature have changed, of course, since every man in Faulkner country wanted to kill the last bear in the woods, and Alaska—which still has a ratio of one bear to every six people—has always been a long way from Mississippi. The Kustatan bear, thankfully, was not the last bear in *these* woods, though it may have been the last to be associated with shamanism. Nonetheless, the changes taking place at Kustatan a hundred years ago were surely as significant as anything happening in Faulkner's time and place. It's entirely logical that such big changes were connected to a big animal: not only to *ggagga*, the most powerful and respected of all animals, but to a *ggagga* of extreme strength and ferocity, inhabited by not one but two shamans.

Real bear or symbol, it doesn't matter. What matters is what the people say happened, and then what happened after that, and then, and then. History is a series of reactions; culture is the whole stew of thought. The Kustatan bear, if it was larger than life, was first a bear.

That as much as anything is what holds my interest in the story—bear as bear, and the awe I feel before the natural (never mind supernatural) world. No matter what any person believes about the individual power of bears and the instruments through which they may operate, and no matter how destructive and even deadly bears may sometimes be, the fact that this world can hold such creatures and that we occasionally can be aware of their presence is miracle enough for me.

❖ ❖ ❖

I come at last to the *other* Kustatan bear, the one of our own experience.

On the day we saw it, Ken was returning from somewhere, flying in to the lake above our camp. I waved from the cabin porch and went on with whatever I was doing, but Ken kept circling the lake and the bluff, around and around. I worried that something might be wrong with the plane, and then I wondered if Ken was signaling for me to meet him and help carry a load. I began to walk up the creek.

I hadn't gone far, and Ken was still circling, when I looked up. In the late afternoon the draw was entirely in shadow, but bright sunlight spun across the top of the bluff. There, amidst the flaming leaves and grasses, stood a golden bear. It was bigger than any bear I'd ever imagined, as immense and fantastical as King Kong. For an instant as it stretched upright, its head and chest filled the sky like the blazing sun itself. It possessed the place with a straight-out look of quiet authority, with movement as fluid as waving grass, and then it was gone. As it turned, I saw a dark and glittery stripe that began at the base of its neck and ran like a part down the center of its golden back, and then I turned away, too.

When I remembered to breathe I could feel every molecule of air that entered my chest, could hear every drop of blood that pulsed up my neck and across my temples. It wasn't fear that so tightened all the strings of my senses; the bear and I were separated by a chasm of uncrossable space. No, it was something different. I was caught in a kind of acute awe, pinched by beauty, strung out by grace. This must be, I told myself, how true believers feel when they think they've seen the face of God.

All this time, Ken had been watching the bear. He'd initially landed on the lake and been startled to find, grazing nonchalantly in the reedy area next to where he would park the plane, the largest bear *he'd* ever seen. He took to the air again and watched the bear as it left the lake and strolled down the trail, and then he decided he'd better continue to watch it until it was beyond where he might meet it on his own walk through the woods. After it paused at our draw it kept heading north, and Ken landed and came home.

We haven't seen the Kustatan bear again, but we like to think it's up there somewhere, deep in the woods, probably back along the river. I have only to close my eyes to see its tremendous, haloed head rising over the bluff, and in the wind I think of its fiery fur parting along its back, sparking one way or another along that dark stripe.

✧ ✧ ✧

These, then, are my stations: that spot on the top of the bluff, the sunny slope beside the beaver pond, a jumble of rocks down the beach, the creek-crossing area, the still alders behind the smokehouse. And these are my visitations: bumps in the night, gobs of chewed weed, a sudden flash between leaves, smeared paw prints, tracks in the sand. They remind me always of the ways we share this world, the ways in which things of this world are bigger than we are. Each glimpse recalls other bears, past bears, possible bears—bears to be pitied and bears to be feared, bears to be admired, mythic bears, bears that are like us in their weaknesses and strengths and yet are utterly *other*. Bears live on the back side of the wardrobe mirror, and every reflection we catch tells us something about ourselves and our own capacities for pity, fear, admiration, respect, desire, and love, for knowing beauty and grace when we see them.

In the end, there is also belief.

Ken and I speak of the Kustatan bear and we don't mean the one inhabited by evil shamans and defeated by blessed bullets. We don't mean the colossus we both saw that one day. We speak of the Kustatan bear as a part of our own mythology, one that incorporates what we can understand about those other bears, one that approaches bear-ness with a sense of possibility. The possibility is not just of bears, not just of what we might see looking down from the sky or up from the creek bed or out from the cabin window at night, but of all the world. We believe in the Kustatan bear. It's all that's big and golden, half-terrifying, and in possession of a power that reaches far beyond physical strength.

Beluga Days

Day One

The north wind pushes the ebbing water in against the shore, smacking it into the sides of boulders and sending up spray to mix with the cold rain. There are few fish to be caught in a north wind, and our nets are nearly empty. After a midday break and some hot food, Ken and I trudge back down the beach to where we've left the skiff anchored behind our point.

I'm so intent on watching where I put my feet that I almost stumble into a beached beluga, twelve or fourteen feet of adult white whale. It's not the whiter-than-white shoe-polish perfection of the belugas we see cruising the inlet, their backs rising like whitecaps from the sea. This one is dead and beaten, bloated and discolored, patchy with gray and yellow and pink. Still, it's startling—something so large and unexpected, so close to life.

We look it over, checking for a clue to its death. Only Native subsistence hunters can legally kill belugas. Perhaps twenty beluga are taken for food each year out of a Cook Inlet population thought to lie somewhere between eight and twelve hundred animals. Perhaps a few more are struck and

lost during hunts. The only other predator of the beluga here-
abouts is the killer whale, which rarely ventures this far up the
inlet. Elsewhere in the world pollution kills belugas, but the
limited studies here have found very low levels of toxins in the
whales' fat.

There's no wound that we can see, just a raw place on the
whale's side where it wore against rocks as it washed ashore.
The skyward eye is missing, leaving only a hollow filled with
dimpled rainwater. Its mouth, ajar in what looks like a broad
grin, is crenellated with pointy white teeth—not so worn and
broken as they might be if they belonged to a whale that had
simply reached the end of a long life. The matter of the animal's sex is settled by a penis, skinny and wrinkled, hanging
toward the sand.

"Let's go," Ken says. We're late to move a net. The last thing
I notice is the water pooled below the beluga. It's oily, as
though we'd just spilled a cup of salad oil, and pink with
blood.

Downwind, the smell is strong, fetid, unpleasant without
being nauseating. There's a thickened sweetness to it that's almost cloying, like something that will stick.

Day Two

The tides are falling for the next week. We're stuck with a
dead beluga high on our beach, a quarter mile from our camp.

Tracks of a small bear circle the whale. There are chew
marks along the tail and around one flipper and one long
swipe of claw scratches on the tail, but it's as though the bear
couldn't figure out how to break through to something edible.
All around, the sand is patterned with the prints of bird feet.

Ken tugs on a tooth and asks if I want him to pull one out.
I don't. It doesn't seem right—to take to this animal with pliers and pick, like stealing gold teeth from a corpse.

The only beluga tooth I've ever handled was at an archaeo-
logical dig I participated in. In my square of the excavation, I
discovered—along with the usual bits of worked slate,
clamshells, and fire-broken rock of prehistoric Eskimo tradition—a two-inch-long beluga tooth, brown with centuries of
age and carved with delicate, decorative rings.

That tooth is in a museum now, where I go to look at it on
display. What I like best about it is that it had no purpose.
That is, so far as the experts know, it wasn't part of a tool; it
wasn't designed for any use beyond ornamentation and, perhaps, good luck. It may have been worn as a necklace, tied
around the groove in its base end, and it may have brought its
wearer some of the beluga's grace or fishing ability. It is, in any
case, proof that for a long time there's been more to human
life than food, clothing, and shelter. Some person took that
tooth in hand, admired it, and worked into it a pleasing design. The rings suggest to me the whale's own roundedness and
smooth, surface-cutting movements. Surely the artist found
inspiration in the animal itself and in the place that owned
it—a place, like this, of fish and fish eaters, pummeling seas
and ragged mountains, seasons turning one to the next.

Day Three

George comes to see the whale. He tells us that small animals
will clean a dead beluga from the inside out, hollowing it out
within its skin. Once, he said, he came upon one in the winter. When he knocked against it with his snowshoe, it boomed
like a drum and an entire menagerie of "varmints" ran out, including a red fox.

Two eagles sit in spruce trees on top of the bluff and squawk
down at us like chickens. The eagles, along with ravens and
seagulls, have been pecking at the whale; a large area on top
of it is raw, picked over, and sandy from many hopping-on-

and-off feet. Guano streaks the whale's side like vandal-thrown paint.

Beluga, or belukha, as some prefer. The word is Russian—*byelukha*, from *byelo*, for "white." In Dena'ina the name is *qunshi*. Aside from providing the traditional people with a major source of their meat and oil, the beluga was valued for its sinew, made into ropes—and its stomach—used as a container for oil. The Dena'ina packed other foods, such as clams and ground squirrels, in oil-filled beluga stomachs to preserve them.

In the days before hunting was done with motorboats and rifles, the Dena'ina here planted driftwood logs upside down—the narrow end deep in tidal-flat mud, the spreading roots providing a high platform—and secured it to stakes with sinew ropes. A hunter would wait among the roots for the tide to rise and belugas to swim past and then throw his harpoon. Eskimos hunted from boats, but the Dena'ina beluga stands made good sense in the fast currents around which they lived.

It wasn't unusual for belugas to pass within a stand's harpooning distance. The whales often swim so close to shore that they stir the bottom with their passage. Their sonar systems are perhaps the most sophisticated of all marine mammals', allowing them to navigate through shallow water—where they can escape killer whales—and narrow channels and to locate fish in the inlet's mud soup. Although they normally have no trouble avoiding fishing nets, once a cow and calf sailed right through one of ours, leaving side-by-side matching holes that took me a whole day to mend. We didn't actually see the collision—only a pod traveling close to shore and then, when we checked a net they'd had to pass, the unmistakable holes.

Before whale hunting was limited by the 1972 Marine Mammal Protection Act, George hunted belugas on a few occasions. Every summer across the inlet, town folk used to cel-

ebrate something called Beluga Days. As George has described
it, the event was mostly about money, hosted by the Chamber
of Commerce to draw people to town. Instead of roasting hot
dogs or a fattened pig, they cooked up beluga muktuk. Those
in charge weren't very adept at whale hunting, so they sometimes asked George to get them their whale. George has told
me how he'd maneuver seaside of a whale and herd it into
shallow water, where his crew would shoot it with a rifle and
finally strike it with a thirty-pound harpoon.

Another time, in the 1960s, George was hired by Sea World
to capture three belugas for its aquarium. The whales had to
meet certain age and size specifications—weaned but not
much older or they'd be too big to carry south by plane. Although George repeatedly cut individual whales from a pod
and surrounded them with net, he says he never could get
ones that were the right size. His son, Buck, once told me that
they did catch a right-sized whale, but by the time they did,
he—Buck—had lost all stomach for the harassment and the
idea of sending any beluga to a zoo, so they'd let it go.

That bit of local hunting and capture, though, is minimalist
compared with the commercial harvest that took place at one
time just to our north. In the early 1900s and again about
1930, whales that had ascended the Beluga River on high
tides were corralled with nets and made to strand when the
tide fell. As many as thirty whales were taken in this way on a
single tide. The fat was rendered into oil for sale, and the hides
were processed into glove leather. At neither time did the operations prove to be commercially viable, and both were abandoned before the whale population was sent into a tailspin.

Day Five

As we pass back and forth in the skiff, tending our nets, I pick
out the beluga onshore. It's more rounded than the boulders it

lies among, and it's darker now, gray and a color like burnt-desert orange. Behind it, the lower slope of the bluff glows with yellow monkey flowers and a few fireweed stalks lit just by their top, final blossoms. Eagles and ravens loiter, flapping between rocks and posing on treetops. The sea, on this calm day, smells like dead fish and freezing water.

The seals race us for fish as though they, too, feel the end-of-season pressure, the need to get what they can before there's nothing left. Once, Ken reaches for a gilled salmon just as a seal grabs it from beneath the surface. For a second, they're in a tug-of-war, and then Ken pulls the torn and wrung-out fish into the boat. "Catch your own fish!" he yells.

I don't know how many salmon a single seal can eat, but I've read that belugas eat about sixty pounds of fish each day, roughly ten salmon. I do a little math in my head. If there are a thousand belugas, and if they rely almost exclusively on salmon May through September, we could be talking about one and a half million inlet salmon eaten just by belugas. Or, to look at it another way, one beluga may be eating as many inlet salmon as Ken and I catch. If all animal relationships were as neat and tidy as accounting, I could say that the one dead beluga on the beach has just freed a summer's worth of salmon for such as us.

I don't mention these numbers to Ken. He's still grumbling about the seal. Besides, there may not be anywhere near a thousand beluga in the inlet, and they may eat a much more varied diet than I suppose. Hardly anyone knows anything about these whales, a fact that's particularly surprising, since they've been living adjacent to the majority of Alaska's human population and in among the fishing boats and oil rigs for so long—and so visibly. Aside from not having a good count, biologists don't know whether their numbers are increasing, decreasing, or staying stable. They don't know where these belugas go in the winter or what they eat then. DNA

samples show that the inlet belugas are genetically different
from the belugas of western Alaska, which indicates that
they've been isolated and evolving separately since the re-
shaping of landforms by the last ice age, some ten thousand
years ago.

Day Six

Flies buzz around the whale. The teeth look larger now, starker
and whiter, as the flesh pulls back from around the mouth.
The eyehole swims with grease. The hide is torn away along
the tail and side, exposing meat and dripping white fat that
looks like Crisco.

I think about how much life and death this one beluga
might have seen in its twenty, thirty, maybe forty years of life.
It may have witnessed the coming of the seismic ships and the
oil wells as well as the end of most hunting by men in boats.
It probably escaped its share of killer whales, and it very likely
spent time lying high and dry on beaches, as often happens to
belugas—with no apparent ill effects—when they're caught
short by the fast-moving tides. It certainly ate plenty of fish,
and it most likely passed on its genes to another whale generation.

Forty is old for a beluga, but belugas are young among
whales: two bowheads recently taken in subsistence hunts
along Alaska's Arctic coast were found to have buried in their
flesh jade harpoon points identical to those collected by an-
thropologists in the same area in 1881.

This morning there are new bear tracks in the sand—two
sets, one larger than the other and softened by an earlier rain.
I follow the tracks backward and see where the bears came
down the bluff and walked along a driftwood log at the top of
the beach, where one slipped and left a wide streak of muddy

footprint. The bears didn't feed; their tracks go past the beluga and then disappear below the tide line. Perhaps they were hoping for salmon instead, looking for dropouts from our nets. Perhaps there's too much human scent here or too much smell altogether, too much rot.

Day Seven

In the evening, I walk again to the whale. The tide is ebbing, but the beach is narrow, and I feel pressed uncomfortably close to the bank. From a distance, the beluga seems less, smaller, and very dark—orange gone to brown, purple like bruises on its enormous chin.

When I get close, I see what's different. Where the whale's back had risen, now there's exposed skeleton—bone sticking into the air like paddles raised above a kayak.

The bears have eaten.

I approach slowly, stopping every few steps to look for movement, half expecting a bear to rise up from where it's been sleeping off its meal. I watch grasses waving at the foot of the bluff and angle closer to the water, as though running into the inlet might save me from a charging bear. I come to the first of several huge, pebbly mounds of feces, black as loamy earth.

There's no doubt what went on here: an orgy of eating and carousing. The sand is as scuffed and beaten as on the most popular bathing beach; gobs of meat and fat and strings of sinew lie scattered like messy sandwich remains. The bears feasted exclusively on the beluga's choice lower back—as much bulk, I calculate, as my entire self, more than a hundred pounds. About four feet of backbone, licked clean, lies exposed, as does a long pile of unbroken, shiny, swollen intestines as thick as my arm. They are careful diners, then, these bears—able to pull away the intestines without puncturing them, to thoroughly clean meat from bone. I revise my mental image of slashing claws and teeth, indiscriminate gorging.

Before bed, from outside our cabin, I train binoculars on the beluga. A dark bear moves around it, a bear I identify by shape—long neck, small head, stretched-out body—as a black. I watch it move around the whale, now on its back legs, now walking off to one side. I've forgotten again just how graceful bears are, not a bit clumsy. This one seems nervous, lifting its head, standing, as though the breeze is carrying my scent.

And then, at the edge of the frame, there's more movement—more bears, bigger bears, lighter fur, extra bears bunched around the whale. Three brown bears have come down the bluff, dirt still spilling after them. The black bear scampers away, stopping to look back from a safe distance. The arrivals, muscular shoulders rolling, begin to eat. One is larger than the other two: a sow with twins. I expect them to settle in around the beluga like dogs at dishes of food, but they keep moving, stepping up and moving back, changing places, one disappearing behind a boulder and then reappearing. Each time the black bear edges too close, they run at it. Finally, they all move off down the beach and disappear into the dusk.

Day Eight

From offshore, as we pass in the skiff we see a clear, trammeled bear trail that falls steeply from the top of the bluff to the hollow just behind the dead beluga. This new trail, a hundred feet high, is beginning to be a highway.

The beluga itself shows up clearly on the beach—its bony back now exposed for most of its length—looking like a dinosaur skeleton among the rocks. The rest of the whale has shrunken to a low brown pile, like a pool of melted-down fat.

It reminds me of the bad witch in *The Wizard of Oz*. Each time we pass in the boat, the sticky, oily sweetness wafts out to us, making us catch our breath.

Day Nine

The dinosaur look is gone. The bones of the back have been knocked apart to lie in pieces in the sand, three-lobed vertebrae like outboard props, rib bones licked clean, a scapula. Guts are piled to one side of a nearly leveled mess of wet red flesh. Only the head remains intact, the ragged hide drawn back around it like a dirty cloak. But even the head is molten looking, blackened and shapeless, the eyehole less distinct, the mouth tighter. In the rain, it all has a wet, vinylized look. A rivulet of water runs over the sand; a whitish piece of viscera is caught in it as though in a whirlpool, spinning around and around, fast. A wave smacks a rock behind me, making me jump.

Day Twelve

The tides are bigger now, reaching the beluga, but the water has been coming in calm, riding up over the remains and then washing back out. Near high tide, a group of seagulls paddles over the area, feeding on whatever scraps float up.

When the tide recedes, there's little to see. The skull and what's left of the tattered hide have been washed to the top of the beach. The part of the hide that has pulled off the skull is studded with teeth; this confuses me until I realize that the shrinking hide still gripped the teeth as they loosened in the flesh of the jaw. Other bones, bare except for a greasy slickness, are spread over the beach, stuck among rocks. I find what remains of a flipper—a ball joint, like the ones in our shoulders. The smaller bones are gone, though I know, from look-

ing at a beluga skeleton in a museum, that the bone structures
of beluga flippers are just like hands—jointed bones that form
five fingers. A flipper may be just a blunt appendage, but inside—why all that careful finger articulation? The ancestors of
all whales were land mammals; they're carrying with them yet
those residual body parts they haven't needed for millions of
years. I learned something else from that museum display: the
beluga is the only whale whose top vertebrae are not fused—
the only whale with, in fact, a neck that allows it to turn its
head.

Ken finds the lower jawbone with a few teeth still in it. He
brings it back to the cabin, sets it on a log, and pulls a tooth
loose. He soaks the tooth in a cup of Clorox to clean it.

Day Sixteen

A pod of belugas passes today heading south, the first group
we've seen in weeks. They're close enough to shore, and the
water is calm enough, that I can hear their breathing, like the
beating of hearts. *Phooof.* They exhaust their breaths with
thin sprays of water that hang like crystals in the air.

"Sea canaries," belugas have been called, for the wide range
of singing sounds—including grunts, clicks, chirps, and whis-
tles—they're known to make. Yet as often as I've watched
them pass, I've never heard anything but the businesslike
sound of their traveling breaths. One calm day, I promise myself, I'm going to be ready at the end of the reef when they
come along, and I'm going to put my ear to an overturned canning jar and hear whatever I can hear.

The adults passing me are stunning in their crisp whiteness,
the blue-gray calves harder to spot. Just as a bald eagle takes
about five years to fledge its white head, belugas take about
twelve years to lighten to whiteness, each year stepping up
one more shade by rubbing off their old skins against rocky

shores. This is unique among whales, apparently—this yearly shedding.

Only a fraction of the whales are visible at any one moment, which is why they're so notoriously hard to count. The experts say belugas can stay underwater for six minutes or more. When they're traveling like this, though, they seem to rise and fall at a regular pace, and I guess that in any snapshot of time I may be seeing a fifth of what's passing me. That would put this pod at about a hundred.

I follow one animal, watching its sleek, white roll and then moving my eyes ahead, anticipating its next rise, the rhythm of its motion, its breathing, again and again. I try to see it in wholeness—its length and shape—but always there's only the brief arc it cuts through the water. At best, I make out the bulbous forehead—the "melon" that holds its sonar equipment—and the slight hump and indentation behind it, a certain ribbed look along the back. The beluga has no dorsal fin—or, rather, the dorsal is reduced to a low ridge along the back's midline. Most of the world's belugas live in ice-covered waters, so a dorsal fin would only be in the way.

One whale, instead of smoothly rolling, flips its tail cleanly out of the water, showing me the darkened underside of its flukes. It does this not just once but repeatedly; it's the only whale in the pod to exhibit this odd, extraneous behavior. I wonder if it has an itch it's trying to satisfy, or if it's expressing pique or delight about something, or whether it's just a whale swimming to a different drummer. Why should a whale bother to be different? Why not?

Day Twenty

Neighbors far down the beach have visitors from California. We see them on our beach, looking at what remains of the whale. Only after they've recrossed the inlet do we learn that they took the beluga's skull with them, wrapped tightly in layers of plastic. I try to picture it in California, hollow eye sockets pointed at someone's swimming pool.

Day Twenty-Five

It's too stormy to fish; huge rollers pound the beach. We tie a short net to our running line to get an idea of what we might be missing. When we check it, there's only one rubbery silver salmon, dozens of sticks, and a beluga rib, the knob on the thin end wrapped so tightly in web that it takes me several cold minutes to work it loose.

In the cabin I reach to unclip a washcloth from the line behind the woodstove, but the back of the clothespin is being used as a holder for Ken's beluga tooth. I forget the washcloth and take the tooth in my hand instead.

It's so white and almost delicate: the root end is hollowed and thin walled and is ringed with distinct ridges, growth circles like tree rings. The shape flares forward from the root before tapering to a hard enamel point, solid as ivory and slightly yellowed. There's a chip out of the end the size of a small fingernail—or it may be not a chip but a hollow worn against an opposing tooth. A network of spider-thin lines etches the point end with a history of hard, gritty eating. Perhaps, after all, this tooth belonged to an elderly whale.

I hold it to my nose. There's no sticky smell left, only—very faint—something like dust, like chalk powder.

I turn the tooth again and again in my hand, feeling the rightness of its shape, the fit in my palm, the weight. Any way I turn it, it's perfectly itself, true to its own aesthetic. I think again of the carved tooth I'd dug out of the ground and of the jade harpoon points found in centenarian bowheads; they are wondrous expressions of the ancient connections between our species and the fine artistry visited one upon the other.

This tooth is only a plain tooth, made souvenirly hygienic. The whale to which it belongs is dead and scattered, washed to the sea, turned to new flesh, and retired in part to California. We took one ordinary tooth, but it seems at this moment that what I hold is not so much a tooth from a whale but the near opposite. My hand clutches a beluga's tooth, and in the tooth is the whale, abiding.

Epilogue

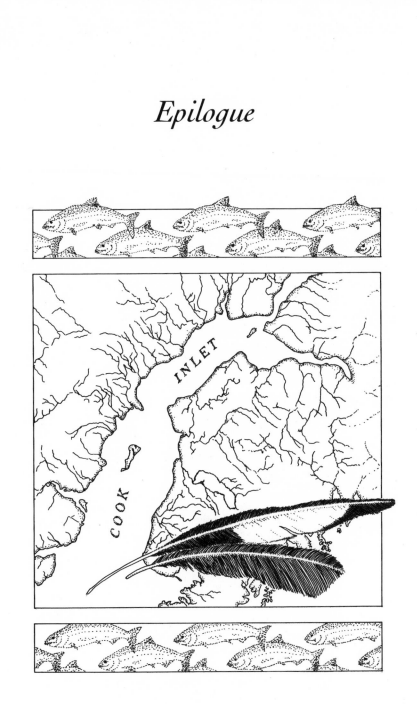

At camp each year, the king salmon pass, and then the sockeyes and silvers. The fireweed blossoms climb their stalks. Inky cap mushrooms poke up overnight beside the trail and dissolve almost as quickly. One day the wind blows cold from the north, laying the grasses flat and stripping alders of their faded leaves. The ocean carries a solemn smell of dead fish: spawners washed out of the rivers, ghost salmon going back to sea in their old clothes. The muddy inlet continues its incorrigible widening and filling, its geological journey.

Ken and I catch our last reddish, toothy, and tatter-finned fish. On a cool day in September, the Dena'ina month of Leaves Turn Yellow, we coil up our water hose and board over the cabin's windows. We leave fishcamp with both reluctance and readiness. What we do there is essential to us, but when the fishing season is over, our lives demand an expanded circle.

From our winter home on the roaded side of the inlet, we watch noisy flocks of sandhill cranes spiral into the sky to begin their southward flight. With friends, we dig potatoes from cold ground. We attend plays and art openings and meetings, meetings, meetings. We send faxes to our senators in

Washington, D.C., and travel by jet across four time zones to visit family. We are, both of us, social and political creatures. In our "good citizen" seasons, engaged in the larger community, we pay attention to bigger fish and to waters even muddier than those of the inlet.

✧ ✧ ✧

On a winter day when snow drifts past my windows like feathers, I moor myself in a sea of paper. I page through the latest salmon market report, skimming news about competition from farmed fish, oversupply in Japan, and new pink salmon products—sausages and hams, spreads and fast-food nuggets—that might or might not catch on with consumers. I sort through pleas to help fight a ballot measure that will allocate more salmon to sport fishermen, to attend an oil lease sale hearing, to write more letters on federal fisheries legislation. I read about problems in the Pacific Salmon Treaty negotiations with Canada and how Alaskan fishermen are being asked, again, to pay the price of dam building, deforestation, and urbanization in western Canada and the northwestern states. I ponder the confusion of so many people who think that because salmon runs in abused places are endangered, all wild salmon must be endangered.

Alaska's salmon, after going near the brink in the 1960s, are today well managed, their runs at historic highs. Even so, new threats develop daily. Our state legislature, increasingly dominated by urban interests, has stepped up the schedule for logging state lands at the same time it's eliminating the jobs of habitat biologists. Both state and federal governments have proposed new oil lease sales in Cook Inlet while the inlet's existing tanker traffic comes and goes without any tug assistance, any safety margin. The oil industry continues to dump millions of tons of pollutants into the inlet.

I set my paperwork aside and address an envelope to George, who is wintering now in Nebraska. I have photographs to send him that were taken in the summer, when a museum curator visited his camp and marveled over its history. Here's George standing by his bluestone tierce, the last of the big wooden barrels used in his cannery days for disinfecting linen nets. Here's George beside the huge, old retort—taller than he is— that pressure-cooked his hand-packed salmon fifty years ago, and the steam engines that powered it. With its black iron and a silver wheel on the front, the retort looks like a vault, and these days he uses it as exactly that—to store his rice and flour and cases of outboard motor oil. Here's a picture looking into the rafters in the back of the cannery, where George still keeps several of the early "nines"—the 9.9-horsepower outboards that were the first used in silty Cook Inlet, motors that had to be invented without water pumps.

I don't know what will happen to these relics—junk to the uninitiated eye, and much of it too heavy to be relocated easily. Gradually, though, George has been shedding himself of the old place, cleaning and packing, taking across the inlet the tools and tokens he wants to keep and putting others up for sale. He may, he thinks, even have a buyer for part of his fishing operation: "one of those people that puts you to sleep"— an anesthesiologist.

We want George to be able to get out of fishing with something for his retirement, of course, but this news of a wealthy doctor as his potential buyer sticks uncomfortably in my gut. There's no money in fishing anymore—not this kind we do, not in the place we do it—so no "real" fisherman could possibly afford to buy George's place and still make a living. Only someone with plenty of spare income to begin with, someone who didn't expect a return on his investment or need to make a living from fishing, could justify such a purchase. The doctor, George has said, is looking for "lifestyle," for something he can do with his family when he has time off.

This, then, may be the cold reality of modern-day fishing, the future we behold. The trend already has become apparent to us—more lawyers and schoolteachers and other professionals buying up at inflated prices fishing permits, boats, and beach sites as supplemental sources of income or tax deductions, for something like recreation. Individually, they're perfectly fine people, as neighborly and kind and as fond of their lives and children as any. And yet. For them, fishing is not *primary*, and a living conducted by those for whom it is not the most important thing becomes, I fear, only an avocation, a hobby, a sideline—no longer truly necessary.

Fishing's not, in this sense, essential for Ken and me, either. If the fish disappeared, if our seasons were closed, we wouldn't end up in unemployment lines or retraining schools as have the beaten-down fishermen of the North Atlantic. We can do other work, and we do already, piecing together both livelihoods and a wholeness of life. None of this other work is steady, none of it's assured, and most of it isn't even paid, but all of it fits, one way or another, around a center of fishing.

The work does all connect. We know these sacred truths, east and west, in our bones: *everything has a life of its own, but nothing lives by itself*. And *there's no picking out any one thing without finding it hitched to absolutely everything else*. For the eight months we live away from fishcamp, we never cease knowing it as home. We inhabit it as we inhabit our clothes— making it a habit, the custom and everyday practice of our lives.

Today, the prices we're paid for salmon are lower than when we started fishing. The world is industrialized, and the marketplace is global. Fish farms, where salmon are raised in pens and fed on pelletized protein, have proliferated from Norway to Chile to Maine and now provide as much "product" as do fishermen who catch salmon at sea.

Farmed salmon, most of which are Atlantics—only distantly related to the Pacifics and closer to trout—can be harvested in a very consumer-friendly way. That is, they can be taken from their pens in agreeable serving sizes all year long and rushed fresh to stores and restaurants with nary a disturbed scale. That these fish are less tasty and healthful than well-muscled salmon that have eaten a varied, natural diet in a clean, cold environment is less important to consumers than their convenience. Farmed salmon are taking over the market and driving down prices.

Just as most Americans reject the juicy, golden peach handpicked at its moment of ripeness by the small fruit farmer in favor of the hard, cosmetically red peach that packs and travels well, they reject the seven-pound, firm and fatty wild salmon with net marks on its head for the pale imitation that packages well. In the process, they reject as well the small fruit farmer and the fisherman and the sustaining work that such people do.

A friend of mine, a woman who fishes for salmon in Bristol Bay, recently volunteered in a salmon-marketing project. She visited urban supermarkets in the Midwest, giving out cooked samples and talking to people about the reasons they should buy Alaskan salmon. She and her husband repeatedly spoke with shoppers who wouldn't believe they were salmon fishermen, people who didn't seem to comprehend that salmon could be caught in the ocean and that men and women actually did the work that brought salmon steaks and fillets to stores. Some of them didn't even know what a salmon was.

I want people to know that salmon exist, as food and more than food. I fear less the future of individual fishermen, myself included, than I do a future in which people don't know or care what a wild salmon requires, a future in which we don't do what we must to ensure that rivers run clean and unimpeded, that oceans be nurseries instead of strip mines and dumps. Only when we provide for salmon will they provide for us—will we live in a world where it's possible to continue. Native Americans whose lives were intimately tied to salmon knew this. Commercial fishermen, with our own bonds and salty knowledge, understand this as well, even—or especially—as we see our places in the salmon's world evolve and diminish.

✧ ✧ ✧

I stuff George's photographs into his envelope and then look for a minute at another—one of Ken and me, taken at the beach with water and sky behind us. We look pretty good, I think—tan and fit, squinting into the sun. There's gray creeping through our hair, but we like to think we're getting smarter as well as older, that we've learned over the years to fish harder with our heads than with our bodies. If we can have another twenty years . . .

The phone rings and I answer; it's a conference call for a committee I'm on, to talk about computer mapping of marine habitat. One hand clutches the receiver to my ear, but the other goes about fielding beach agates from the corners of my desk, setting them into piles, and clinking them together. I turn a favorite one as I talk, fondling it with the soft pad of my thumb and rubbing its rough side, its sharp edge, a smooth, glassy curve. I feel the life in my fingers, the strength to pick fish and the patience to mend nets, and the power and the need to do the other work to keep fish and fishing alive, to do what I can to bring together history and heaven.

Suggested Readings

The following books have been particularly informative, instructive, or inspiring to me as I thought about my relationship to the place where I live, at fishcamp and in the world.

Burks, David Clarke, ed. *Place of the Wild*. Washington, D.C.: Island Press, 1994.

Carson, Rachel. *The Sea Around Us*. New York: Oxford University Press, 1951.

Childerhose, R. J., and Marj Trim. *Pacific Salmon*. Seattle: University of Washington Press, 1979.

Dauenhauer, Nora Marks, and Richard Dauenhauer, eds. *Haa Shuka, Our Ancestors: Tlingit Oral Narratives*. Seattle: University of Washington Press, 1987.

Dillard, Annie. *Pilgrim at Tinker Creek*. New York: Harper's Magazine Press, 1974.

Ehrlich, Gretel. *The Solace of Open Spaces*. New York: Viking Penguin, 1986.

Eiseley, Loren. *The Immense Journey*. New York: Random House, 1957.

Fobes, Natalie, Tom Jay, and Brad Matsen. *Reaching Home: Pacific Salmon, Pacific People*. Seattle: Alaska Northwest Books, 1994.

Haines, John. *Living Off the Country: Essays on Poetry and Place*. Ann Arbor: University of Michigan Press, 1981.

Halpern, Sue. *Migrations to Solitude*. New York: Pantheon Books, 1992.

Kalifornsky, Peter. *A Dena'ina Legacy: K'tl'egh'i Sukdu*. Fairbanks: Alaska Native Language Center, 1991.

Kari, James, and James Fall, eds. *Shem Pete's Alaska: The Territory of the Upper Cook Inlet Dena'ina*. Fairbanks: Alaska Native Language Center, 1987.

Kari, James, and Priscilla Russell Kari. *Tanaina Country*. Fairbanks: Alaska Native Language Center, 1982.

Kari, Priscilla Russell. *Tanaina Plantlore: An Ethnobatany of the Dena'ina Indians of Southcentral Alaska*. Fairbanks: Alaska Native Language Center. 1991.

Kittredge, William. *Hole in the Sky*. New York: Knopf, 1992.

Kizzia, Tom. *The Wake of the Unseen Object: Among the Native Cultures of Bush Alaska*. New York: Henry Holt, 1991.

Leopold, Aldo. *A Sand County Almanac*. New York: Oxford University Press, 1949.

McKibben, Bill. *The End of Nature*. New York: Random House, 1989.

Matthiessen, Peter. *Men's Lives*. New York: Random House, 1986.

Nash, Roderick. *Wilderness and the American Mind*. New Haven, Conn.: Yale University Press, 1967.

Nelson, Richard K. *The Island Within*. San Francisco: North Point Press, 1989.

———. *Make Prayers to the Raven: A Koyukon View of the Northern Forest*. Chicago and London: University of Chicago Press, 1983.

Norris, Kathleen. *Dakota: A Spiritual Geography*. Boston: Houghton Mifflin, 1993.

Osgood, Cornelius. *The Ethnology of the Tanaina*. New Haven, Conn.: Human Relations Area Files Press, 1976. Reprinted from the 1937 edition.

Pyle, Robert Michael. *The Thunder Tree: Lessons from an Urban Wildland*. Boston: Houghton Mifflin, 1993.

———. *Wintergreen: Listening to the Land's Heart*. New York: C. Scribner, 1986.

Rockwell, David. *Giving Voice to Bear: North American Indian Myths, Rituals, and Images of the Bear*. Niwot, Colo.: Roberts Rinehart Publishers, 1991.

Ross, Rupert. *Dancing with a Ghost: Exploring Indian Reality*. Ontario, Canada: Octopus Publishing Group, 1992.

Sanders, Scott Russell. *Staying Put: Making a Home in a Restless World*. Boston: Beacon Press, 1993.

Schofield, Janice J. *Discovering Wild Plants*. Anchorage: Alaska Northwest Books, 1989.

Shepard, Paul, and Barry Sanders. *The Sacred Paw: The Bear in Nature, Myth, and Literature*. New York: Viking, 1985.

Sherwood, Morgan, ed. *The Cook Inlet Collection: Two Hundred Years of Selected Alaskan History*. Anchorage: Alaska Northwest Publishing Company, 1974.

Stafford, Kim. *Having Everything Right*. Lewiston, Idaho: Confluence Press, 1986.

Teale, Edwin Way, ed. *The Wilderness World of John Muir*. Boston: Houghton Mifflin, 1954.

Thoreau, Henry David. *Walden*. Princeton, N.J.: Princeton University Press, 1971.

Acknowledgment of Sources

Some essays in this volume have been reprinted, in most cases with modest alterations to bring their substance up-to-date, and with permission of the publishers, from the sources listed below:

✧ "Beach Time" first appeared in Mānoa, Vol. 8, No. 2, 1996 (special Seeing the Invisible issue).

✧ "Two Lakes" first appeared in *Alaska Quarterly Review*, Spring 1994.

✧ An earlier version of "A Crying Country" first appeared in *Left Bank*, No. 2, Summer 1992 (as "In the Country Above").

✧ "First Fish" appeared in *We Alaskans* (the *Anchorage Daily News* Sunday magazine), Feb. 25, 1996.

✧ A portion of "Creek Culture" appeared in *Left Bank*, No. 7, Dec. 1994 as "Drop." The entire essay appeared in *Connotations*, the journal of The Island Institute, Vol. 3, No. 2, Fall/Winter 1995–1996.

✧ "On Not Being Alone" appeared in *Witness*, Vol. IV, No. 2, 1995 (special Rural America issue).

✧ A shorter version of "Beluga Days" ("Beluga") appeared in the Nov./Dec. 1991 issue of *Sierra*.